THE FOOD STYLIST'S HANDBOOK

THE FOOD STYLIST'S HANDBOOK

DENISE VIVALDO
with CINDIE FLANNIGAN

GIBBS SMITH
TO ENRICH AND INSPIRE HUMANKIND

First Edition
14 13 12 11   5 4 3 2
Text © 2010 Denise Vivaldo
Photographic credits on page 258

Published by
Gibbs Smith
P.O. Box 667
Layton, Utah 84041

1.800.835.4993 orders
www.gibbs-smith.com

Designed by Debra McQuiston
Printed and bound in Hong Kong
Gibbs Smith books are printed on paper produced from sustainable
PEFC-certified forest/controlled wood source.
Learn more at: www.pefc.org

Library of Congress Cataloging-in-Publication Data

Vivaldo, Denise.
  The food stylist's handbook / Denise Vivaldo with Cindie Flannigan. — 1st ed.
    p. cm.
  ISBN-13: 978-1-4236-0603-1
  ISBN-10: 1-4236-0603-5
 1. Photography of food. 2. Food presentation. I. Flannigan, Cindie. II. Title.
  TR656.5.V592 2010
  778.9'96413—dc22
                          2010011370

We dedicate this book to the culinary students and aspiring food stylists we've met and taught from around the world. We appreciate their passion, talent and tenacity.

CONTENTS

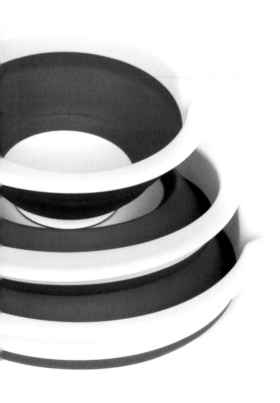

Acknowledgments

I had a dream in 1988 to write a book about how to become a food stylist. I even had a publisher interested for a second. That book never came to fruition and now I know that was a good thing. I didn't know enough about food styling to write such a book back then.

Fast-forward twenty-two years and here it is. It has been a joy, stinky hard, and a huge challenge to write this book. It only came about because of Cindie Flannigan. She supports me in all my wild and crazy dreams.

Cindie came to Food Fanatics as an intern in 2001, after graduating from my alma mater with honors (they taped *my* diploma together) and has never left. I am so grateful for her. Cindie makes work fun and energizing, and, best of all, she is extremely talented. I get to learn from her. I love being a chef, food stylist and author, and having a creative partner to work with every day has helped me survive, prosper and enjoy the ride.

A few years ago, Cindie suggested I start teaching food styling workshops. It came out of the thirty or forty emails we get every week asking us how to break into the business. I told her, no—too much work, too costly to run, too many working weekends. Blah, blah, blah . . .

Well, Cindie said she'd help and eventually we gave it a try and the workshops have been booming ever since. Not only are they fun and we make a few bucks, but best of all, we have met incredible stylists, students, and photographers from all over the world that come to our classes.

Our workshops taught us that the culinary community needed this book. We are privileged to have the opportunity to publish it.

I have a brilliant agent named Lisa Ekus of the The Lisa Ekus Group. She's a legend in the culinary world. (I'm still amazed that she represents me.) At an IACP conference a few years back, over a pork chop in New Orleans, she handed me a cocktail napkin with the name Gibbs Smith and a phone number. "Call him when you're sober." She's always there with good advice.

The mission statement of Gibbs Smith publisher is: To enrich and inspire humankind. Gibbs is a tall man who has created a successful and distinguished publishing company. So, over lunch at IACP, I tried to explain my idea for a food styling book. I met his daughter and several of his A team. I was talking a mile a minute; I have no idea what I said, but I was sober. A few months later, we signed a contract.

To Lisa, Gibbs, and everyone who works at both these cherished companies, I thank you.

Michelle Witte of Gibbs Smith was assigned to this book. Her calm and quiet manner brought this book to life. Madge Baird took over the task of navigating the project. I've said it more than once, it takes many hands to publish any book. Thank you, ladies.

And to the designer: Debra, you exceeded my expectations. Our book is beautiful!

I will always be indebted to Charlotte Walker for introducing me to food styling; Maggie Waldron for telling me she could "see a little talent in my work"; and to Kit Snedaker, "Kid, if you want something, you just get up every morning and put one foot in front of the other."

Cindie and I would like to thank the photographers whose work appears in this book. Our photographers did not get paid. They released these photos to us because they believe in us. If we had had to pay them for their services, this book would never have happened. They helped us because not only are they gifted photographers but they are also dear friends. In alphabetical order: Matt Armendariz, Ryan Beck, Victor Boghossian, Kent Cameron, Rachael Coleman, Edward Covello, Jack Coyier, Anita Crotty, Jon Edwards, Laura Edwards, Ben Fink, Kim Hudson, Jeff Katz, Diana Lundin, Ed Ouellette, Jerome Pennington, R. Pratima Reddy, Jeff Sarpa, and Heather Winters.

We'd also like to thank the prop stylists whose work is displayed in many of these photographs: Robin Tucker, Laurie Baer, Brian Toffoli, and Kim Wong.

A huge thanks to Jenny Park for sharing her experiences and to Jeff Parker for great suggestions and that last, crucial read-through.

And, finally, thank you to all the great food stylists, assistants, interns and students we've been privileged to work with over the years!

Our best to you,

Denise Vivaldo
Cindie Flannigan

FOOD STYLING AS A CAREER

I'm betting you've seen beautiful food photography in cookbooks and magazines and thought to yourself, "I want to know how to do that!"

You see the dazzling settings, the beautiful light, the expensive linens and tableware, the delicious-looking food, and you love it, critique it, and might even try copying the styling and experimenting with the recipes. The fact that you are reading this paragraph proves that you care about food presentation.

In 1984, I was struck by a passion for food styling. I was a culinary student in San Francisco and found myself hooked after a food stylist taught a weeklong class at my school. The class took us to a photographer's studio and taught us about recipe writing, designing a photograph, and prepping food for a shot. The information was everything I had wondered about when I would read a cookbook or magazine. That course changed my life.

Today, food styling is a relatively small niche market compared to other jobs in the food industry. But it's a growing market with strong international appeal. Both of those trends bode well for food styling.

When I began working in the business, getting information about food styling was almost impossible. Stylists in the field were few, and they were reluctant to share their information. There were no books on food styling, and no World Wide Web.

I want to change that. So, after twenty-five years of working as a food stylist, I, along with my creative partner and fellow stylist Cindie Flannigan, have decided to write a book about every important aspect of food styling that we have learned long the way.

We hope you find it useful and enlightening. Please write to us when you get work.

—Denise Vivaldo
dvivaldo@earthlink.net
www.FoodFanatics.net

What This Book Covers

The book takes a comprehensive look at food styling, both from a business and an aesthetic point of view. Among other things, we:

- Describe the details of food styling. What exactly is food styling? What are the tips, tricks, and techniques used to create beautiful food?
- Deal with the financial and production aspects of your food styling business:
- Explain how to write a business plan. What elements belong in a food styling business plan? Have you run your own business before?
- Tell how to market your business: Describe the unique characteristics of your food styling business and explore how to pay for your marketing strategy.
- Discuss how to quantify the size of your business, the amount of startup money you may need, and how much profitability you can expect.
- Explain using apprentices and assistants to help your business grow.
- Describe the main categories of food styling customers.

- Detail how to create a portfolio that showcases your work and outline what food styling customers and other professionals look for in a portfolio.
- Detail how to break into the business.
- Describe the work behaviors and professional practices that are expected from a food stylist that will increase your chance of success when dealing with other professionals.

From this book you will gain an excellent overview of the rewards and pitfalls of the food styling industry. We give you the tools to get organized and the information to get started. We tell you how to create your first portfolio pieces and how to market yourself. We share personal stories from the front lines of food styling, many of them humorous and all of them illuminating; We've been as candid as possible to give you the most realistic idea of the profession of food styling. This career isn't for the faint-of-heart, but if you love daily challenges and treasure offbeat experiences, then this job is for you!

At the end of this book you will find resources for stocking your own styling kit, a short dictionary of culinary terms, and a few suggestions to create a diversified and exciting food styling career.

What a successful food stylist does
is help produce a photo that sells a dream, brand,
product, plate, lifestyle, chef, or restaurant.
We style everything connected to food. Think of it this way:
every picture tells and sells a story.

WHAT A FOOD STYLIST DOES

What a successful food stylist does is help produce a photo that sells a dream, brand, product, sandwich, plate, lifestyle, chef, or restaurant. We style everything and anything connected to food. Think of it this way: every picture tells and sells a story.

It fulfills something deep within our souls to produce a beautiful photo, food buffet, or show segment for everyone to see. Food styling is an art form where food is our medium.

Different people will have reason to hire you as a food stylist—photographers, producers, and art directors among them. The job has different definitions depending upon the client. Nevertheless, what all jobs and clients share is a need for someone to wrangle food in front of a camera, whether that camera is digital, film, HD video, or live television.

The actual styling of the food, when you put all the separate pieces together, is the smallest—but also the most important—part of the job. This is where food styling experience truly counts.

the food on a plate doesn't get there without a food stylist.

These steps are part of any food styling assignment:

- Initial contact with a photographer or client.
- Getting hired by a photographer or client.
- Discussing the needs of photographer or client.
- Making a shopping list and getting petty cash.
- Shopping and possibly prepping the day before.
- Schlepping products and equipment to the location.
- Setting up your workspace, which includes your kit, disposables (foil, plastic wrap, resealable baggies, small cups, plates), work tables, cookware as needed (bowls, skillets, pots, colander, sheet pans, utensils, etc.), equipment (possibly rental, if not already available at the shoot location) such as a stove, refrigerator, freezer, sink with running water, and even trashcans with liners.
- Prepping and cooking the food.
- Styling the food.
- Refreshing the food on the set.
- Perhaps making the same food again . . . and again until the client feels it is right.
- Cleaning up.
- Disposing of any opened and possibly contaminated product.

- Packing out all unused product and dropping off to a food bank, shelter, or otherwise distribute to someone who can use it.
- Packing out all your supplies, kits, and cleaned equipment.
- "Tail lights" as they say in TV productions—the drive-away time that ends your budgeted day, the time at which you stop getting paid.

As you can see, there's a lot more work to food styling than arranging parsley on a plate. Are you still with us?

A Brief History of Food Styling

A long time ago in kitchens far away, there were tales of food stylists that started as home economists employed by large corporations as recipe developers and testers. While selling appliances or new products, like the cake mix, they were drafted into food styling simply because there was no one else to do it. They worked in uncharted waters. Even if they did manage to make something look nice for the camera, the photographer probably had no idea how to light it. See for yourself: go to any used book store and look at the photos in books and magazines from the 1930s, 1940s, 1950s, 1960s, and 1970s.

The incongruous use and overuse of props was a constant theme from the '50s all the way through the '80s.

Photos of food looked the way they did mostly because the food looked that way. Printing methods of the time didn't help either, as they didn't accurately represent the colors of the food, and props were used with little or no logic (one of our favorite old photos shows a roast beef on a platter sitting on fake grass with a duck decoy next to it). Also, in the '30s and '40s, molded foods were popular: lots of domed salads and meat recipes

being exposed to artfully presented food. Julia Child and James Beard began educating the public about great food, and as a society we became more interested in food and cooking. Photography and printing improved, as did the presentations.

Slowly, food images started to change. Food photography started getting better, the lighting, framing, and propping improved, and the food began looking truly edible in the 1980s.

with thick, shiny sauces. It was often impossible to tell what the food had started its life as. Cultural changes influence food, so, after WWII household kitchen equipment began improving and becoming more readily available. Household help in America was disappearing, and Mom became the cook. She needed recipes; they came with pictures. Grocery stores sprung up, making every kind of food easier to purchase, prepare, and store. Those '50s coffin-like freezers made once-a-week shopping the norm and changed how America ate and looked at food. Together with prosperity and an economic boom, eating out became more common, and increasing numbers of diners were

We styled a series of award-winning photos for an International Association of Culinary Professionals (IACP) photo styling contest in 2003. The theme of the contest was to reproduce the styling techniques and photography used during different decades. The title of our series is "My Life in Cheese," and it chronicles the decades of food presentation and styling that I have lived through.

The incongruous use and over-use of props was a constant theme from the '50s all the way through the '80s. The '60s and '70s tended to show food in the context of entertaining. (That fondue pot in the '70s shot was a wedding gift the first time I got married. I got it in the divorce settlement,

• **How do I break into the food styling industry?**

Research what food-related industries are in your area. Research the food or packaging photographers in your area. Who shoots the billboard photos? Who shoots the bus shelter ads? Who shoots restaurant menus and menu boards? Who shoots food ads in the local newspaper? If you live in a small town, figure out how far you are willing to travel for a job. Small markets may not have enough work to support even a part-time food stylist.

• **How do I break into the food styling industry as an intern or an assistant stylist?**

There are several ways to get involved in the food styling business as an intern or assistant. A good way to begin is browsing the Internet. There are websites that offer directories of different food stylists nationwide, providing names, phone numbers, and websites as sources of contact and information. If you are a student or alumni of a culinary school, take advantage of the resources and learning tools that the school provides and has to offer; many culinary schools have agreements with many different restaurants, companies, and people involved in the food business (like food stylists) that allows the school to contact them if a student is interested in beginning an internship with the particular company.

• **How do I prepare to work as a stagiaire with a food stylist?**

"Stagiaire" is the French term for internship or vocational training. When we use that term in food-

related work, it refers to working for a day or up to a week for no pay so that you can see what a job is all about. This also gives people you are staging for a chance to see if they like you. When preparing for a day of staging, you should make sure you have the right professional attire (chef's pants, kitchen shoes, comfortable top, apron), tools such as a well-sharpened knife kit, and a positive attitude.

• **How do I behave as a stagiaire to ensure I get asked back?**

It's always very unnerving to start a day of apprenticing without knowing what to expect, but not to worry; there are a few things you can do to help ensure the success of the overall day as well as getting asked to work with the company/stylist again.

It's important to make sure you find out what the shoot is about, what they would like you to do, and then get to work quickly and efficiently on any task asked of you by the stylist or the assistant. If you need clarification about what they want done, ask and be sure what you're doing is correct. It's also important to remember that the stylist is busy prepping and finishing plates as well as working on the set, so you should be anticipating the next step or task rather than standing around waiting for someone to tell you what to do. As long as you work hard, don't disrupt the shoot, and show your ability to work well under pressure, you should have no problem getting asked to work with a stylist again. If you feel like there is nothing to do at the moment, you can always wash dirty dishes, clean up messy work counters, take out the garbage, or tear stacks of paper towels. There's always something to do. Being idle on the set is a definite no-no.

• Are there food styling classes or workshops offered anywhere to enhance my skill and technique levels?

There are several places that you can learn about food styling. We teach our own classes in Southern California. When looking for instruction, find teachers that are currently working as stylists, as it will do you little good to learn out-of-date styling techniques used in pre-digital photography times.

• What are the main duties of an assistant stylist?

The job of an assistant food stylist is to aid the lead stylist in whatever he/she needs, relative to the job. This includes much shopping, staying on top of the prep work, and keeping up with the overall organization of the kitchen area. You will often have to do two or more things at once. You will often be required to drop everything and start on something completely different.

• When can I begin to book my own jobs?

When you develop a list of potential clients and feel confident that you can handle the job.

• What is the most surprising aspect of the job for people getting into food styling?

When people first get involved in food styling they are often surprised at the amount of work that goes into preparing for a job. Many people expect to cook a few dishes by following a few basic recipes,

dress them up to make them look pretty for the camera, and go home. People don't consider the time it takes to shop as well as transport all that food, along with your kit and equipment, to each location. People are also often taken aback at the number of different styling tricks and techniques necessary for the success of a shoot. Newbies are amazed to find that clients can be finicky, difficult, and often petty. Have we mentioned defensive? When all of the above comes into play at the same time it makes for a very long day.

• What are some tips to staying successful in this business?

Develop a thick skin and a sense of humor, and charge enough to make it worth your while.

• What are other important things to consider?

Be a good team player. Even though you are a freelancer, if a client or photographer enjoys working with you, they will consider you part of their team and will call you first when jobs come up.

• How do you maintain a good working relationship with the lead stylist, clients and photographers?

During the heat of a long shoot, when everyone is suffering from low blood sugar and is cranky and wants to go home, don't say things you will regret. Cindie's motto, which she often mutters under her breath on difficult shoots: "This will all be over in a couple of hours."

thus proving my point that if you keep something long enough, you'll be able to use it as a prop.)

Beginning in the eighties the emphasis was on lavish entertaining. People started paying more attention to food, especially gourmet food. An empty wineglass on its side was a frequent prop; we still don't know why.

In the late '80s and early '90s there was an emphasis on busy, tiny garnishes and lots (and lots and lots) of height. Why? You'd have to ask Charlie Trotter. As a leader in the '90s food scene, Charlie's food presentations became legendary and were copied.

The late '90s brought towering food to the plate, dwarfing the food from the '80s. Food became architectural in scale. The closer the camera got to the food, the fewer props were needed. Although the food often looked fussy and silly, this change, along with better photography and

In the nineties people started showing food in provocative ways. *InterCourses: An Aphrodisiac Cookbook*, by Martha Hopkins and Randall Lockridge, took food photography into a whole new realm.

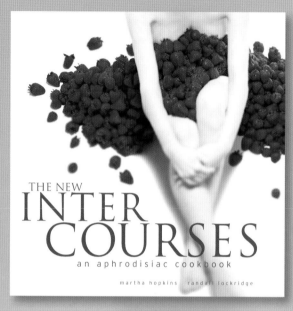

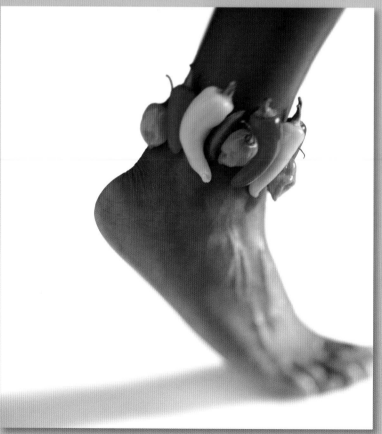

printing, meant that you could actually see the food close up, making the profession of food styling an ever more necessary one.

In the nineties people started showing food in provocative ways. *InterCourses: An Aphrodisiac Cookbook,* by Martha Hopkins and Randall Lockridge, took food photography into a whole new realm.

The nineties also brought healthy foods to the forefront. Later in the decade the simple, clean, and well-lit food photos became very popular through magazines and books from Donna Hay and Martha Stewart. From the late nineties and continuing to today, beautiful realism is the

Traits of a Good Food Stylist

Food stylists today come from a variety of backgrounds. Not all have culinary experience, but we've found that they all love food. Stylists can think about food, talk about it, work with it, look at it, and eat it twenty-four hours a day. When we're not working with food we're taking classes or reading books and magazines to learn more about it. Food is our happy and safe place.

Successful stylists have the *ability to look at food with an artist's eye*; to see the beauty (and the photograph) in the food that's in front of them. They keep an open mind; preconceived notions are limiting.

THIS SANDWICH is built to last! The scaffolding holds up the bread layers so the other product can be easily replaced.

popular look. Food bloggers who are also talented amateur or working photographers are reaching millions of people around the world, influencing the industry in ways yet to be seen.

When looking at decades of food photography we ask ourselves: Does life imitate art or does art imitate life? We think it's a little of both. Food is trendy and its changes are reflected everywhere in our society—magazines, restaurants and television.

Since this job requires working some strange hours in even stranger locations, the *ability to work under any circumstances* is necessary. Most shoots last ten to twelve hours a day, and some productions go into overtime. How well can you tolerate sixteen-hour days? How well can you tolerate sixteen hours bent over, crouched under, or twisted around sets, lights, tables, cables, and props?

Successful food stylists are *masters of improvisation*. A stylist can solve just about any problem

Food Stylist
Personality Profile

Answer the questions below and see if you have the skill set and personality for a food styling career.

1. Have you been to culinary school?
Yes ___ No ___

2. Do you have cooking experience outside the home?
Yes ___ No ___

3. Do you have an unnatural attachment to food?
Yes ___ No ___

4. Do you have any experience in photography?
Yes ___ No ___

5. Do you have any art or design experience?
Yes ___ No ___

6. Do you work well under stress?
Yes ___ No ___

7. Do you mind being smelly for hours on end?
Yes ___ No ___

8. Can you solve problems quickly?
Yes ___ No ___

9. Can you work long hours?
Yes ___ No ___

10. Can you do six things at once?
Yes ___ No ___

11. Are you good at taking directions from others?
Yes ___ No ___

12. Are you a good manager or leader when necessity or a situation presents itself?
Yes ___ No ___

If you answered yes to ten or more of these questions, then the bad news is: you have the right personality for a career in the exciting world of food styling!

with a little Vaseline, some duct tape, a bamboo skewer, and a cotton ball. Every shoot presents multiple puzzles and challenges. Problem solving is often the highlight of our day.

Being *able to do many things at the same time* is an absolute must for the food stylist.

A little Attention Deficit Disorder wouldn't hurt. Neither would a dash of Obsessive Compulsive Disorder (Denise has ADD covered; Cindie is all over the OCD).

A food stylist must be *able to give their client what they want*, not what the stylist thinks is best. It is, after all, the client's product, invention, or vision, not yours. You can suggest options if you think something could be improved, but it is not normally up to you to make final decisions. A good stylist knows when to speak up and when to keep quiet. You learn how to pick your battles or you will exhaust yourself and everyone you work with. We frequently hear horror stories from new clients who had fights with previous food stylists. Don't fight with your client; it's a bad career move.

A good stylist also *knows how to stay focused on the message being sold*. Is it the lobster? Or is it the

CAN YOU FIND the sponge hiding in the bok choy? This is the back side of the photo (above). Notice how the bok choy is supported to make it look natural to the camera in the final photo (right).

lobster pot? Is it the crackers? Or is it the cheese? Or is it an editorial piece that is touting the health benefits of the spring water being served with the lobster? *Know what you are selling.*

A good stylist *knows where to put the effort.* She/he doesn't waste time on the back of a cake if no one is going to see it. Or on fine details of a garnish that is going to be quickly panned over in video. Spend your time and energy where it counts; this will be different for every job.

The Importance of a Culinary Background

Since a food stylist works with food, everything they know about food is a plus. Completion of a comprehensive culinary course at a cooking school is the fastest way to gain this knowledge. Experience working in restaurants or catering can also provide a good background. Home cooking and entertaining are not excluded but by themselves do not give the amount of preparation needed.

Food styling is not just arranging food on a plate. You need to really understand food and how to make it do what you want it to do.

Culinary school gives you a working knowledge of food terms and cooking techniques. Much of the time as a stylist you will be working with recipes supplied by a client; understanding how a recipe works is vital.

This skill is especially useful when the recipe is poorly written. We've had clients ask if our perfectly styled cake was made from their recipe. "Yes, of course," we say and later we hear them say, "Wow! Most of the time that recipe doesn't work." Yeah, thanks; we found that out when we made it yesterday and it bombed. Luckily we had a cake mix and were able to fake it. As a stylist, you have to save the shot, whether it's a photograph or a television segment, your job is to make sure the specified food is ready for its close-up at the scheduled time.

You'll get recipes from television chefs, food editors and cookbook authors that don't know how to cook and can't recognize their own recipes. The wider your food knowledge, the easier it will be for you to alter or correct recipes so they'll work. Having a culinary background will also help you understand how food reacts under different conditions: how does food react when it's chilled, when it's hot, and when it's at room temperature? You need to know this so you can fix the recipe if something goes terribly wrong. Or know what to substitute if an ingredient is unavailable.

And finally, in today's marketplace, you are not going to make money as a food stylist unless you can move fast. Moving fast means having good production skills, meaning hands-on training that cooking schools or working in a restaurant will give

Culinary School As Background for Food Styling

Jenny Park came to Food Fanatics as an intern, having graduated from culinary school, and has been with us since 2008. Here she shares what she found valuable about her culinary school experience.

"Although I don't think culinary school is necessary to succeed in the food industry, specifically within food styling, I think people who have attended an organized culinary institution hold an advantage in the kitchen over those who have not. Through my own experiences I found culinary school to be helpful to my career in food styling in a variety of ways.

"Getting a broad knowledge of food and ingredients—both locally grown and raised as well as from around the world—has been invaluable.

"At my school's career center, I could speak with a guidance counselor about my goals and obtain assistance and useful information from the career center about anything culinary.

"Most culinary institutions also offer various skills classes at no extra charge. I took advantage of this by attending as many of them as I could. Not only was I able to practice many of the basic techniques like braising, searing, roasting, knife cuts, making sauces, etc., but I was also able to learn additional skills and techniques not part of the standard curriculum, such as making sushi and learning about molecular gastronomy. Going to culinary school has given me the opportunity to meet and train under some of the hardest-working and most talented chefs in the industry, as well as some talented chefs-in-training (my classmates) who I still keep in touch with today.

"I even found my first restaurant job through a chef instructor who had given me a great recommendation. It was my first experience networking within this competitive industry. From there I was able to apply to Food Fanatics as an intern and have been working as an assistant food stylist ever since.

"On the whole, I feel that culinary school has given me a jump start over people in this industry who have not attended culinary school."

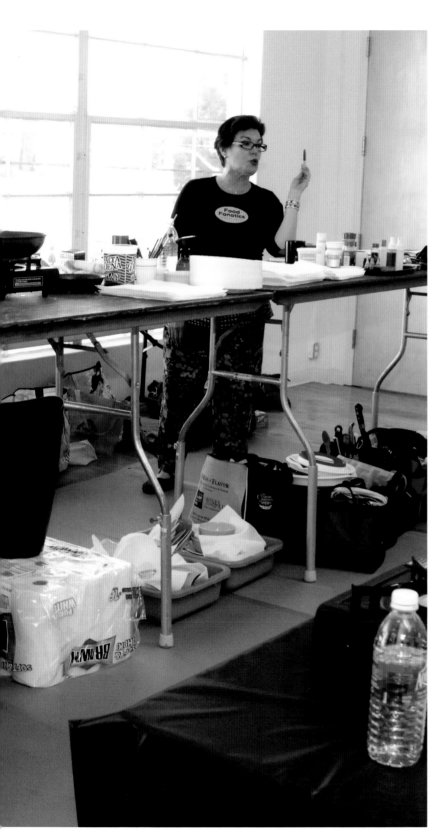

you. With experience, you'll develop an intuitive sense of everything going on in the kitchen: what needs to be checked on, what assistant is ready for a new task, and which assistant is falling behind. You'll learn to anticipate the next shot . . . and the one after that. And then, in your free time, you'll style the beautiful, finished food (called the "hero plate"), work the set, and handle the client.

We find that culinary graduates usually work out best as interns because we can teach them to style but do not have time to teach them to cook.

Where to Learn Cooking Basics

Culinary schools like the Culinary Institute of America in Hyde Park, New York, the California Culinary Academy in San Francisco, The Institute of Culinary Education in New York, the Art Institute and the CEC Group/Cordon Bleu (many locations), and many more offer complete culinary programs, short courses, and weekend seminars for beginning, intermediate, and advanced students. *The Guide to Cooking Schools,* published by Shaw Guides, has the most comprehensive listing of schools and classes, covering all areas of the globe. www.ShawGuides.com. Check it out.

For single classes, many markets, such as the Central Markets in Texas, offer two- or three-hour classes, as do some culinary and restaurant supply stores and also some restaurants. Many cookbook authors, chefs, and food writers teach classes out of their homes. Look around your neighborhood to see what's available.

We teach our own classes at our studio classroom in Southern California and, less frequently, in different cities around the globe. We have classes that focus on areas of concern for food stylists, photographers, art directors, chefs, project managers, writers and bloggers, packaging designers, and culinary students. Check our website for information: www.CulinaryEntrepreneurship.com and www.FoodStylingWorkshop.com.

Who Hires a Food Stylist?

People from all different industries need the services of food stylists. Some will contact you directly, usually off the Internet. We have found that our presence on the Internet gets a lot of attention from potential clients. New clients often ask us to recommend photographers. This is a relatively new development, but it helps us justify the amount of money spent on our website upkeep. We use our site not only to advertise our services but also to educate potential clients about what it is we do and the importance of the food stylist for a variety of different jobs. (A chapter on marketing begins on page 98.) Potential clients that contact you will have wildly varying needs. We have organized a list to give you some idea of what to expect if you are contacted by one of the following:

Photographers

Often a client will hire a photographer, expecting the photographer to hire a food stylist. The photography can be for cookbooks, magazines, ads, editorials, product packaging, brochures, point-of-purchase materials, and just about anywhere an image with food is needed.

Public Relations Firms and Advertising Agencies

PR firms and ad agencies will often assemble a team to produce photos or a commercial for a client. For example, a PR firm representing the California Avocado Board hired us to style a commercial for the holidays and photos for their website. Another PR firm representing a national turkey packager sponsored a satellite media tour featuring Dr. Steven Pratt, author of *Super Foods*. Not only did we make and bring all the food, we were also responsible for bringing all the props and for decorating the set. A PR firm representing Kahlua and San Pellegrino hired us to appear on a satellite media tour, using my background as a Hollywood caterer, cookbook author, and stylist to show people across the country how to use these products to enhance their parties.

Authors and Publishers

An author or publisher might contact you about styling food for a cookbook. As you will be making dishes based on the author's recipes, you'll be in a good position to offer your services as a recipe tester, too. Authors often have cooking demonstrations booked on local television shows, as well as satellite media tours and public appearances where they need food and samples prepared for them. We provided food for Dr. Howard Shapiro when his book *Picture Perfect Weight Loss* was published. His publisher arranged with us to bring and set up food for Dr. Shapiro at local morning shows, at the *L.A.*

Times Book Faire, and on a cable TV book show. A book tour can produce several jobs for one stylist. A sign of the times: more and more publishers are requiring authors to pay for their own photography, forcing authors to hire a food stylist or photographer directly. Make sure you give every author or publisher you come into contact with your card; maybe you'll get hired for the next project.

Product and Appliance Manufacturers

Anything that has to do with food, even in a roundabout way, can require a food stylist's services. A product manufacturer might hire you to work with a spokesperson or talent on television shows, commercials, infomercials, satellite media tours; a photographer for ads, packaging or the Internet. Recently, Richard Simmons had a product developed for him by Salton, Inc. (maker of the George Foreman Grill, among many other nationally known brands) called the "Steam Heat" Steamer. Richard referred us to his manufacturer, who hired us to provide the food for his many television appearances, product photography, photos in the accompanying cookbook, and for developing additional recipes for the website. Thermador hired us to make gorgeous food to put in and on their stoves and ovens for product photography. Bradshaw International, Inc., a huge maker of kitchenware, hires us to suggest, make and style the food that appears on the product packaging and labels.

Package Designers

Package designers can be either a company employee or an independent contractor. They help to bring a new product to market or to improve the packaging or sales material for an existing product. Generally, designers have a good idea of what the client wants and will have an example or template of the packaging to use as a guide. Some of the companies we've shot packaging for are Ventera Ranch, Trader Joe's, and many products in the refrigerator and freezer cases at Costco, Wal-Mart, and Sam's Club. We style photos for the actual products the consumer gets when they buy it in the store. Not a lot of room for tricks. Our job is to make the products look as great to the camera as possible. Experience teaches every stylist how to fool the camera's eye.

TV Show Producers

A production company (often with no food show experience) may be hired to film an entire season of a cooking show. The producers need somebody to run the backstage kitchen and to act as a liaison between the backstage kitchen, the set and the talent. They might need someone to block out the recipes and segments (also called "stepping out the food"). They may need someone to teach the talent how to look like they know what they're doing. They often need someone to tell them how much and what kind of food and equipment they will need. Whether they call you a food stylist or a culinary producer, this is a big job—also time-consuming, exciting, and career-building. We've spent many months in different cities working on television shows for various networks. As long as the talent is willing, it can be a very rewarding and lucrative experience. We give more detailed information on what TV productions are like later on in this book.

Prop Masters

Whether for movies or television, a prop master will call you if he has a scene or segment that requires food. It could be a large wedding buffet for a movie scene, food for street vendors on a TV show, or producing the demonstration food for the guest chef on a talk show. Food Fanatics has styled food for many television shows in years past, *The Ellen Degeneres Show* being one. Whenever there is a cooking guest scheduled, the prop master calls us and goes over what he needs for the segment. Shows with decent budgets, like *The Ellen Degeneres Show,* ask us to bring enough food to make the recipes several times because they always start with a rehearsal. On a show like this, the food segment often changes minutes before going on air. They expect the stylist to deal with it. The single most important thing for the stylist to remember is that this is not a food show: it is *The Ellen Degeneres Show.* The guest chef and the food are props for Ellen. As long as the pans on the set are hot and the food sizzles when it goes in, that's all they really care about. The segment, actually the entire show, is Ellen's opportunity to make the audience laugh. (Finding out that the segment is all about Ellen is often a surprise to her guest chef.)

Chefs and Owners of Culinary Businesses

Often, the owner of a culinary business like a bakery or restaurant will hire a stylist because they are unhappy with the way their product looks in their advertising or on the menu. Natalee Thai Restaurant had never had professional photos of their food before, and they had been in business for twenty years in Los Angeles. Even though the restaurant is only a mile away from the Food Fanatics office, they found us from a photographer who in turn was found by a designer fifty miles away. After years of success, the owner wanted to improve the appearance of his menu. We helped him do that, and he even ended up using the photos as art on his walls. A national restaurant chain with fifty locations hired us to photograph its new line of frozen foods based on the restaurant's most popular menu items. We worked right in the busy restaurant kitchen, next to the hot line, doing our prep. The owners were so happy with the results that they referred us to another restaurant chain. Repeat and referral business from successful campaigns can become your best accounts.

Later in this book we break down exactly what you can expect on different types of jobs, the equipment you will need, the product and disposables you will need, and what should be in your styling kit. We also give you equipment lists for different types of shoots and other information you might not know, but we know you need to know.

How to Get Started: Beg, Call, and Beg Some More

Different cities will require different methods of finding your first styling jobs. Big markets like New York and Los Angeles have hundreds if not thousands of food manufacturers, businesses, photographers, and PR firms. Smaller markets are much more limited, making it necessary to get creative, possibly expanding your definition of what you consider "local." Below we describe different ways to go about reaching people who could hire you.

Test Shots

A test shot is when a photographer or stylist needs a certain type of shot, possibly to show to a potential client. One contacts the other to take some practice shots with the understanding that they will hire each other if they get the work. The photographer takes care of all his expenses and supplies you with a digital file or copies of the photographs.

The stylist purchases the food and styles it. Or a new stylist and a new food photographer help each other out by shooting some test photos for their respective portfolios. We've always thought of this as a way to "test" each other to see how you get along. Working in a studio with someone you don't get along with makes for a really long day.

Above are some test shots we took with photographer Martin Mann. Johnnie Rockets had suggested to Martin that he submit some tests. They supplied us with their product and we went to work. No job came of this test, but it was fun and we had great burgers for lunch from the extra product.

Unless you go out and work as a stylist on test shots and see what it means to be the lead stylist, you are never going to understand the entire job. Each of us brings our own personality and style to any photo we work on, so it is important that you do the work to develop your own style. We encourage our assistants to test with photographers so they can better learn their craft.

Working as an Intern

The best way to start is to find established stylists already working in the field and ask to intern. Since many stylists are protective of their clients, they might not want to introduce you into their arena, where you could be a threat to their future

After working as an assistant food stylist for about a year, I got together with a new photographer and decided to try my hand at getting some of my very own shots. I wanted to put all of my food styling knowledge to use. I also wanted to see how well I could style a plate by myself. After brainstorming different ideas with the photographer, we decided to create a classic (and easy, or so I thought) roasted chicken shot. Not knowing how we would work together, I thought it was best to start with one shot.

Before the big day came, I looked through my kit to make sure I had the necessary tools. I made my list and went shopping. When I unwrapped the chicken I ran into my first problem: there were slight rips in the skin between the breast and thigh on both sides. (What I should've done was buy two, but I was paying for this myself and I thought I would be fine with one.) I tried pulling the skin to cover the holes and ripped it even more. I've seen Denise and Cindie fix worse, so I ignored the tears and threw it into the oven.

My next mistake came when I started on the vegetables. I wrapped the cut pieces in several sheets of damp paper towels and stuck them into the microwave for a minute, then sprayed them with browning spray to give them a cooked look. I should have put them into the oven for a bit so they got that wrinkled roasted look.

MY FIRST TEST SHOOT

Jenny Park, intern

When it came time to set up our overall shot, the photographer was very keen on doing the prop setup himself, so I let him have at it: my third mistake. I should've given my input. He felt the un-ironed tablecloth gave our shot a more rustic look. I thought a lime green tablecloth with tiny pink flowers was an odd choice for rustic. I probably should have chimed in at some point and said, "Maybe we can compromise and take some shots with a wrinkled tablecloth and then iron it and take some more shots." He was so enthusiastic that I didn't want to step on his toes. I won't make that mistake again. The only thing I see now when I look at the photos is that wrinkly tablecloth.

We were lucky to have great natural light that day, and the photographer and I ended up working very well together. All in all, I'd say it was a somewhat successful day. The photos were much less than perfect and I could see a dozen little mistakes I could've prevented, but that's what test shots are for: to learn from your mistakes and move on. I was happy with the overall end results. Although I know the shots weren't perfect and I wouldn't be seeing them in the next *Saveur* or *Bon Appetit*, it was such a great experience, it only pumped me up and had me looking forward to the next time.

It is much easier to find intern opportunities in a major metropolitan area that has a big food photography business.

income. This was truer in the past, when most stylists didn't have a culinary background and were defensive about their lack of knowledge. They liked to think that their styling secrets really were secret and not something anyone with culinary experience and a little imagination could come up with on their own. While this makes interning problematic, it isn't impossible. Be polite and assertive.

It is much easier to find intern opportunities in a major metropolitan area that has a big food photography business. This way you can find several stylists to work with, as most might not have enough work to support themselves, let alone a new assistant. The key to getting asked to assist is to be persistent but not needy, extremely helpful but not a nuisance. How's that for walking a fine line? Once you find someone willing to take you on, here are suggestions for making the best possible impression:

Tips on Having a Successful Internship

- Always show up to jobs on time or a few minutes early.
- Be precise and meticulous when shopping. Read the list and ask questions before going to the store.
- Always dress appropriately for the job.
- Behave in a professional manner.
- Always do what you're told by the lead stylist.

It is very important that you follow the chain of command. If someone on the production team asks you to do something for them, talk to the lead stylist first; your job is to assist the food stylist, not to do the production team favors, especially favors not food related.

- Be prepared for long working days standing on your feet, and then get used to the long working days.
- Don't complain.
- Work quickly and efficiently.
- If the lead stylist needs anything, drop what you're doing and assist.
- Be prepared for (and get used to) an ever changing schedule and for working in strange places.
- Be organized.
- Never throw anything away unless told to by the lead stylist.
- Always ask questions; if you're confused about shopping, prep, etc., always ask the lead stylist instead of plowing ahead and possibly doing it wrong. Mistakes cost money, time and labor.
- Keep your car clean and empty; you'll be loading it and unloading it with a number of different items . . . over and over and over again
- Take care of yourself; with the amount of physical work that goes into this job, it's a good idea to stretch and exercise your back and legs.
- Don't take things personally; it's good to have thick skin.

We have so many people contact us about interning with us that we posted this information about interning on our website. It may sound harsh and a bit scary, but it saves us time and energy by weeding out the faint-of-heart.

Food Fanatics Info for Prospective Interns

• What are the prerequisites for an intern-/externship?

A credit card. You will be doing a lot of shopping. It is not unusual to purchase $700 or more of groceries in a day. You will be reimbursed that same day, but you must have the credit necessary to make the purchases in the first place.

A car in good running condition. We will be relying on you to be on time and to complete errands.

A cell phone. We'll often need to add items to your shopping list after you have already left for the store.

A local place to stay. We are located in the western part of the city of Los Angeles, south of West Hollywood and north of Culver City. Your residence needs to be no more than a 30-minute drive from our studio. We have had interns/externs from farther away and it does not work. Our studio classroom is in Long Beach, about 20 miles south of Los Angeles. If you are staging with us only for a class, we suggest you stay within a 10-mile radius of Long Beach.

Money to live on. Even though this is a paid intern-/externship, it does not pay much. Anyone considering this career needs to have money saved or another source of income. It takes five to seven years to build a client list large enough to support yourself. This is assuming you aggressively market yourself. Most new stylists have some other work or income that they rely on.

• What can I expect to get out of an intern-/externship at Food Fanatics?

Interning/externing with us will give you a chance to see exactly what goes into keeping a small culinary business afloat. While you are with us you may have the opportunity to work on photo shoots, commercials, and TV shows. Your time with us might coincide with a cookbook we're developing. You might be assisting us when we teach food styling classes. For someone who wants exposure to alternative culinary careers this is an excellent intern-/externship.

• What kind of hours can I expect to work during my intern-/externship?

It is quite possible that one week you will work only 20 hours and the next week you will work 40 hours in three days. Some days you might work from 10:30 a.m. to 2:30 p.m.; other days work might start at 2:00 a.m. and end at 3:00 p.m. This is not a misprint, the hours can and do vary widely. We need interns/externs that can accommodate a chaotic schedule.

• Will I work weekends?

Most weekends you will not work, but there is a chance that a particular client will book us to work over a Saturday and/or Sunday.

ARE YOU FIT FOR AN INTERNSHIP?

• **Is there a possibility of full-time employment after my intern-/externship?**

No. Due to the nature of this business, there aren't many full-time food styling jobs. Most stylists also work as recipe developers or testers, writers, personal chefs, caterers, or cooking teachers to make an income they can live on. Anyone looking solely at food styling as a career needs to have a very entrepreneurial personality, the tenacity of super glue and the ability to create a huge network of loyal clients.

• **What kind of work will I be doing?**

Shopping, errands, washing lots and lots of dishes, keeping work areas clean, schlepping loads of stuff back and forth, prepping *mise en place*, and generally jumping in and doing just about anything with good humor. Some office work is also required, so you will need to know, at the very least, how to use Microsoft Word on a PC; any additional computer knowledge is a plus.

• **What other type of knowledge is a plus?**

❧ The more you know about food the better.

❧ The more experience you have with a wide variety of cuisines the better.

❧ Photography and/or design experience is a great thing to have.

❧ Knowledge of sets and productions is valuable.

❧ Having a MacGyver-like personality and being able to creatively solve problems is a tremendous help.

❧ Being able to write well is helpful.

• **How physically demanding is this work?**

There is a common misconception, mostly among chefs and culinary instructors, that food styling is not hard work. If you've ever run your own catering business you will know how physical this type of work can be. This is not for the weak or the slow. When a media production company is waiting on you and every minute of their time is costing them

tens of thousands of dollars, you'd better move fast. When on a shoot or a show, you will be on your feet for anywhere between ten and fourteen hours. The fourteen-hour days are few and far between but they do happen, and you must be physically able to do the work.

• **What type of personality is ideal for this type of work?**

❧ People who can't sit still and need to be constantly busy are a great fit.

❧ Lazy people who like to complain when things get rough are a bad fit.

❧ The more you know about and love food, and the more interested you are in the whole process, the more you will give and get from this opportunity.

❧ If you can join the "we're all in this boat together" group and work together when everyone is tired; then we welcome you. If you bitch when you're tired and ask to go home early, then the only thing you're accomplishing is to remind the rest of us how tired we are, making the job that much harder for the rest of us.

❧ You should be able to find humor in just about any situation.

❧ You should not take things personally.

❧ You should not be a picky eater, as food choices are limited.

• **Is there anything else I should know?**

❧ This is a physically and intellectually demanding intern-/externship. We must stress the importance of being able to work fast and think on your feet.

❧ When on the set of an expensive production, we are very low on the hierarchy. Our job is to simply do what we're being paid to get done without drawing attention to ourselves. These productions are run with an almost military chain of command, which means the privates don't speak to the general unless directly addressed. If you were to come to their attention by acting out, being loud, or offering your unasked-for opinion, they will find out whose fault it is that you are there and ask that you not come back. This reflects very badly on our business and we cannot afford this. If you need attention and constant feedback, then this is a bad intern-/externship choice for you.

🐾 It is important that you don't use work time for personal calls or to take care of personal errands.

🐾 Much of our work is proprietary and confidential; our clients expect confidentiality from us and often require us to sign a statement to that effect.

Please consider carefully the information above before applying for an intern-/externship with us. We will all get more out of this if you know what you are getting into beforehand. Nobody likes unpleasant surprises!

THE DIFFERENT NICHES OF FOOD STYLING

Different food styling jobs require different skill sets, different shopping and prep, different questions, different behavior, different assistants, different experience. We address the differences in this chapter.

Digital and Film Photography

The mainstay of our food styling business is digital photography for print. The images end up being used in ads, in cookbooks or on a package. Television shows, commercials, infomercials and an occasional movie make up the remainder. Below we describe different types of jobs you could be hired for.

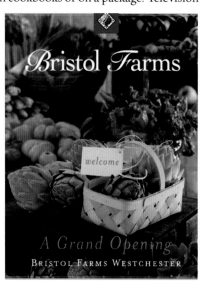

Advertising and Print Ads

Images used for advertising need to fit into predefined spaces. Magazines, billboards, newspapers, vehicle wraps, wherever the image is used it will have to be taken with the exact dimensions in mind. The art director or designer will let the photographer know what the size is and whether

Delectable Gourmet
Magazine

Tempting Strawberry Shortcakes
Amazing New Recipes for the Desserts Everyone Loves!

Plus-

"The Food Stylist's Handbook" Review

New Wine Tour Adventures

More How To's in the Kitchen

When Jobs Collide

Some jobs are a combination of more than one. The reasoning being (from the producer's or client's point of view) that since you are styling food for the commercial anyway, they might as well bring in a photographer to take still photos of the food at the same time; this way they don't have to pay you twice. What they are not taking into consideration is that the food made for television is different from the food made for print. After the food has been used for the commercial, it will need to be re-styled and refreshed because the still camera will get a lot closer and see much more detail than the video camera did.

So, if you are expected to style food for two sets, to make this job work, you'll need a second stylist or at least an assistant stylist to work with you. We've had to do this for several national clients in the last year. In addition to the two of us (Denise running the backstage kitchen and Cindie running the still photo set), there was also a third stylist on the video/commercial set. Food Fanatics hired another experienced stylist to work with us, and we had a ball. We also had two assistants with very strong production skills just cooking with Denise in the kitchen. The trick is to sell the cost of the extra stylist as a cost-saving measure. We did and it worked. We were able to shave three or four days off the entire timeline of the project.

Delectable Gourmet *Magazine*

Tempting Strawberry Shortcakes
Amazing New Recipes for the Desserts Everyone Loves!

New Issue on Stands Now!

Get Your Copy Today!

EXAMPLE OF images used for a magazine (previous spread), billboard (above), and bus wrap (facing, upper).

Also shown is the final image used on a truck wrap (facing, center) and the original photo before being finished in Photoshop (facing, lower).

it's a vertical or horizontal shot. This isn't something you need to worry about except as it defines the space you have to place your food in.

See the Delectable Gourmet photos for an example of one basic ad idea used three different ways.

Publishing and Cookbooks

It's a real treat to work on cookbooks. You get a chance to help create a beautiful book, something you can actually hold in your hands and show people. Cookbooks also give you the opportunity to diversify. Sometimes we function as the art director, prop stylist, recipe developer, and/or recipe tester. Look for opportunities to sell related culinary services to current clients.

The publisher or author will send you the recipes to be photographed. Look over the recipes as soon as you get them to see if there are any obvious problems, such as all the food is brown, or the recipe calls for pomegranates and your shoot is in May. Early communication about any such challenges will make for a smoother shoot.

For well-budgeted cookbooks, in addition to you and the photographer at the shoot, there can be an art director or designer, a prop stylist, the author or talent, and a representative from the

publishing company. If it's a "big name" cookbook and the "big name" is going to be in the shots, there will also be someone (or several people) present for hair, makeup and wardrobe. The "big name's" publicist, manager or even their shrink might also be there.

Food Product Packaging

An image used on food packaging needs to accurately represent the product it is selling. Where the product is being sold will also influence how you represent the product. Large chain stores sell enough product that their buyers can dictate what packaging they like and what they don't like. The buyer might decide whether or not side dishes can be in the background or on the same plate and if garnishes can be used, or even suggest the color of the plates they think the manufacturer should use. Your client should know all this information and be able to explain it to you. Your client wants and *needs* the buyers to like the images on their packaging as well as the product inside.

Editorial and Magazines

Editorial work traditionally meant a writer or editor producing an article for a magazine, usually including recipes, and a food stylist hired to

Some of the cookbooks we're proud to have been part of

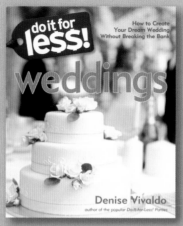

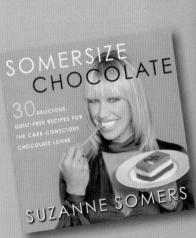

thai chicken and lemongrass soup

We love Thai food, and we never tire of this soup. Each of the dozens of restaurants in Los Angeles's Thai Town has its own variation of this delectable soup. Try it at your local Thai joint and then try to make it better at home. To bruise lemongrass, gently crush the stem with the flat of a knife to release its flavors. If you can't find fresh stalks, look for tubes of lemongrass paste in the produce department and add a bit to the soup.

prep time: 10 minutes | *cooking time:* 30 minutes | *yields:* 6 servings

Set a Dutch oven or large saucepan over medium heat and add the oil. Sauté the onions until translucent and soft, 4 to 5 minutes. Add the bamboo shoots and sauté another 2 minutes. Add the chicken broth, fish sauce, lemongrass, and ginger. Simmer 15 minutes to let the flavors meld.

Add the chicken and let simmer 3 to 4 minutes, or until just cooked through. Stir in the coconut milk and lime juice, remove the lemongrass stalks, and serve hot.

ingredients

2 tablespoons canola oil
1 medium onion, thinly sliced
½ cup sliced bamboo shoots
6 cups low-sodium chicken broth
2 tablespoons fish sauce
2 stalks lemongrass, cut in half and bruised to release flavor
1 tablespoon finely minced fresh ginger
2 skinless, boneless chicken breasts, thinly sliced
1 can light coconut milk, shaken
Juice of 1 medium lime

variations

For a spicier soup, experiment with sliced or whole Thai or serrano chiles, removing the seeds and the membranes. Add Jasmine rice for a complete meal.

soups 59

PROFESSIONAL
FOOD STYLING 101

The secret's out! Denise shows us how she does her work using some of the most popular items photographed for books, magazines, and advertisements. See how pros shape the perfect picture.

POULTRY

1 Choose a bird with a nice, full shape; preferably organic.
2 Pull flap of skin down and under bird. Secure with pins or sew shut. Using kitchen twine, secure the legs close to the body. Tuck wings under if that style is called for.
3 Spray bird with cooking oil and place on a greased baking sheet. Bake in the oven at 350°F for about 30 minutes, depending on size. Skin should start to get a tightened look. Remove bird from oven and let cool.
4 Paint chicken with Kitchen Bouquet, a bottled cooking condiment that functions as a browning agent (*available at The Landmark*). Continue until desired color is achieved.
5 Layer light coats of color on the bird rather than paint it with a single dark coat. Coating it lightly with paprika or torching it also helps.

BURGER

1 Use the fattest ground meat available. Place hamburger patties on a tray lined with wax paper and place in freezer until well-chilled but not frozen solid, about 40 minutes. Cook semi-frozen patties on a well-seasoned grill or a nonstick cooking surface. Cook until a nice brown color is reached. Use a torch to add extra color. Place on tray and adjust color with Kitchen Bouquet and water. Cover lightly with plastic wrap until ready to use. Burgers will hold for 30 to 45 minutes.
2 For the buns, spray the inside surface of buns with a fabric protector like Scotch Guard to keep them from soaking up the condiments.
3 Build a burger by placing curly leaf lettuce on a bun. Add the patty. Follow with a slice each of cheese, onion, and tomato. Cover with the "crown" or the top bun. This order may vary.
4 Condiments are added with a syringe, eye dropper, or squeeze bottle. This is usually done when the burger is in front of the camera.

THIS IS AN excellent example of an image out of your control. This burger photo shows the hamburger from the side, not the front, and the bun top needed retouching.

interpret or style photos to accompany the recipes. An example would be an article on Texas Chili, with a photo of a big bowl of red chili in the center of the page, surrounded by the raw ingredients and some spurs or rope or a cowboy hat in the background. Editorial work can be a great career builder, especially if you get a professional credit, but traditional magazine or newspaper markets are shrinking. Sometimes ads in magazines resemble editorial content; the only difference is that the word *advertisement* appears in small type across the top of the page. These ad layouts, called soft sells, are really advertising, not editorial.

Here's an example of an editorial. This article about Denise's Food Styling Class in Singapore appeared in *Yummy Magazine* in 2009.

ICE CREAM

1 In an electric mixer with the paddle attachment, beat together 1 pound powdered sugar and 1 cup shortening until smooth, about 10 minutes. Add cornstarch as needed to adjust consistency.

2 Food color should be added at the start. Always add a small amount of color then let it completely incorporate into the fake ice cream before adding more.

3 For realistic looking drips, use white toothpaste colored with food coloring.

4 For the chocolate topping, mix chocolate fudge sauce with chocolate sauce. Or keep the topping of choice chilled and spoon on at the last minute.

NOW IT'S YOUR TURN...

What can a home cook learn from a professional food stylist? Try these handy tips from Denise.

Explore fresh herbs as garnish on any food
An example: Mint leaves on ice cream will add freshness to the dessert. You can also place sprigs of fresh rosemary beside a whole roasted chicken or leaves of fresh basil atop puttanesca pasta.

Use simple plates for food presentation
Think of white as a canvas. A busy patterned plate will look messy, not pretty. That's why many of the top restaurants you visit stick to white, as it lets you appreciate the food more. The fancier the plate, the more the attention is taken away from the dish itself.

Think about contrasting colors when cooking
That beef stew needs bright orange carrots or roasted red tomatoes as a side dish. Bland-colored fried calamares can be made more visually interesting with splashes of yellow from lemon wedges on the side. Or try a drizzle of sour cream on tomato soup.

Develop different textures
Think about offering your guests a layered experience. If you're serving creamy soup, for example, garnish it with crispy croutons. Other ideas: Top a dish of ice cream with crunchy, roasted nuts; sprinkle herbs on a pool of sauce; or dust confectioners' sugar on lemon bars.

Light candles at dinner
Everything looks better in candlelight! No need to spend much on this easy upgrade. Simple candlesticks or votives will do. In fact, avoid scented candles so they don't interfere with the smell—and taste—of the food.

Internet

The Internet has become one big marketing tool. Many companies are using their websites to provide recipes and product information to generate business. Generally speaking, these are simple shots with minimal props because Internet images are displayed small. These photos need to clearly convey information about a particular recipe or product without being confusing.

Restaurant Boards, Menus and Point of Purchase

Images used on menus and restaurant boards are often also used in advertising pieces, on websites, and on Point of Purchase (POP, for use near cash registers, in store aisles, and on tabletops). When dealing with chain or franchise restaurants there are product blueprints to follow so that the images represent the actual food being sold; the food stylist must use the in-store product

provided and work with the correct portion sizes. When the shoot is at a studio, the chain will often send a Food and Beverage manager or a chef to work with the stylist in achieving the correct balance of real and styled food. When food is being shot on location at the restaurant, the stylist often styles food prepared by the restaurant kitchen. In these cases, we ask for extra cooked but unassembled elements of the food to use in styling: extra garnishes, side dishes, sauces, and extra pieces of ingredients that are visible in the finished dish.

Television

Television can be very confusing; there are so many people involved in getting a show or segment on air, most of whom have nothing to do with you. Be friendly, smile, and refer to the lists on the next few pages to see who is responsible for what. If you need something, ask. That said, don't ask stupid questions.

Each person you need to concern yourself with has his/her own role in getting a segment on the air.

Whose Job is That?

There can be as many as seven people involved in getting a food segment on television that you need to be concerned with:

- A host/network or show talent.
- A talent/guest/spokesperson.
- The talent's publicist.
- A food company representative sponsoring the segment and/or their publicist.
- A segment producer.
- A prop master/art department representative.
- A food stylist.

Sometimes the product publicist and the company representative are the same person. Sometimes the host is also the segment producer. Only on bigger, well-funded shows will you be lucky enough to have a prop master. If there is no prop master or art department, then providing the on-camera props will be your responsibility. Your client may or may not be willing to pay for props, so you need to find out all this beforehand.

And since we are on the subject of prop masters, be sure you give your card to any prop masters you come across. They are often in need of a food stylist but don't know where to find one and so end up doing the food styling themselves, which will make them appreciate your competence all the more. When they find a reliable stylist, they will remember them and use them whenever the necessity arises. We have worked with some prop masters for over fifteen years and they use us whenever they need food for a show.

Each person you need to concern yourself with has his/her own role in getting a segment on the air. It will help you to know what those roles are. There is a hierarchy—and guess what? You are at the bottom.

The job of the publicist or public relations representative:

- Initial contact with the show/producer.
- Provides producer with product information.
- Books the talent.
- Discusses segment goal with the talent.
- Gives show and host information to the talent.
- Hires food stylist.
- Discusses segment goal with food stylist.
- Gives show and host information to food stylist.
- Puts talent and food stylist in contact with each other.
- Sends product to food stylist.
- Sends product to producer or brings to show.
- Keeps talent and food stylist informed of changes.
- Provides travel arrangements for talent and, in smaller markets, may ask stylist to help with talent transportation and act as a media escort.

The job of the talent/guest/spokesperson:

- Researches company and product.
- Researches show and host.
- Suggests demo ideas to publicist.
- Writes up any recipes used in demo.

- Provides recipes to publicist and producer.
- Discusses demo with and provides recipes to food stylist.
- Discusses bumper (or tease) and timing with food stylist.
- Discusses look and theme of the segment with food stylist.
- Suggests wardrobe with publicist and producer.
- Confirms travel arrangements.
- Arrives at show early to go over prep with food stylist.
- Checks hair, makeup, wardrobe.
- Verbally goes over segment with producer and, if time allows, maybe pantomimes a rehearsal.
- Meets host, briefly goes over segment, if possible.
- Clearly and pleasantly states product messages.
- Acts natural.
- Is prepared to shorten or lengthen segment.
- Is pleasant to everyone.
- Thanks everyone.

The job of the food stylist:
- Gets budget approval.
- Researches show and host.
- Researches company and product.
- Contacts producer about set specifics.
- Contacts producer about rehearsal: is there one that will require more product?
- Contacts producer about how early the setup can start.
- Confirms with producer the availability of a pass to drive onto the lot.
- Discusses demo with talent and publicist.
- Draws a rough sketch of table/set and blocks out or organizes the prep and props in order of use so that the flow of the demo is easy and natural.
- Has publicist send product.
- Buys food and any approved props.
- Brings appropriate flowers/vase/basket of fruit/veggies to prop table.
- Brings any necessary small appliances, tabletop burner and fuel.
- Preps food prior to segment.
- Preps extra for talent to use during bumper or tease.
- Brings finished edible hero (finished and styled dish/recipe, also called the "hero").
- Brings extra copies of recipes.
- Brings any extra items or product that might be used.
- Packs everything securely.
- Gets to the set as early as possible.
- Checks in with gate security.
- Has producer's name and cell number in case gate doesn't have a drive-on pass.
- Asks where to park to unload.
- Checks in with studio security and asks where to find a cart.
- Finds out where to set up near the set.
- Introduces himself/herself to the producer and publicist, if available.
- Is nice to everyone.

- Finds out who the go-to person is on the set.
- Knows where the bathrooms, green room, and craft service are located.
- Styles table and sets up demo as soon as possible.
- Places product on table where camera can see it.
- Goes over segment with talent.
- Lets talent know if there were any substitutions or changes.
- Makes sure prep and hero looks the way the talent wants it to.
- Gets the set electrician to provide power/gas for appliances needed on set.
- Covers all food with damp paper towels to keep it fresh until segment.
- Lets talent know they have stylist's support and can ask anything.
- If there is no show support for talent, offers to brush or comb hair, check make-up and wardrobe.
- Makes sure he/she is present during run-through with guest and producer and is prepared to make changes.
- Is always ready to make last-minute changes.
- Makes sure power/gas is on, if needed.
- Heats up hero, if necessary.
- Runs through pantomime and makes sure everything is where it should be, if time.
- Provides damp and dry kitchen towels within easy reach of talent and host.
- Makes sure talent and producer know if anything is not edible.
- Removes damp paper towels from food.

- Puts hero on set.
- Turns on heat under any pans being used.
- Refreshes demo food with spray water or spray vegetable oil.
- Clears set immediately when segment is finished.
- Leaves all edible product for crew.
- Cleans up and packs out.
- Thanks everyone and passes out card or portfolio disc.

The job of the host:
- Meets talent.
- Goes over segment with talent and publicist.
- Interacts with talent and facilitates demo.
- Shows interest and asks questions.
- Keeps segment on message.
- Shows enthusiasm for product.
- Gives final product pitch and thanks talent.

The job of the producer:
- Chooses segment, recipes, ideas, on-air guests/talent.
- Coordinates segment.
- Makes sure everybody concerned knows what they need to know.
- Is the liaison between host and guest/talent.
- Is the boss, as far as the food stylist is concerned.

The job of the prop master (if there is one):
- Makes sure the set is decorated.

- Makes sure power/gas is turned on.
- Moves set tables onto set.
- Provides props.
- Moves props and tables off set.
- Makes sure the producer and host are happy.

The job of the food company representative:

- Makes sure their product is represented correctly.
- Writes the checks.
- Drinks coffee.
- Critiques everything.
- Bosses everyone around whether it's appropriate or not.

Styling a Cooking Segment for TV

One of the jobs a food stylist might be hired for is styling a cooking segment for television shows. Some of these shows are live (like morning news shows), and others are taped (most talk shows). The process is the same whether it's live or taped, but live shows don't stop for retakes unless something really awful happens.

Who hires a food stylist for a television segment?

- A publicist working for a publishing company with a book to sell, or working for a corporation with a product to sell.
- An author with a new book to sell.
- A producer or prop master with a food segment to produce.

Points to keep in mind when styling for TV:

- You're helping to sell a product. Be sure you know what that product is.
- Prep the food in accordance with the length of the segment. For a longer segment, the guest might have time to demonstrate some of the cooking or prep processes; for a short segment, everything has to be ready so that talent can just finish the recipe.
- The type of show, .i.e., news, talk, entertainment, or lifestyle, will influence the setup and personality of the segment.
- The theme of the segment or show influences your choice and colors of props, etc.
- You are to prepare what your client wants. If they ask for your ideas, you have another chance to impress them.
- Blocking out the segment is crucial.
- Never assume anything. Double- and triple-check because there is no going back.
- It's good to have a job sheet to refer to (example on page 57).
- Remember that the main reason you are there is to make the author/talent/spokesperson look good. You are their extra pair of hands. Don't bring your personality into it; it's not about you.
- Talent/guests have differing levels of comfort cooking on camera. Determine how cooking savvy your guest is and adapt to him/her. A professional chef will be very confident, but your talent might be more comfortable with simple tasks or just talking and pointing rather than actually interacting with the food.

Homeland Security and You

If you are hired to bring food to a television station early in the morning, make sure (this is very important) that the segment producer leaves your name and the name of your assistant (if you are bringing one) at the security gate for a drive-on pass. Make sure you also have the producer's name, the name of the show, and the producer's cell phone number. It looks really bad if you get stranded at the gate for the hour, resulting in the talent going on air with their food only half done. In many large cities you will not be allowed to drive onto station property without authorization. In the case of morning shows, you will be arriving before everyone else gets there.

As for flying to far-flung locations, you will need to overnight ship your kit or check it in as luggage. Be sure to remove any lighter fluid, cans of butane, and anything else stored under pressure. Since baggage compartments have air pressure that varies wildly, you will also want to remove any liquids. Arrange to pick up necessary replacements once you arrive at your location. Research what supplies you will need so that you can have your clients cover the cost.

Look in a monitor to see how much of the set is actually being seen. Adjust your props and prep so everything looks as beautiful as possible.

When providing food for television it is best to get as much information as possible, since TV people are extremely difficult to get in contact with. You might only be interacting with one person on the production—probably the producer—but maybe also with the prop department, depending upon the specific show.

For most four- to five-minute segments, there is enough time to demo one recipe. Guests/talent often think there will be time to squeeze in another demo, but there rarely is. We always bring the prep for another recipe just in case. Sometimes the talent will do all the cooking and sometimes the talent will get the host to help. If recipes are complicated, parts of it will have to be made ahead of time. We always bring the demo food in every stage of prep so the talent can decide what he or she wants to do.

Another thing to keep in mind about television is that, more often than not, there won't be any props for you to use. You will need to bring every single last thing for your prep and for the set table. Television stations will usually have the table but double-check, don't assume! Here is a sample of a job sheet we fill out when contacted for a television styling job:

FOOD FANATICS
Food Styling Job Sheet—TV Segment

Contact: Denise Vivaldo, 310-836-3520, dvivaldo@earthlink.net, www.FoodFanatics.net

CLIENT INFO

Client or company name:	Marks & Davis, California Fresh Produce
Client address:	1000 Main Street, Los Angeles, CA
Sponsor's product or book title:	Produce grown in California
Client contact:	Stephanie
Client phone/fax/email:	310-555-1212
Guest name:	Chef Windy Seabreeze
Guest phone/fax/email:	310-555-1213

LOCATION INFO

Location name and address:	Raccoon Studio on Bundy Avenue
Location parking and unloading:	Unload at entryway, park in visitor's parking
Time client/guest arriving at location:	Stephanie @ 7 a.m., Susan @ 8 a.m.
Our arrival time:	6:45 a.m.

SHOW INFO

Show and host name:	Great Morning LA, Ed Stephens
Producer/director name, phone/fax/email:	Nicky, 310-555-1214
Art dept/prop master name, phone/fax/email:	Benny, 310-555-1215
Rehearsal?	No
Bump/tease times:	8:30 a.m., 9:00 a.m.
Segment time:	9:20 a.m.
Kitchen to prep in?	No
Bring set props?	Yes, bring everything
Bring set décor?	Yes, bring everything. Bright summer colors.
Station providing:	Set table and worktable

Other items to bring: Baskets, 2 tablecloths, 2 portable burners with fuel, flowers, disposable plates and utensils in bright color. Bring disposable baking dish to leave food behind for crew.

Recipe 1 name:	Enchiladas Fresca
Demo:	Yes
Hero:	Yes
Twin:	Yes

Other instructions: Bring salsa prep and finished, enchilada sauce prep and finished, bring whole ingredients (avocados, peppers, garlic, onions, etc.) for table décor. Bring plated hero and twin finished in baking dish to pull out of on-set (fake) oven.

Recipe 2 name:	Chilaquiles
Demo:	No
Hero:	Yes
Twin:	No

Other instructions: In addition to hero, bring enough to fill a large skillet in case Chef Windy wants to plate and serve.

On the following pages we will walk you through the step-by-step process of how to plan and execute a food styling job for a demo on television. We'll refer to a real-world example from a segment Food Fanatics styled for *The Ellen Degeneres Show.*

How to Prep and Block a Food Segment for TV

THE STYLIST NEEDS TO:

STEP 1

Set up the terms of the relationship (financial arrangements) with the publicist, producer, or prop master that contacts you. In this case, we were contacted by the prop master and put in touch with the guest's publicist.

STEP 2

Discuss with the publicist what you are selling. The guest was Chef Eric Ripert of La Bernadin in New York. The point of the segment was to publicize his cooking and his restaurant. The point for the show producers was the opportunity for Ellen to be funny, which is her thing.

STEP 3

Receive the recipes and make sure they have been approved. The publicist sent the chef's recipes to the producer, the prop master, and us. We double-checked that the producer and the prop master received and approved the recipes.

STEP 4

Contact the guest and discuss what they are comfortable doing in front of the camera. As Chef Eric was on a plane, this wasn't possible, so we talked to his publicist instead.

STEP 5

Contact the producer and prop master and find out:
• What time the segment goes on air.
• What time the rehearsal is scheduled for.
• Where we prep and whether there is a work-table for us.
• If we can style the set table and move it onto the set, or whether we need to style it on set.
• What time constraints there are to setting up (i.e., do we have to set up only during commercial breaks?)
• If there is a drive-on pass waiting for us at the security gate.

STEP 6

Wait for a final go-ahead on the recipes before shopping for product. Under most circumstances, when the guest is an experienced cook, we shop for the amount to make the recipe three times: one for prep, one for a hero, and one for oopsies. For *The Ellen Degeneres Show* it was four times because the producers and guest went through a full rehearsal.

STEP 7

Prep the demo the day before. We do this by putting pre-cut and measured product in the correct amounts in small glass bowls, covering with damp paper towels (to preserve the freshness of the product where necessary) and securely wrapping with plastic wrap. We cut a little bit extra to have on hand, and always have uncut product for the talent in case he/she decides to chop anything on camera. We also make heroes of the recipes (if they will last overnight), cover and refrigerate, and make any necessary twins (a second finished and styled hero).

STEP 8

Arrive at the studio with all prepped food and any needed cooking equipment and props, then go to work. We find out where our prep area is and what table we are styling and putting the demo on for the segment. Sometimes there is a kitchen with equipment; sometimes there isn't even a microwave or sink. We then prep all last-minute stuff and set up the table for rehearsal. We add props to the table (any extra ingredients like whole fruit and veggies, or sponsor's product, flowers, etc.) and place burners, cutting boards, prep bowls with ingredients, knives and utensils on the table.

STEP 9

Have everything ready for a full rehearsal. Write down any changes.

STEP 10

Go back to the prep kitchen to make changes, then prep the set/demo table for the segment. We protect all food by spraying with oil or water and covering with damp paper towels. Place damp towels for talent's hands under the table.

STEP 11

Hurry up and wait . . . wait . . . wait . . .

STEP 12

Double-check that set table is perfect. Get ready to follow the art department when they roll the table out to the set during commercial break. Make sure burners are on, pans are hot (and anything else that is supposed to be hot is, in fact, hot), remove the damp paper towels and be sure everything looks good. Wish the talent good luck, then move off camera to watch the segment on a monitor.

STEP 13

Congratulate the talent and break down. Tell talent the segment was great and they were wonderful. Follow the art department as they move the table back to the prep area, then break down the table and throw away inedible food. Place any edible food in disposable containers (it will be eaten!) to leave behind. Pack up and drive away.

STEP 14

After you get home, verify with the producer or prop master whom to send your invoice to.

Other Food Styling Jobs

Print photography and television segments are the most common jobs, but they aren't the only ones. Here are descriptions of the other projects you might be hired to work on.

Satellite Media Tours (SMTs)

SMTs are quickly replacing traditional media tours, as they are much less expensive and have the potential for much bigger audiences. Instead of a media tour that involves weeks of expensive travel and help, an SMT takes only one day and one location. A studio with a special satellite hookup is booked, and morning shows across the country are scheduled to interview the talent live for a few minutes. They generally start with the East Coast shows at 6:00 a.m., that's 3:00 a.m. if you are on Pacific Time. They can schedule anywhere from one to three dozen interviews, with as little as a minute (or as much as forty minutes) between interviews.

SMTs can have one sponsor or several to spread the costs around. Sometimes the talent won't cook anything or touch any of the food, and your job will be to dress the set table with beautiful food and keep it looking good until the end of the day, refreshing and replacing when necessary. Or you could have Wolfgang Puck for talent and he'll want to keep cooking every minute he's on screen. In this case, you'll need to constantly have prepped food ready for him to use. When the time between interviews is under a few minutes, you'll only have time to do the bare minimum of finishing on the display.

Cooking Shows

If you are hired to run the backstage kitchen of a cooking show, you will be producing prep for demos, heroes and twins for every recipe featured. You will need to have enough demo food prepared for several takes (a "take" is every time the same action is repeated). Experienced chefs rarely need more than one take, but you'd better have two just in case. Talent with little or no culinary skill will require many takes. Your job is to have enough prep so that taping doesn't stop due to lack of food. It is also your job to have all food required for that day's show ready to go. You never want to be the cause of a delay in taping.

Your presence will be required on the set to get each segment set up. You will also be required in the backstage kitchen, prepping for upcoming segments and the next day's food. Unless you can be in two places at once, you will need at least one assistant. We suggest two: someone with strong styling and cooking skills to run the backstage kitchen and an assistant to help you on set, help in the backstage kitchen, and act as a go-between to both. More elaborate shows will require more pairs of hands. In today's market, production companies try to shoot between nine and twelve segments (three to four half-hour shows) in the space of two days.

Your job is to have enough prep food so that taping doesn't stop due to lack of food

Infomercials

Infomercials for kitchen appliances are huge productions. There are often multiple locations with limited space for prepping food. The last one we worked on we had five pairs of hands. The first days were spent on a sound stage and the last day we cooked out of a cube truck fitted with kitchen equipment, with a second prep area closer to the set.

The item that will ultimately be sold probably doesn't exist yet, so you will be working with prototypes, meaning there will be a limited number of the appliances available. This means that every time a scene has to be redone, the used appliances need to be replaced with clean ones. Make sure that this job does not fall to your people, as you will have enough to do wrangling the food. A scene can have as many as twenty takes, which is a lot of cleaning. Each time a scene needs to be redone, the food has to be redone too. We have the producers arrange for a PA (production assistant) or two to take care of the appliance cleaning.

Since infomercials require days of shooting, they also require someplace to keep all the food. If you need to, order reach-in refrigerators, freezers, speed racks and sheet pans to keep your product and prep fresh and organized. (Read more about location shooting on page 148.)

Commercials and Interstitials

More and more commercials are being shot in one day, so there isn't a need for lots of refrigeration. Unless it's a hot day, you might not need a refrigerator at all. On longer commercial shoots, budget-conscious producers will often arrange to film all the food scenes on a single day to cut costs. You'll need a very clear shot list to prepare for this. Commercials vary widely in what they require laborwise and equipmentwise. It's a good idea to bring an assistant in the event of script changes (requiring more or different food), and to help with set-up and clean-up.

Interstitials are soft-sell short commercials that don't look like commercials. For example, a car company might run an interstitial on the Food Network (FN) that shows people having a picnic out of the back of their car, thus tying together the channel's lifestyle with the product.

Feature Films

There are stylists who specialize in preparing food for the film industry. It's rare that a production can schedule a food scene with any accuracy; they are dealing with hundreds of scenes, and the schedule of everything depends upon what goes on before. If you are hired (usually by a prop master or production designer) to provide prop food for a movie element or a restaurant scene, you will need to find out if anyone is going to be eating it and, if so, if there is refrigeration to keep it safe. If the principal actors in a scene are eating food, that food will need to be edible and look pretty (check on actor's food restrictions or preferences). If extras are eating food, you can usually arrange

I've known Bonnie Belknap for decades. We started in this business about the same time, and although we handle very different kinds of jobs, we love sharing war stories!

"Working on feature films normally allows us the luxury of time to prepare and organize in advance—unlike TV, where it is standard practice to be called the day before a shoot. It's also crazy, with last-minute changes and enormous amounts of food needed for retakes.

"One of my recent projects was a major motion picture. The first scene up was "Honeymoon – Mexican Resort – Luncheon," filming at a beautiful hilltop estate in Malibu. My directions were "light lunch, upscale." Great time to try out this chef with great credentials who had been wanting to assist me. It was an impressive menu and it needed to be edible as well as beautiful. The chef was to purchase beautiful product from Santa Monica Seafood, our go-to place for anything from the ocean.

"I prepared everything else and packed all the equipment. The chef was to meet me at my studio at 5:00 a.m. I got a call at 5:15 that he was running late—and he was lost. We arranged to meet in the parking lot of a supermarket near the shoot location. My stomach sank as he got out of a taxi with grocery bags that looked as crumpled as he did. Nothing was packed on ice. The scallops were so overcooked they looked like golf balls; the shrimp was bay shrimp (how do you confuse bay shrimp with prawns?!). At least the supermarket was open. I ran in and bought the best substitutes I could. The scene went well but with no thanks to my helper. That was stress I didn't need.

"The next food scene was shot at Hummingbird Nest Ranch in Simi Valley. What each actor would eat on camera was decided on long beforehand. I had specially ordered big beautiful lobsters for some of the actors to eat. I guess they looked really good, because one of the actors decided she also wanted lobster, which meant a mad dash to every grocery store in Simi Valley looking for lobster. We finally rounded up three dozen, which we then had to kill and cook.

"The shoot for this scene went on for two long days, plus travel time, unloading, cleaning and restocking. The second day actually went until 6:00 a.m. the following morning. And then we still had hours of cleaning up and packing out.

"When the movie came out I went to see it and the luncheon scene got lots of play but the enormous two-day dinner scene was cut drastically. All that work and not a single close-up of our beautifully styled food."

SEX AND THE CITY THE MOVIE

Bonnie Belknap,
of Gourmet Proppers

a plate of food, not necessarily edible, and put a piece of edible something-or-other out of sight on the plate that they can eat. Whatever the food is, be prepared to wait around (sometimes days) doing nothing until your scene is ready to shoot. (*See* "When the Food Has to be Edible, pg. 143)

Food Special Effects

Part of prop food for television and movies is special effects food. There are people who specialize in this sort of thing, usually part of the art department. The fact that it's edible is really secondary to whatever it is that it's supposed to look like. We once made pieces of "edible" tires—out of dyed fondant with tread marks that we made by rolling over a real tire! In the movie *Splash*, someone came up with a fake lobster shell that Darryl Hannah could bite into. The often-used shot of cream and melted chocolate swirling together is also considered a special effect. The shot has little to do with food styling and more to do with the actual machine used to swirl the two liquids together. If you are very creative and have an engineering bent, you might find the challenges in designing culinary special effects right up your alley.

Street Scenes, Office Scenes and Other Light Food Scenes

These types of scenes typically have little food and are used more for atmosphere than anything else. The food is usually simple: something you can purchase, arrange and drop off—like hot dogs and pretzels for street stands, food for that office potluck lunch scene or on a simple picnic, sandwiches at a meeting, or Chinese take-out or pizza for office or home.

Typical TV

Make sure you have a clear idea what is being asked of you, since the request is often originating from the director, going through the producer, then to the prop master before finally getting to you. We had a prop master ask us for a "hippy-looking" wedding cake, three tiers but homemade. When he found out the cost of a three-tier wedding cake (they needed two identical cakes), we were able to talk him into a fourteen-inch one-layer cake, four inches high. That's actually a pretty big cake. This was for a flashback scene and was supposed to look early-1970s flower child, but not really, as the flashback was actually from 1994. Confusing? Oh, yes, but this is clearer than much of our information. Our instructions were to "have two cakes for us and I'll call you the night before we need them. Deliver them to the set of *The Cleaner* before 7:00 a.m." This doesn't leave time to do much, so we ordered two cakes from a great local bakery, had them minimally decorated, and put them in our (thankfully empty) fridge. When the call came on Thursday early evening to deliver the cakes on Friday, we picked up fresh flowers and met at our kitchen at 5:30 a.m. to decorate the top with "hippy-looking" flowers. By 7:00 a.m. we were dropping off our beautiful cakes. Here's where it gets typically television: we get a call on Monday saying "the cakes were beautiful! They didn't get to the shot so we ate them. Can you bring us two more on this Friday?"

> The camera usually won't linger on anything, so you can concentrate on the look rather than what the food actually is.

Home Scenes

The prop master can usually handle a cup of coffee and a bowl of cereal, but what if the scene requires a family dinner? You'll want to find out how many takes they are planning for and how many people will be in the scene. A scene that has ten people sitting around a dinner table that needs six takes equals sixty servings of food. You will also be providing hero platters of the food for the table. If the scene has an actor cutting into a roasted chicken, you will need six roasted chickens if the prop master tells you to bring enough food for the scene to be shot six times.

Grand Displays

A grand display is usually a buffet set on a table or series of tables. Find out from the prop master what the food is being displayed on: it could involve six curved eight-foot tables or three small occasional tables or anything in between. The serving platters are usually much bigger than you'd think, so you'll need lots of food to fill them. Most of the food will not have to be edible and no one will be touching it. Find out from the prop master if anything is going to be touched so you can supply extra to replace any ruined food. If cost is an issue, and it usually is, suggest that the edible items be crackers, cookies, raw veggies, or small fruits like grapes and strawberries. These items stay looking good and will remain edible all day long.

Displays are more about the overall impression than about single items. The camera usually won't linger on anything, so you can concentrate on the look rather than what the food actually

is. Go for color, like displays of fruit, breads, and vegetables. Stay away from greens that will wilt, fruit that will turn brown, or anything so unusual that it isn't immediately identifiable.

Weird and Ugly Food

Every once in awhile you will be asked to make something . . . well, odd. These are some of our favorite jobs. When we were styling the food for our favorite prop master for the television series *Related,* we were often asked for strange food, as one of the regular characters was an enthusiastic but very bad cook. We did a really sad Thanksgiving dinner with lopsided, burned and ugly food. We made gnocchi that looked like a scrotum (because the producers asked for it, not just because we wanted to). We made Jell-O molds that looked like toxic waste and pancakes that were Dali-esque. For the series *Method & Red* we made sushi that closely resembled genitalia, both male and female, and were surprised it made it past the censors. (Again, not our idea. Our minds go to some pretty strange places, but they never would have gone there without a request from a producer.) You can't make this stuff up!

As you can see, every food styling job is different. Some food stylists decide to specialize in certain areas. Many food stylists won't take live television jobs, working only with still photography. Many won't take movie work. Some won't work with ice cream. Only you can decide if a particular job is worth your time, effort and expertise. In the next chapter we address what it means to work as a food stylist.

Be prepared. We get serious here.

STARTING A FOOD STYLING BUSINESS

As creative as food styling can be, it is, first and foremost, a business. I have supported myself for twenty-five years as a chef, caterer, and food stylist. It hasn't always been easy, but it sure has been fun. Making money as a stylist has been the hardest. Why? Because it takes years to establish a client base large enough to make a living at this. The idea behind this chapter is to get you to ask yourself a lot of questions, for us to give you some answers, and for you to have the business information that will enable you to decided whether food styling is a good career fit for you.

I've known many talented food stylists in the United States over the last twenty-five years; some made it and some didn't. The common denominator wasn't a lack of talent; it was usually a lack of cash flow, or in simple terms, making enough money to sustain a career and grow a food styling business. If you can't support yourself by running your own business, you will be forced to take a nine-to-five job. There's no shame in that, but if you have the desire to be your own boss (it can be fun and rewarding) you do have to prepare yourself and plan for it. Keep reading.

The Most Common Mistakes New Food Stylists Make

- Not seeking and receiving professional help. (Join professional organizations for culinary professionals, small businesses, and local businesses. Take advantage of Small Business Administration www.sba.gov)
- Not assisting and learning from an established stylist. (Volunteer to work for free so you can have a few days on a real shoot.)
- Not studying your craft. (Learn as much about food and food science as you can.)
- Not estimating your budgets and costs accurately. (Learn your costs, figure gas and mileage, and decide on an hourly rate. Keep up with current prices.)
- Starting out with debt or accumulating it. (Don't purchase equipment on credit. Use marketing methods that take more elbow-grease than cash. Have a steady source of income or savings to pay your living expenses for six months.)
- Not setting up a bookkeeping system for billing and accounts receivable. (Keep track of every expense and income in a simple accounting program.)
- Not keeping adequate financial records. (Every penny going out needs to be entered into your accounting program. If this amount of bookkeeping is beyond you, then the services of a professional bookkeeper or accountant become a necessary expense.)
- Not projecting a confident and professional public image. (Your clients should feel relieved by your presence, not like they made a mistake hiring you.)
- Under-pricing your services in the hopes of getting more. (Undercutting prices compromises your integrity as well as the food styling community as a whole. People who dangle the promise of future work in exchange for significantly reduced rates will not call you for more work. Please trust us on this one.)
- Not staying current on food trends and photography. (Don't let your style get dated. Know what's hot and what's not.)

Make a Business Plan

A business plan is the document that helps you to express your plans for your business, both immediate and long-term. It is a great way to gather all your thoughts and ideas about what you expect and organize them in one place; in other words, to get your ducks in a row.

You won't create a business plan in a couple of days. I suggested to my UCLA culinary students that they write a business plan, which caused lots of grumbling and groaning. The point was, "You can't afford *not* to ask yourself these questions and make a plan!" How do you achieve what you want if you don't write down clear goals?

If you are thinking about making food styling a career, go to the library, look up food styling, and find any information that might be of value to you. Do you know how much the average food stylist makes in a year? Do you know how much money you need to make in a year? Have you researched classes or who the working food stylists are in your area? Go to the library or get on the Internet and spend some time doing the necessary research.

Writing a business plan is the single best way to clarify your vision for your business. You will be able to measure your success against it, and it is an important tool in helping you to make decisions.

Questions to Ask Yourself about Starting Your Own Business

Do You Need a Business License?

Depending on where you live, you may or may not need a business license. In Los Angeles (where

Be a partner in your client's success.

we live), the moment you become a vendor to another business (this will happen if a client pays you through their business or with a business check rather than with a personal check), your name will pop up on a business list and the city or cities involved will track you down and request your business license. Why? Because this is how cities in California make their revenue.

We know of several food stylists who live in cities and states outside of California that do not require them to have a business license. When I first started out, my business license only cost $100 for one year. Now, it's over $3,000 yearly. The fee is based on a percentage of yearly gross sales. For $30 my accountant takes care of the paperwork and I just sign the check. The cost of your business license is a yearly business tax deduction, as are almost all accounting fees.

If you choose to operate your office (you are going to need an office) out of your home, you should find out if you can legally operate *any* business office out of your home. Home offices are regulated under the zoning laws in your area. As an example, in Los Angeles, we can have a home office as long as it doesn't create any extra foot traffic or parking problems. You can inquire about a business license from your city clerk's office. Even if your city doesn't require it, you may want to get one anyway, because without a business license you might not be able to get product liability insurance. Oh, yes, styled food gets eaten on TV sets and movies, and your client might insist on you having product liability insurance and prove it with a certificate of insurance.

We also recommend applying for a DBA (Doing Business As). This protects your personal name for the future should you experience any difficulties with your business. Hope for the best and prepare for the worst!

Your accountant can advise you about a Federal Tax ID number if you want to open a business bank account. Which brings us to:

How Do I Keep Track of My Money?

Again, this is about running a business. Do you want to just operate out of your personal checking account and use your social security number as identification? We think that's fine if you're the only person using that checking account. But if you are married or living with a partner who has access to your checking account, we recommend a separate business account. It's clearer and cleaner. And when it's time to pay taxes, you have your business checking account and credit card statements as a record of your business income and expenses.

I hate accounting but learned if I do a little bit every day and keep accurate records in my accounting software, I am aware of each penny I have and every penny I spend. Slowly but surely I learned to manage my money better. My husband gave me the gift of bookkeeping when he bought me a Microsoft Money program, installed it on my computer, and said, "Use this, my sweetheart. Make our lives easier." My bookkeeper does almost all of my accounting in ten hours a month. Advantage: I use much less of my time and energy. I highly recommend hiring a bookkeeper or an accountant to keep your finances in order if you are unable or unwilling to do it yourself.

Bookkeeping is simple math. Know how much you spend and how much you make on every single job. Your day rate as a food stylist and as an assistant is going to vary from job to job. You are going to have to learn to negotiate with clients—it's part of cutting the deal. With that said, your profit or bottom line will vary from job to job.

Why Do I Need Insurance?

You need insurance to protect yourself, your clients, and your future. Should something unforeseen happen (someone eats the food and gets sick, your assistant trips over something and breaks her ankle, you get hurt and can't work for a time), insurance protects you and your assets.

Food product liability insurance is sometimes offered through membership in organizations like the United States Personal Chef Association (USPCA.com). We've found that the closest thing to running a food styling business is running a personal chef business. They are very similar, as it's one person providing a service and being paid for completing that service.

Because food styling is still a small business community, many insurance companies will have no idea how to handle your needs. Plan for confusion and be ready to explain to a busy agent exactly what it is you do. Here's an overview of a small business insurance package so you'll know what to ask for and what to discuss. Larger companies, like State Farm, have begun to offer customized packages designated for small home businesses. You might find their website informative: www.statefarm.com.

Types of Coverage

Property Insurance: Beyond just your homeowner's or rental property insurance, make sure your insurance agent is aware of your office equipment and any other equipment that you use for your business. Is your home office equipment covered? Is your styling kit covered? Here is a thought to kick around: it takes years to get a styling kit together (ours, by the way, fills the entire trunk of our cars). Their values could be between $4,000 and $5,000. The thought of having to replace our knives, tool kits, spatulas, tweezers, heat gun, and thousands of paintbrushes, to name only some of the items, makes us break out in a sweat! It takes many jobs to build a complete kit. You never stop building it, really. What would happen to *your* business (income) if your laptop or your kit were stolen while you ran to the market? It could take months or even a year to financially recover without insurance.

Personal Liability Umbrella: What happens if you damage something that belongs to your client? Will this policy stretch to cover product liability? What if something you prepare makes a client or the client's talent sick? What if they have to visit a doctor or an emergency room? Obviously a photography studio, a production company, or producers will have insurance, but when the dust settles their insurance company will be looking for your insurance company to reimburse if they decide the problem was your food. Yep, insurance policies are like playing musical chairs: don't want to get caught without one when the music stops.

It's easier to control the styled food at a still photo shoot. But often, when you are working on a TV segment or sitcom, the food will sit out under hot lights for hours. When the scene starts moving again, the director will want the talent to taste something. Is that food still safe to taste? Was your budget big enough for you to have brought extra food? Did you have a refrigerator? Or has the extra food been sitting offstage, next to a heater?

Loss of Income/Disability Income: What happens if you get hurt and can't work? How do you pay your bills? Working in kitchens or at a photography studio, on a busy set, or at an outside location can be much more treacherous than working at a desk. You need to look into disability insurance as a small business owner. Having supported myself in this career, I have always purchased private disability insurance. I had to know that if I got sick or hurt I would still be able to make my condo payment and feed my cat. I slept better at night.

What Kinds of Written Agreements Do I Need to Make?

A written contract for a client may seem unnecessary, but writing down details will nip most misunderstandings in the bud, since most arguments arise out of miscommunication. You don't have to call it a contract or an agreement if you don't want to, but you should create some sort of written "deal" memo or a very complete email with all the facts clearly written out.

The deal memo needs to clearly state:
- What services you are providing.
- What props or equipment you will need.
- A description of the location where you'll be working.
- Who is responsible for providing what.
- How much time is involved for shopping and transportation.
- How you get petty cash.
- Your deposit or cancellation policies.

Give the client an estimated total of how much this shoot, segment, or satellite media tour is going to cost. You need to establish your policies and rules now. Later is to late.

An experienced client will ask about a cancellation policy. Nothing is worse for a food stylist than to hold a date for a client for two weeks, then have the client call the night before and tell you the shoot is cancelled. Without cancellation being discussed at the time of booking, you will have no recourse. Not to mention perhaps having turned away another client, loosing the opportunity of that income.

Another potentially sticky cancellation situation is the cost of the supplies you've already purchased. What if you already shopped for props or groceries? Hopefully you got petty cash up front. If not, who owns those groceries now and what happens to them? We are very aware of how every change our client makes (before, during, and after the project) affects us. Every change costs our time, which translates into our money. How do you guard against such a loss? Get a deposit for every job you can. Our deposits run 50 percent of the estimated total we've given them, and we get all our estimated petty cash up front.

Getting the most information from your clients before arriving at any set or studio will make your job easier and the whole day go more smoothly, with as few "uh oh" moments as possible. After nailing down all this information, you

Contact: Denise Vivaldo, 310-836-3520, dvivaldo@earthlink.net, www.FoodFanatics.net
Client Info:
Client / Company Name:
Client Address:
Client's Product:
Description of Product:
Client Contact Name:
Client Contact Phone/Fax/Email:
Photographer Info:
Photographer Name:
Photographer Phone/Fax/Email:
Studio/Location Address:
Location Parking and Unloading:
Call Time: Time you are told to arrive for a job.
Styling/Fee/Rate: Based on a 10-hour day. Lunch is included in print work, not included in television, commercial, and info-mercial work. Your lunch hour in television will be deducted from the ten hours. Meaning you most likely will be at the studio for 11 hours. If you have shopped for a one-day job the morning of a shoot, shopping time is deducted from the 10 hours, meaning your day started when you started shopping.
Overtime Pay: 1.5 hourly rate after 10 hours, double time rate after 12 hours
(To arrive at an hourly rate, divide your day rate by 10 hours.)
Number of Shots Anticipated:
Shopping and Prep Time Needed:
Assistants Needed:
Assistant Rates:
Image Use: Are the images for packaging, website, tear sheets, cookbook or all of the above?

LIST OF SHOTS:
Shot 1: Plate of fettuccini with client's sauce on top.
Garnish/Background: Fresh herb garnish, glasses wine in background.
Context: Single serving on dinner plate, second plate out of focus behind.
Instructions: Prepare day of shoot, client bringing sauce.

Shot 2: Slice of 2-layer birthday cake with client's sprinkles on top. White cake with pink and white frosting.
Garnish/Background: Prop stylist bringing party stuff for background.
Context: Close-up of cake slice on party table.
Instructions: Buy cake already made in bakery with only crumb coat of frosting. Frost and decorate on shoot day. If you have to, order un-frosted cake layers from bakery and pick up the day before.

Shot 3: Plate of chocolate chip cookies with milk.
Garnish/Background: No garnish, lunch box in background (prop stylist).
Context: On corner of kitchen table or kitchen counter.
Instructions: Buy large home-made looking cookies, extra chocolate chips, use cream for milk.

Shot 4: Platter of client's baby back ribs in barbecue sauce.
Garnish/Background: Stack of red and white checked napkins. No garnish.
Context: On picnic table, ribs on wood platter or cutting board.
Instructions: Client bringing pre-cooked ribs, heat at shoot. Bring extra sauce.

Shot 5: Client's stuffed and pre-cooked chicken breast.
Garnish/Background: Herb garnish, bread or rolls in background.
Context: One breast thickly sliced on dinner plate with veggie and/or starch.
Instructions: Client bringing chicken breast. Buy green beans, rice pilaf, broccoli, small red potatoes.

FOOD FANATICS FOOD STYLING JOB SHEET

will be able to determine if one or more assistants are necessary and if a day of prep is needed beforehand.

Everything you have to plan for on a project translates into a cost or charge to your client. Sometimes we charge for a day of prep and the prep is simply renting a van, calling assistants, finding that special cake, making a trip to the florist, and going to the mall for a certain color tablecloth. Sometimes that day is making shopping lists, shopping, and cooking everything we possibly can.

You need to write down every detail and keep track of your time. It will impress your clients. When we spell out for our clients all it takes to make a successful shoot, they realize it's not as easy as we make it look.

Take a look at the sample client worksheet for a photo shoot on the facing page. Not only does it keep track of everything you need to remember, but it also gives you a script for selling your services and closing deals.

When you've had several conversations with a prospective client, write the information you've gathered in the appropriate spaces on the job sheet. Each time you speak to the client or the photographer you can fill something in. The more information you have, the better the service you will provide. By demonstrating your business skills to your client from the very beginning, you are inspiring trust in your professionalism.

Keeping track of every communication you have with clients will help you to manage your schedule and stay on track. Notes from conversations, copies of emails, anything that has to do with your client should all go into a client folder. We put one together for every single job or shoot. It's not unusual for us to have five or six shoots in a week. That's a lot of shopping and details to keep track of.

Pre-production meetings, deal details, questions, and phone calls are all devices to avoid problems. Here's our favorite kind of surprise: all of a sudden the client is asking for "steam" on their bowl of soup, but we don't have a microwave or a clothes steamer (the two ways we generally make steam). We immediately go back to our pre-production notes to see if steam was brought up, then mention to the client that this had not been discussed. Now the real question is: Can we provide steam with what we have or not? Is it even a good idea? Clients will often ask for steam for print work out of the blue, without thinking it through.

In print, steam can fog up the camera lens, making a blur on the image. Steam is visually effective in video or films where the camera can capture the motion. Also, steam must be shot against a black or very dark background to be seen. We've found that when the client starts asking for things that were never discussed beforehand, instead of getting defensive or nervous or saying no (which just annoys them), it's better to meet their question head-on and tell them exactly what it will take to solve it. When they find out that the solution will cost lots of money or slow down the production, they often let the issue go. Sometimes they still want to try it. But they will appreciate you trying to solve their problem.

Hiring Assistants

We've mentioned the hiring of assistants a few times already. It's an important issue that can make the difference between getting a job done on time and going into costly overtime. No client likes paying overtime. But clients will present you with a shot list that is enough work for two days instead of one, or just plain unrealistic. When this happens, educate them about how long each shot will take. Count up the time and put it in your 10-hour day. When this happens we suggest hiring an assistant. A lead stylist is going to get much more done with an assistant than working alone.

Look at it this way (and you can explain this to the client): two hours of your overtime will probably cover the cost of an assistant.

When digital photography became the norm in food photography, clients started pushing to get more images done in a day than was previously possible with film. We now get twice as many images done per day as in previous years. In order to work at the speed we need to shoot at, we find it necessary to bring an assistant to nearly every shoot. The cost of the assistant is billable to the client. Having an assistant can make everything on the shoot run more smoothly and the cost of the assistant being fairly low compared to the rest of the shoot expenses makes it an easy sell.

Having an assistant to work with you, when you have a busy day or week, not only saves you time and energy but can make the difference between enjoying your shoots and feeling like you've been hit by a truck. You have to protect yourself in order to continue on.

Assistants often shop the day before the shoot, help prep the food, run to the store when plans change, keep work areas clean, and protect the product to keep it fresh until ready to shoot. The assistant is there to assist the lead stylist. A good assistant is worth her or his weight in gold. Nothing is nicer for the lead stylist than to be on the last shot of the day, walk back to the kitchen, and find all the dishes done, the counters wiped, and extra groceries bagged to drop off at the food bank.

Most of the assistants we use come from our food styling classes or our internship program. Assistants we hire are independent contractors. They may work two days a month or ten days a month, according to how busy we are or how long the project is. They need to provide their own tools or small kit, have their own business license, be responsible for their own taxes (we send them a 1099 at the end of year), and accurately invoice us for their services.

Working as an assistant to a food stylist will give you the opportunity to see if this is a career choice that works for you. We've had assistants work with us who were amazed to find out that it's just as hard being a food stylist as it is working in a restaurant. We've had assistants who couldn't get beyond the fact that no one cared what the food tasted like. We've had assistants who came in with no professional culinary knowledge and amazed us with their knack for the job. We've had recent culinary school graduates that must have been sleeping during class. You can never tell where good assistants are going to come from.

Having a descriptive business plan is an important part of organizing not only your new business, but also your thoughts, hopes, and dreams. Answering the questions below will get you thinking about all aspects of your business, some of which you may not yet be aware of, as well as keeping you motivated. A business plan will make you consider the long-term success in this business. Answer these questions, flush out the sections, and you will have a great start on a business plan.

Below is a standard business plan structure. I have included something similar to it in every culinary business book I have written. I hope the reader will use it!

Step 1: The Summary Statement

Your company name.

Your primary location.

As Los Angeles–based food stylists, we work mostly in Southern California but often travel nationally and even internationally. If the client will pay for plane tickets, hotels, a per diem and meals, we're there.

Who you are and what your credentials are.

Insert your bio here. If you don't have a bio, start by answering these questions:

What is your background: are you a chef, a home economist, an artist?

What makes you think you can do this job?

What makes you different or interesting, or what sets you apart from other food stylists working in your area?

Think about the primary market you want to target, without limiting yourself to that market.

Step 2: Type of Ownership

Typically a food stylist business is a sole proprietorship. Other types of businesses include limited liability corporations (LLC), but these are not generally used for food stylist services, and corporations (Inc.). The type of business you decide to have also depends on what assets you have. If you've got nothing, you've got nothing to protect. If you own property and don't want to lose it in a possible product liability lawsuit, you should speak to your accountant and attorney and ask them, "How should I hold the title or structure my business?"

I ran my business successfully for years as a sole proprietorship. As it and my assets grew, my accountant and attorney advised me to incorporate. It was easy. I called a company that offers incorporation services, and voila, I was incorporated. The cost was minimal. We have had students who did the paperwork themselves. Being a corporation makes your bookkeeping slightly more complicated. My advice is to befriend a good accountant. Many clients prefer paying us as a corporation so they don't have to put us or our assistants through a payroll service. That saves them time and energy and all of us a lot of bookkeeping. Whether as a sole proprietor or corporate president, you are the owner, your own boss, the lead stylist, marketing department, bookkeeper, dishwasher, and ambassador of goodwill. You will learn to juggle all these different hats and (hopefully) enjoy them.

Will a sole proprietorship work for you? Or will you need to incorporate?

Step 3: Defining Your Services and Your Competition

Define your boundaries as a food stylist: how much (or how little) do you want to work?

How many food stylists are currently working in your area?

Can your community support another food stylist?

What niche are they filling?

We know several food stylists who work television but not print. They target their marketing efforts solely to TV shows. We are experienced and comfortable in every sector of food styling, so we market to all different markets. This was my plan from the start—to diversify and work as much as possible.

List the other food stylists and what they specialize in:

How do you differentiate yourself from them?

How can you compete with them?

Is there a niche in your location that no one specializes in?

Get all the information you can about your competition. This is where assisting other stylists can be important. You will learn first hand what happens at a shoot, how stylists react, and how important client relationships are.

Are there production companies or a production agency in your area that offer food styling services that may have an edge on you?

Or could you introduce yourself to them and find out if there is a way to market your services through them?

Are you planning on being a food stylist only, or increasing your income stream with teaching gigs or food writing as well?

Who do you plan to target as your clientele?

Consider authors, television and movie producers, local product photographers. Without totally limiting yourself to a single clientele, have an idea who you are going after so you know how to market yourself and your business. Tap into your entire network for potential clients. An example: say you are a supervising nurse who has worked for fifteen years at a local hospital and you want to make a change. There might be two hundred people you've been working with on a regular basis. Make a flyer stating your new intentions and pass them out; cut down your nursing hours to keep your benefits, and start your food styling business. Your fellow coworkers already know and trust you. Out of two hundred people, some of them know people working in the food industry, or writing books, or working in television. Ask for their help and contacts. Make a name for yourself in your community by developing relationships that get you noticed. Go out and meet and greet people who can use your services as a food stylist. Increase your exposure so people begin to know who you are and what you do. In the food world, referrals are critical and have to be nurtured. There are quite a few stylists married to prop masters or photographers. How convenient! In the words of a very smart friend of mine, "nepotism never hurt nobody."

Step 4: Organizing and Supporting Yourself

Many new stylists are surprised by the physicality of this work. You will need to decide how many days out of the week you are physically able to work on a shoot (usually 10 to 12 hours) then balance that with how much you need to make to support yourself.

How many 10+ hour days can you realistically work in a week?

If you work alone, never take more jobs than you can handle. Stay organized and focused by developing an operating plan based on a day-by-day, week-by-week, or month-by-month schedule that shows you when jobs start and end. This makes for more efficient scheduling and may protect you against burnout. If you have styling dates five days a week, what day do you take care of your accounting and office work? If the money is good enough for you to be able to support yourself, retain the clients that you style for on a regular basis and on whom you can count for regular work. Only say yes to the people and jobs you know you can take on. Clients that understand your policies, payment schedule, fees, and services are clients that won't waste your valuable time.

How will you pay your bills if work is slow?

Always have a backup plan. It's best to start every business with at least six months of expenses in the bank. With that said, I didn't have more than a wish and a prayer when I started my first business, but I did learn the valuable art of getting deposits. And you will, too.

Who can you hire to help or assist you on big jobs?

In the event that you have more work than you can handle and you need to hire someone to help you shop, prep, or style, make sure you inform the client of your help's credentials and culinary history, and why you are using him/her for that occasion. If it gets to the point where you have to choose between canceling a job and paying for a helper out of your own pocket, then find a helper. Never flake out on a client at the last minute when they may not be able to find someone else to replace you. Don't lose someone who could become a regular client. Try to establish a reciprocal relationship with another food stylist in your area. If you have joined any of the organizations we have suggested (see Appendix D, page 257), you might find a business friend in a chat room or discussion forum. We all have a wealth of information to share, and sharing strengthens everyone's business.

Step 5: Describing Your Culinary Skills and Experience

List where you have worked and the experience received that relates in any way to food styling.

In your personal bio, emphasize your special talents and include an updated resume. Your bio and resume should include people and companies you've cooked and styled for and your years of experience in the culinary field, including any work experience that will impress. It need not be only food styling or culinary experience. For instance, experience in the business industry (which illustrates to potential clients that you not only know how to style food but also have business savvy and know

> Writing a business plan will enable you to measure your success—an important tool in decision making.

how to run your own business), and anything else you think might help your chances of gaining a client. Experience in design, photography, television, ad agencies, packaging, or marketing are all industries with relevant experiences.

Step 6: Developing Your Marketing Plan

It's crucial that you let people know about your business. You can't just sit back and expect them to find you.

Once you've created a name and business for yourself, work toward referrals and word of mouth based on your good reputation to do the advertising for you. (For tips on how to get word of mouth going, see page 109.) Not only are referrals free but they are also the most effective selling tools that a food stylist can use. Remember that bad word of mouth travels ten times faster than good, so run your business wisely and ethically.

Who do you know that you can you give business cards to?

Begin advertising by giving friends and relatives your business cards to hand out. Unlike some other businesses, you might not organically run into people who could hire you directly; however, they may know someone who could.

Who else can you give business cards to?

Start speaking about your work with the people you already have a relationship with, and remember that asking them to keep you in mind is not annoying to them. Most people want to help you out.

Who can you put on your postcard mailing list?

When you start making enough money to advertise, make a postcard that showcases your latest work and mail it out to your leads. We do this every few months. Postcards are a great way to stay in touch with existing clients, solicit new clients, and sell our services. Postcards require the cheapest postage and, if you provide a recipe or helpful hints on the card, busy people might want to keep it—all the better. A beautifully styled picture on the postcard speaks volumes.

What other services can you offer?

When marketing, include what kind of services you offer. Although you are targeting food styling clients, if you also moonlight as a personal chef or cooking instructor, mention those as well. You never know what people will need.

Step 7: Creating and Maintaining a Portfolio

A portfolio of beautiful food that you have styled is the strongest marketing tool you can have. The easiest way to display your portfolio is on a website. Much of your experience can become information for your site. Unless you want to design it yourself, there will be costs associated with setting it up and keeping it current. The Web is the fastest and easiest way to grow any business. Document your jobs in photos and writing and share selected tips to help establish your expertise.

Think of your website as a letter to a friend who you want to fill in on all your good news. Keep reading: in the next chapter are suggestions and ideas about developing a website for your business, which, honestly, is a must-have in today's market.

Are you able to create a website yourself?

Do you know anyone who can help you create a website?

Step 8: Crunching the Numbers for Profit

Being realistic about costs and expenses is your only chance of long-term success in any business. Start simply. You have to know how much money it takes for you to live each month. With computers, accounting software, and good advice from a friendly accountant, budgets and finances are easy to create and understand.

Do you have good accounting practices?

Is your checkbook balanced and accurate?

Your business accounts have to be. Don't let these business questions scare you; it's way harder to style a perfect photo than it is to balance a budget. The easiest place to start is a personal income and expense statement.

How much is your monthly income? List all sources:

What are your monthly expenses? List all:

How much do you owe on loan balances or debts?

How much are your monthly loan or debt payments?

Can you figure out a way to work part-time at your old job and still start your new business?

What benefits do you loose if you quit your job?

Can you afford to start a new business?

Does anyone else depend upon your income besides you?

If you have a partner or family, they need to express their feelings about you starting a new business. You owe it to them. Open communications will help solve problems.

For books on writing business plans see Appendix C, page 255.

Starting any business takes planning, research, and thought. The questions we've asked you in this chapter were intended to inform and prevent your being blindsided by the many aspects of running your own food styling business. Starting and running your own business can be one of life's great journeys, and we think it's important to enjoy the ride.

> When you start making enough money to advertise, make a postcard that shows your latest work and mail it out to your leads.

BUILDING A STYLING KIT

Food stylists build their own kits according to their specific work requirements, their personality, and the tools they are most comfortable with. Every stylist's kit is different, and typically food stylists are curious about the tools other food stylists use. We have an assistant who seems to have everything in the trunk of her car so she can run out and get it whenever we need it. In this chapter we'll tell you what kit items you need to get started, what stuff you'll need to buy yourself, and what to ask your clients to pay for.

A Food Stylist's Basic Kit

Everything you buy, whether starting as a food styling assistant or eventually working on your own, will become a business or tax deduction. You'll want to start keeping every receipt and enter it into an accounting system for your business. This may seem daunting at first, but if you can balance your checkbook or even have basic computer skills, you will be fine. In the chapter "All About Money," we give you some information, tips and forms for accurate accounting.

There are some items that every stylist should have. We include an annotated list on the following page.

BASIC ITEMS THAT EVERY FOOD STYLIST SHOULD HAVE IN THEIR KIT

- **Apron.**
- **Angostura Bitters**—an orange-brown coloring agent for food or beverages.
- **Bamboo skewers**—to move small pieces of food onto and off of a plate or adjust food once on the plate. Skewers can also be used to hold different foods together (example: for matzo ball soup, after false-bottoming a bowl of soup with something like shortening, you can push the matzo balls onto the skewers and then push the other ends into the false bottom to give the soup a more even and natural look so all the balls of matzo aren't floating or sunk at the bottom).
- **Can opener.**
- **Cookie cutters**—round, in various sizes.
- **Cosmetic sponges**, wedge-shaped—use as a wedge to help angle and adjust pieces of food for the camera. Dipped in a little Windex, vodka or rubbing alcohol, they can also be used to clean the rims of plates.
- **Cotton balls**—same use as above and as non-collapsing stuffing for foods like omelets.
- **Disposable lighter** with adjustable flame, or a barbecue lighter.
- **Exacto Knife** or matte knife—used to cut a multitude of things (example: cutting Styrofoam plates to support layers of pancakes to keep them from drooping).
- **Forks, table and meat.**
- **Fruit Fresh anti-browning powder**—edible white powder that dissolves in water. Dip cut fruit and vegetables into the solution to prevent browning. Also use for reviving wilted greens and herbs.
- **Garnish tools.**
- **Gloves**, tight-fitting latex—for cutting hot chiles or handling stinky food.
- **Glycerin**—use straight or add to water for making long-lasting water droplets (example: controlling the exact placement of water droplets without them moving or disappearing).
- **Graters**—every size you can find. The smaller the better.
- **Kitchen Bouquet.**
- **Kitchen towels, cloth**—buy lint-free bartender's towels, or use old cloth diapers.
- **Knives**—paring, bread slicer, meat carver, and chef's knife are the basics.
- **Ladles**—in a variety of sizes.
- **Matches.**
- **Metal skewers**—heated on a stove and used to create grill marks on different items such as steaks, grilled fillets of fish, chicken breasts, grilled vegetables, etc.
- **Museum Wax, Quake Hold putty or florist clay**—to hold items very securely in place (example: a scene in a commercial where a waiter has to balance a plate of food on a serving tray while it is tipping back and forth. The wax will prevent the food from sliding and can also hold the plate itself to the tray). Museum Wax is our preferred material and we use it on every shoot.
- **Needle and thread**—white, beige, brown and black thread to stitch up tears in meat or poultry before cooking.
- **Piping gel**, clear—can be used as a lightweight food glue or thickener for sauces. You can add Kitchen Bouquet to color it and patch holes and tears in meats.
- **Ruler or tape measure.**
- **Sharpening or diamond steel** for knives.
- **Spoons,** assorted sizes and materials.
- **Squeeze bottles**—for placement of larger amounts of sauces and liquids.
- **Tape**—transparent, gaffer's, electrician's (in various colors), duct, and painter's.
- **Timer,** standard kitchen.
- **Thermometer,** instant-read and oven.
- **Tongs**—in a variety of sizes. We prefer the ones with the heat-resistant rubber covering on the tips so as not to damage the food.
- **Turkey baster**—used to extract or add liquid to a dish, keeping the mess to a minimum.
- **Vaseline**—for gluing food together. Can be colored with Kitchen Bouquet or bits of food to create a food spackle.
- **Vodka**—an excellent cleaner of surfaces, it also slows down the browning of avocados.
- **Whisks**— in a variety of sizes.
- **Windex**—don't leave home without it.

Remember to keep all liquids in resealable plastic bags. One of the food stylist's rules of thumb is that if it can leak or spill, it will.

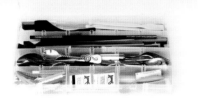

BUTANE TORCH

Adjustable, with extra fuel—to quickly cook the surface of meats or give a melted or charred look (example: to control the melting of the marshmallows and chocolate in s'mores).

BOWLS

In different sizes. We like collapsible rubber bowls, as they are superlight and take up the least amount of space.

PLASTIC TOOL ORGANIZERS

Hold the smaller pieces of our kits. These fit right inside our Husky kits, making it easy to find what we're looking for.

STRAIGHT PINS AND T-PINS

To secure things together, like the layers of a spiral-cut ham, or wayward pasta, or lettuce on a sandwich.

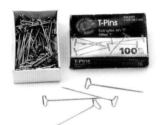

COTTON SWABS

Dip in Windex, vodka or rubbing alcohol to clean small messes.

CHARCOAL STARTER

For creating grill marks.

BRUSHES

Pastry and small paint— to touch up a color or to add shine using Pam or oil on specific areas of a food (example: brushing small amounts of Pam onto the chocolate chips of a chocolate chip cookie to make it look slightly shiny and melted).

FIRST-AID KIT
Antibiotic cream, Band-Aids, aspirin, for obvious reasons.

FOOD COLORING
The standard grocery store brand or gel colors used for cake decorating.

PALETTE KNIVES OR SPREADERS
Straight and offset in various sizes—for spreading sandwich fillings or frosting evenly.

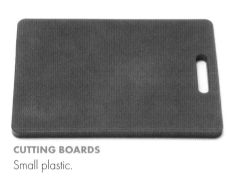

CUTTING BOARDS
Small plastic.

PAPRIKA
Used as a coloring aid to give meats and poultry a browned and roasted look. Paprika can be sprinkled on straight or mixed with water, oil and Kitchen Bouquet, then dabbed onto food.

KITCHEN BOUQUET
A gravy browning sauce we use to color all kinds of foods and liquids. Gravy Master is another brand.

ICE CREAM SCOOPS
Every size you can find, including the 1-ounce portion scoop for scooping butter.

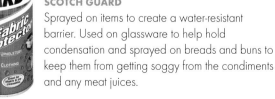

SCOTCH GUARD
Sprayed on items to create a water-resistant barrier. Used on glassware to help hold condensation and sprayed on breads and buns to keep them from getting soggy from the condiments and any meat juices.

MEASURING CUPS AND SPOONS
We like the collapsible rubber measuring cups because they're lightweight and take up a minimum amount of space.

HEAT GUN
Or electric paint stripper—for melting foods on the set or giving foods a quick heat-up.

PAM ORGANIC CANOLA OIL
Cooking spray—to add shine and moistness to almost everything. This brand goes on clear with no air bubbles. The industrial-size Pam that can be purchased at restaurant supply stores is not the same formulation. Other types of Pam and other brands foam when sprayed and are not suitable for photography.

PEELERS FOR VEGETABLES
We carry a couple with smooth blades and one with a serrated julienne blade that makes quick work of julienning firm vegetables like cucumbers and carrots.

PASTRY BAGS AND TIPS

POST-ITS
To label everything you've prepped, cooked and styled. This is the best way to keep organized at shoots that last more than one day (or have more than one pair of hands working in the kitchen). You'll need to tape any Post-Its that will be refrigerated so they don't fall off.

SHARPIE MARKERS AND HIGHLIGHTERS
various colors.

TWEEZER,
In various shapes
and sizes—better to
use than your fingers!

XANTHAN GUM
A super-strength thickening
powder.

GRILL PAN
For making or starting
grill marks without an
actual grill.

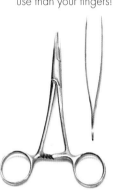

TOOTHPICKS
Used to move stuff around and
to keep food in place.

TWINE
Brown jute and white kitchen.

KARO SYRUP
Light (found in the
baking section) and
dark—thickening,
thinning, and glossing
agent for a variety of
foods (use in place
of maple syrup). Also
makes red meats
appear moist.

ZESTER, CHANNEL KNIFE AND MELON BALLERS
To make garnishes.

RUBBING ALCOHOL
Cleans smudges, fat and grease. A soft paintbrush dipped in rubbing alcohol will clean frosting off of cake.

STRAINERS
Assorted sizes and meshes.

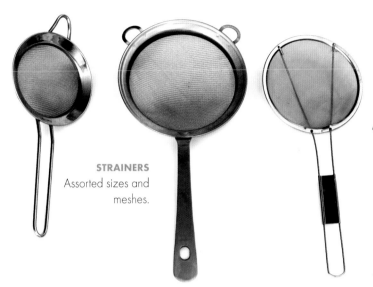

SPRAY BOTTLES
Large and small—for water, vodka, and your coloring sprays. We find the mister bottles of Evian to be great for making a very fine mist of water.

SYRINGES
Medical applicators and eyedroppers— for the exact placement of small to very small amounts of sauces and liquids. Or for controlled drip shots.

SPATULAS
Metal and heat-resistant rubber, every size you can find.

SCISSORS
Every size you can find.

POLIGRIP DENTURE CREAM
An excellent food glue. Can be colored with Kitchen Bouquet or bits of food to create a food spackle.

For convenience, we keep everything in the trunks of our cars, leaving the back seats for packing groceries and props.

Even a basic kit takes up quite a bit of room. We've tried all different ways of transporting our kits over the years. Our new favorite is the Husky electrician's tool bag. It comes in a variety of sizes and has lots of pockets and compartments to hold everything. The important thing to remember when choosing your tool bag or box is that you should be able to easily lift it. The reason we don't recommend the large hard plastic toolbox with wheels is it gets too heavy to pick up. And you will always have to pick it up. Loading and unloading your car will teach you this.

Set Tray and Table for the Lead Stylist

When you get to a set, one of the first things you'll do is assemble a set tray from the equipment in your kit. This saves you walking back and forth from the set to the kitchen or prep area when working with the photographer. A small plastic tray works well to hold everything (inexpensive and readily available at restaurant supply stores). To keep items from sliding around on the tray, line the tray with adhesive-backed cork shelf liner.

Always check with the photographer or producer or whoever hired you to make sure they will have a table or two for you to work on near the set. This is in addition to any prep tables in the kitchen area. I can't start to tell you what a long day it is when nobody has rented or provided the food stylist with a table.

Your set tray should include:

Bamboo skewers
Brushes, small
Coloring spray
Cosmetic sponges, wedge-shaped
Cotton balls
Evian mister
Eyedropper or medical applicator
Kitchen Bouquet
Knife, paring
Pam Organic Canola Oil cooking spray
Paper towels, separated and stacked
Poligrip denture cream
Scissors, small
Spoon, small
Squeeze bottle
Swabs
Towels, lint-free (old cloth diapers work great)
Toothpicks
T-pins
Tweezers

Vaseline

Water in a spray bottle

Windex

Good Things to Have in the Trunk of Your Car

Along with the items to bring with you on every shoot are items that you won't necessarily need every shoot but are good to carry in the trunk of your car or to throw in if you suspect you may need them. We work in dozens of different studios in Los Angeles; some have complete, fully equipped kitchens with prop rooms; other studios can barely scare up a table for us to use.

- Baking sheets—we like the half-size, heavy-duty aluminum available from restaurant supply stores. Usually under $5 apiece, they last forever, won't buckle in the oven, and have 1-inch sides that make them useful for holding prep.
- Blender or food processor—small size. We use a Magic Bullet because it is compact.
- Cake decorating turntable or stand—to raise hero plates up near eye level and make it easier to see all sides. The higher level allows you to stand straighter, thus saving your back.
- Cooler—especially useful if shopping the night before or if you think refrigeration will be scarce.
- Cutting boards—large plastic.
- Electric griddle/grill—griddle for making pancakes or evenly heating oil for eggs, grill for large amounts of grill-marking.
- Extension cord.
- Hamburger press or form—for size consistency, although a 4-inch round cutter will also do.
- Immersion blender, small.
- Mandolin—to slice large amounts of food quickly and evenly.
- Measuring cups—large for liquids, 1-, 2- and 4-cup capacity.
- Mixer—electric handheld with blade and whisk attachment.
- Plastic trays, cafeteria-style—to organize smaller tools and prep for each recipe.
- Portable butane burner and fuel.
- Saucepans, large and small.
- Skillet—large and small nonstick, including a nonstick omelet pan. We usually buy a new inexpensive one each shoot, when eggs or omelets are a critical part of the shoot.
- Spider—mesh ladle for fishing out deep-fried foods.
- Stainless steel bowls—a set of lightweight nesting bowls doesn't take up much room.
- Stockpot—lightweight aluminum.
- Sturdy 4- or 6-foot folding table—Costco carries tables that fold in half and will fit in most car trunks.
- Foam core—very light, thick and rigid cardboard with Styrofoam in between for propping things up, to cut as a template, and to use as spacers for food.
- Florist's wire—can be cut with scissors and is available in pre-cut lengths at craft supply stores.
- Cleaners for copper, silver, stainless steel.
- Lighter fluid—for flames.
- Shortening—for false-bottoming cereal, soup, or salad bowls.
- Sprays, matte and clear—to seal surfaces. Photographers usually have dulling spray.

There are pieces of equipment with combination uses, like the Braun handheld immersion blender that comes with a whisk attachment and a small chopping bowl attachment. These can take the place of several pieces of heavier equipment and they take up less space in your car. We like the Magic Bullet's combination uses: it's a chopper and

a blender, is small and powerful, and has two sizes of work bowls. It also has one of the most successful infomercials ever done—and we styled it.

An Assistant's Starter Kit

Although the lead stylist always has his or her tool kit on every job, when you are working as an assistant it's good to have a tool kit of your own. You may be working in a different area, making it inconvenient to share equipment. On big shoots, there may be several prep or shooting areas. Here are the essentials:

- Apron, clean
- Cotton balls and swabs
- Cutting board, 8- or 10-inch
- Food coloring
- Kitchen Bouquet
- Knives, sharp
- Metal and wooden skewers
- Pam Organic Canola Oil cooking spray
- Pens, ballpoint
- Post-Its
- Rubbing alcohol
- Scissors
- Sharpies
- Spray bottles
- Squeeze bottles
- Tape
- Toothpicks
- Tweezers
- Twine
- Vaseline or Poligrip

As projects and your client list grow, you will find that you can purchase many pieces of equipment on your client's dime. For example, say a cookbook author needs four or five dozen cupcakes for a television appearance. You only have one cupcake tin and so can only bake a dozen cupcakes at a time. It will take you 3 to 4 hours just for the baking. If you buy additional cupcake tins, then you can bake three tins at a time and get them baked in less than an hour. That's 2 to 3 hours less of your time. Which costs more? Three hours of your time or three cupcake tins? The client pays for the pans but saves money on your time and labor for the baking. When the segment is done you can offer the pans to the client, but in twenty-five years of styling no one has ever asked for the purchased equipment back. All of this equipment becomes part of your kit. Later on you can use your complete, extensive kit as a bargaining chip with frugal clients and tight budgets or rent it to other stylists.

Buying New vs. Used Equipment

You can get good deals on items like pots and pans, grill pans, baking sheets, portable burners, and hand mixers. Restaurant-quality cookware

is available at restaurant supply stores, auctions, out-of-business sales (check newspaper listings), and online.

Good-quality cookware for the general consumer can be purchased new at department store sales or at online discounters like Overstock.com or Half.com. If you are a member of a culinary organization like Women Chefs and Restaurateurs or International Association of Culinary Professionals, you can get a 15 to 30 percent discount from cookware and appliance manufacturers when you shop online and use your member number.

eBay is also a good place to find new or lightly used cookware and appliances (pay attention to the ratings and use them as a guide to choosing trustworthy sellers), as are weekly papers devoted to classifieds like Recycler.com (also online). Craigslist.org is an increasingly good place to find used items for sale.

There is nothing wrong with purchasing used pots and pans as long as their condition is good. That being said, we would not advise buying used non-stick pans, as they become less effective with age and most people do not care for them properly.

Specialty Equipment

There will be equipment you'll need on some jobs that you should be able to get your hands on at short notice. Some items you'll already have in your home; others will need to be rented:

- Blender.
- Clothes steamer, professional—can be used to add moisture to food that should look moist, as well as add steam to any dish that needs it for the shot (e.g., steamed vegetables).
- Convection oven, portable.
- Electric cook-top, single or double burners.
- Electric griddle, small (about 12 x 18-inch).
- Food processor, family-size.
- Freezer.
- Stand mixer with whisk and paddle attachment and 2 bowls.
- Microwave oven.
- Propane griddle, large size (for pancakes, eggs, etc.). Approximate size of the industrial griddle and grill are 36 inches high x 48 inches wide x 24 inches deep.
- Propane grill, large size (for meat, fish, poultry, etc.).
- Refrigerator, standard household or commercial reach-in.
- Sink with water heater—specifically for outdoor or remote locations without sinks/running water.
- Speed racks and sheet pans—for organizing, storage, shelving or transporting to or removing food from set.
- Stools—for those few moments you may get to sit down and rest your feet.
- Tables, folding with risers—risers bring the tables up to a better height to prep at, saving you an aching back.
- Toaster oven.
- Toaster—restaurant style works the best.
- Water tanks (and tanks for collecting dirty water, if necessary)—for outdoors or remote locations without sinks/running water.

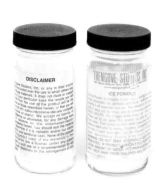

Specialty Tools

You can find all kinds of interesting tools if you know where to look. Medical and dental supply stores carry great items for the food stylist, like medicine applicators (great for exact placement of sauces, condiments, and other liquids), disposable scalpels, and tweezers in a variety of shapes and sizes, scissors in a variety of shapes and sizes, and dental picks. Craft stores, scientific supply stores, and hardware stores all carry items we can't do without. (See page 256, Appendix D for more information on resources.

Special-Effect Supplies

There are certain jobs that require specialty tools and supplies not available at your corner drug store. For these items, see www.TrengoveStudios. com in the resource list at the end of this book.

Some of these really neat, harder-to-find items are:

- Acrylic and glass ice cubes.
- Aqua Frost—will make the outside of anything look frosty cold.
- Aqua Gel—a sticky clear substance that can be mixed with water and sprayed on glasses or applied by the droplet with a toothpick to make very realistic condensation.
- Crystal Ice—mixes with water to make a rubbery mixture that looks exactly like crushed ice

but won't melt or break down.
- Ice Powder—makes a slushy, icy mixture that can be mixed with liquids for granitas and frozen drinks.

Most of these special-effect supplies can be ordered and shipped overnight. Do check out the site and become familiar with their selection and costs. If we order any of these products for a drink shoot or if one of the Trengove products has been requested by the client, we put the receipt for the item in our petty cash. The client pays for these specialty items.

Disposables and Cleaners On Your Client's Dime

These items are on the shopping list for every shoot we're hired for. These are supplies that each client should pay for. Buy them when you buy their groceries. When you are working regularly in any photographer's studio, it's only good manners and good business to purchase extra paper towels or replace any products you use.

- Aluminum foil
- Dish soap
- Dishwashing gloves
- Garbage can liners, large
- Paper plates
- Paper towels
- Plastic cups, small

- Plastic wrap
- Parchment paper
- Post-Its
- Scotch tape
- Scrubbing sponges
- Sharpie markers
- Vegetable or canola oil
- Ziploc bags, various sizes
- Knives

I bought my first good knives when I went to the California Culinary Academy in San Francisco. I still use them to this day. Don't be afraid to make the investment in good knives. A well-designed knife becomes an extension of your hand, gliding through food as if it were butter. A sharp knife is safer than a dull knife, as it will slip less. When cutting with a dull knife, you are putting extra pressure on your hand and elbow, which can cause "chef's"—or what is often called "tennis"—"elbow." If, at the end of a day, your arm and elbow bother you, you should get your knives sharpened and possibly improve your knife skills. It is never to late to take a course in knife skills at a local cooking school.

In the basic kit list, we suggest starting with four knives: the chef's knife, the paring knife, the serrated bread slicer, and the meat slicer. A good chef's knife or santoku will be your most-used knife. An 8-inch chef's knife is the most common but you might find that a longer or shorter knife will be more comfortable for you. Visit a store with a wide selection of good-quality knives and ask to handle them. Choose a chef's knife that feels comfortable and balanced in your hand.

A good serrated bread slicer, a meat carver and a paring knife will round out your knife set, at least initially. We love our knives and often have many more than we need (much like shoes). A cheese-slicing knife (a serrated knife with parts of the blade cut out and a curved tip) is a good one to have on hand, as are a boning knife (long and thinner than a chef's knife, with a somewhat flexible blade) and a pair of kitchen shears. Another handy knife is a utility knife. The utility knife is between 4-1/2 inches and 5-1/2 inches and is shaped like a small chef's knife.

We have found that ceramic knives break or crack when dropped, making them unsatisfactory for carrying from shoot to shoot; but they are wonderful to use in the kitchen. This is why we suggest you purchase high-carbon stain-resistant steel knives for your styling kit (although Cindie swears ceramic knives cut bread better than even serrated knives do).

We carry a couple of cheap (under $5) paring knives with us. They can be kept very sharp with a steel, and it doesn't break our hearts if we leave them behind. Every time you work on a set, you will have somebody run up to you and ask to borrow a knife. In the hustle and bustle to get packed up at the end of the shoot, the borrowed knife is often forgotten. These inexpensive paring knives are just the thing to lend out. Never give anyone your good knives!

As a student, I had all my knives engraved with my initials, and I still do. At the end of a busy shoot, this makes picking mine out of the pile easy. Cindie has marked all her kit equipment with her name in magic marker, and that works also.

A steel to keep your knife honed is also essential, as are knife guards to keep you from cutting yourself and to keep the edges from getting dull. You should also find a good place to have your knives sharpened once or twice a year. If there isn't anything listed under "knife sharpening" in the yellow pages, ask a butcher where he takes his knives for sharpening.

There are many excellent brands of knives. Try out a few and see what you like the best, then keep an eye out for sales. Department stores often have good sales on knives. Among the brands we really like are J.A. Henckels, Wusthof, Global, Shun, Furi and Analon.

Note about knives:
Carbon steel knives are the best at holding an edge, but they stain. Most knives now are high-carbon stain-resistant steel, which is an alloy.

Building a Temporary Prep Kitchen

Some production studios for television and film will have most or all of the kitchen equipment you'll need. If it's a photography studio, make sure you ask whether they have a kitchen. A kitchen for the food stylist is never guaranteed, and we do know how stupid that sounds. If the shoot location doesn't have what you need, you'll be expected to bring it yourself, borrow it or rent it. It is the food stylist's job to tell the people hiring her/him in advance what you'll need and about what it costs. I put all this information in my deal memo. This is the start of your *budget*. We will talk about budgets again. I mention this now so you can get used to this most important word.

In Los Angeles, we call Rick Enterprises (www. RickEnterprises.com), a television and film rental company in North Hollywood, when we need specialty or large equipment. Depending on where the shoot location is—private home, a sound stage, a small studio—there may not be anything existing or even close to a prep kitchen for you to work in.

On a sound stage, for example, the art department will build a "set kitchen," but the "set" is not usually practical. That means it doesn't work or isn't practical. Clever, huh? You'll find out that the sink on the set is not hooked up to water, and the oven can't be plugged in because the grip cut off the cord to fit it in the space. The job of the set is to look beautiful. As the food stylist, you'll need a prep kitchen, an area separate and temporary for the stylists to cook, hold, and store their food. Oftentimes, if there is no room in

There are a lot of hazards with cooking. Always rent several portable fire extinguishers.

the studio or private home for us, we are cooking under a portable tent in a parking lot or backyard. There are a lot of hazards with cooking. Always rent several portable fire extinguishers.

In other parts of the country, where you don't have a place like Rick Enterprises, call a party rental company. They will have portable sinks, stoves, tables, rolling racks, garbage cans, everything you will need for a temporary prep kitchen. This is the same equipment used for private events or caterings. Drivers from the rental company will deliver equipment, set it up, and come back and break it down for pick-up.

At most rental places, they can also outfit a cube truck with stoves, a freezer, a refrigerator, and a sink with water tanks inside. A crew electrician plugs the truck into the power source. If the location is out in the wild, at the seashore, or anyplace else where there isn't available power, the crew electrician will bring a generator. A rental cube truck, tent, or any temporary prep kitchen is usually arranged for shooting commercials, infomercials, films or cooking shows. This is a huge cost to the production; renting the equipment for a temporary kitchen isn't cheap, but it makes the food styling possible. The client or production company is responsible for the cost of renting all equipment. You may place the order, but the rental company must be aware that they are to invoice the production company, not you. We are talking about thousands of dollars; you do not want to outlay that kind of cash when it could take weeks or even months to get reimbursed.

We repeat: always ask whether there is a kitchen for any shoot. You'll be amazed to find out how many productions or producers never think about having a kitchen for us to work in until we ask. We've gone to restaurants for magazine shoots where we had to work in the dining room because we weren't allowed in the kitchen due to insurance issues. It's not that much fun to cook without a kitchen, but you'll be amazed how you get used to it!

Why You Can't Drive a Mini-Cooper

As you can see, you will be hauling loads of equipment and supplies with you on every job. You will also be carting a huge amount of groceries. If you are thinking of purchasing a new or used car, you will want to keep this in mind. Sedans are the most inefficient type of car to haul things in. Some jobs may necessitate renting a cargo van, which should be part of your client's budget, but most of the time a car with generous trunk space, a hatchback, or an SUV with cargo room are your best bets. Trucks with a locking shell will also work.

Building a complete styling kit is a long process, but you don't need to have a huge kit when you're starting out. Much like catering or personal cheffing, it's best to make do for as long as you can until you really need to buy something. If you can, assist an experienced stylist to see what they have in their kit, and to experience the different demands of different jobs. This will help you to understand how every job requires different tools and a different skill set.

MARKETING YOUR FOOD STYLING BUSINESS

When someone needs to hire a food stylist, they will usually ask a photographer for a referral or search for a stylist on the Internet. Often they will do both. We've found that many photographers are searching the Internet for food stylists as they try to expand their networks, businesses or portfolios. Knowing this, you'll want to concentrate most of your marketing energy on your Web presence. Then start a database of people who may have a reason to hire you. Research food people in your area, in the next state, and nationwide. This list should include:

- Food and beverage company owners large and small, their marketing directors, creative directors, art directors, and/or public relations departments.
- Restaurant owners and managers.
- Kitchen product company owners and/or marketing directors.
- Department store public relations departments.
- Producers of any and all local television news and talk shows.
- Owners of production studios.
- Publishers and editors of books, catalogs, local magazines and newspapers, and direct mail advertising.

- Chamber of commerce public relations directors.
- Billboard companies.
- Tradeshow graphics companies.
- Tradeshow public relations and marketing directors.
- Public relations and marketing companies.
- Cooking schools.
- County and regional fair directors of marketing and public relations.
- Freelance graphic designers.

Always search for new markets for your services. No matter whether business is abundant or slow, create continuous marketing and constant promotion for your business. Marketing doesn't always have to be expensive or difficult.

In marketing your food styling business, you are marketing yourself. Remember that you are always your most effective marketing tool. What experiences make you different from other food stylists in your area? What is unique about your background? If you invest the time to learn effective marketing techniques, you'll find that marketing your business becomes second nature. Here's a sample of the ways we market our services at Food Fanatics:

- We use direct methods to keep our name in front of our clients or potential clients by publishing a short monthly email newsletter using Constant Contact (www.constantcontact.com), containing recipes, photos and articles about neat and cool things we've been up to.
- We offer recipes and entertaining ideas to magazines and newspapers, both printed and online. We often supply photos to go with the ideas. Sometimes we get paid, but more often we loan the editors the photos and information to use free of charge. We've done their work for them; of course they like us!
- If you supply a recipe or photo to an editor, you do so with the understanding that you will be given a written credit, appearing with or after the article or photograph, exposing your name to more than a million readers. We create, hire, and pay for artwork for our own books, so we own the rights to these images. Also, anytime we have an extra 15 minutes and a little leftover product, we make a pretty plate and ask our photographer to take a photo of it. We hang onto these images so we have our own photos to choose from when we get calls from editors. Then it takes just an hour or two of our time to write and test the recipe to go with it. Having our recipe read and our name seen by thousands is a long-term investment in marketing. Most photographers love seeing their name credited, but always ask them first.
- If you have been hired to style an image for a photograph, you have no rights to use that image other than as a portfolio or self-promotional piece. To use recipes or photos belonging to a client, you must first get their permission and give them credit (i.e., "Recipe courtesy of Mariel Hemingway"). Most of our clients are more than happy to have their recipes credited. Make sure photographers are always credited. Sometimes the photographer actually owns the image, so check with him/her before offering the use of any images.
- We speak at schools, culinary organizations, charity organizations, chamber of commerce meetings, and private women's clubs. Anywhere we can pass out business cards and talk about our services.
- We sell cooking and entertaining classes to local cooking schools.
- We sell our own food styling workshops: www.

CulinaryEntrepreneurship.com.

- A few times a year we send out postcards that we have printed inexpensively online, featuring a catchy or beautiful photo to drive people to our website. We can print small amounts to target specific types of businesses.
- We update our website regularly.
- We post stories, photos, video, and recipes on our blog, www.FoodFanaticsUnwashed.com.
- We advertise on various online sites: IACP (International Association of Culinary Professionals), WCR (Women Chefs and Restauranteurs); anywhere there is a listing of photographers, especially food photographers.
- We belong to various culinary associations and make use of their member directories to target our marketing and networking. Depending on what project or service we are broadcasting, sometimes we pick and choose from membership lists or purchase an entire group's directory (often available on pre-printed address stickers) and mail.
- We have also paid other food organizations (an example is the San Francisco Professional Food Society; we aren't members but like to keep in touch with them) for their mailing lists so we can send out mass email blasts to their membership a few times a year.
- We donate gift certificates to our classes to charitable organizations and other businesses to use in their auctions or promotional pieces.

Keep in mind that step one in marketing is about putting your name in front of as many potential clients as possible. Step two is turning potential clients into paying customers. The key to a successful sale is having the belief in yourself that you are providing a service to a client that benefits both of you.

Building a Portfolio

The first rule of a portfolio is to never include an image that needs explanation. Every image should stand on its own. Send your portfolio for review to people that can hire you.

Be prepared to accept negative comments. You have to be able to grow from criticism. If you can't handle criticism now, your career will be one long fight after another. That gets old; trust us. Listen to experts in the field and learn how to put your best foot forward.

Invest in a digital camera and take pictures of everything you style. Evaluate your styling. You need to teach yourself how the camera's eye views food. For help and advice on cameras and lighting, read food bloggers' websites, such as www.MattBites.com. We admire both of these photographers and their sites. If you have good photographic or design skills, use your best photos to create your own website. Eventually, you'll want to arrange your photos as a slideshow on a CD to send out to potential clients. Your portfolio offers proof that you can style food for photography. Make sure to include photos of food that are similar to the work you are going after. As an example, if you hope to sell your services to a local sandwich shop, include images of sandwiches. It seems like a no-brainer but this is something that is often overlooked. The sandwich shop owner may love your photos of wild mushroom risotto, but what does that have to do with him? Give potential clients something relevant to look at.

Contact photographers early in their career (search nearby art schools), or established photographers looking to expand into food photography, and ask about shooting test photos together for use in your portfolios. Include quotes from satisfied clients, articles that feature you or your work, or any kind of positive response you have received. See page 35 (chapter 1, Test Shots) for information on arranging test shots.

Targeting Potential Clients and Competition

You will need to define the boundaries of your target area, as it may encompass neighboring cities or even other states. To find potential clients, you will need information on the local demographics of the areas you are targeting. Most chamber of commerce websites have free demographic information available. Join your local chamber of commerce and go to the breakfast meetings, pass out cards and make contacts.

To research your competition, do an Internet search and see who the food stylists are in your area. Will you be the only one or are there already several? What type of work do they do? Look at their websites or work and see how their style differs from yours. Is there something you can offer by way of experience that is unique? Are you a trained chef who can also offer recipe development? Do you have any photographic, design, packaging or marketing experience? Use anything you can to get talking to potential clients.

After you've done some research in your town, you might find out there is little or no work for a food stylist. This means traveling to a busier area. Cities like New York, Chicago, San Francisco, and Los Angeles support many food stylists but, as an example, two hours away from L.A. in San Diego there are only a couple of stylists.

How do we know that? Because we constantly get calls to work in San Diego. Large food companies, photographers, and local authors find us on the Internet and pay for us to travel to San Diego to shoot because they like what they see on our site and feel comfortable with our experience. Several stylist friends of ours live in Philadelphia and commute to New York on a weekly basis to create enough work to support themselves. Remember, the client pays for all of the stylist's travel accommodations and expenses. Once you are established, you'll find your clients will bring you to cities where many great stylists are working, but they'd rather have you!

Your Public Image

The first thing people will see will be your name or logo. Design these carefully, as this is the first chance you have to catch a potential client's interest.

Your Business Name

You can just use your own name as your business name; most food stylists do. But if you hope to expand or sell your business one day, you might want to consider a business name.

If you decide to go with a company name, here are a few things to keep in mind:

- *Make the name simple to pronounce and easy to spell.* If it's long or complicated, or in another language, people won't chance repeating it out of fear of sounding foolish.
- *Avoid names that sound silly, flaky or too cute* as they can be interpreted as unprofessional.

As with all aspects of your business, it is important that you convey professionalism as in attire and attitude.

- *Choose a name that isn't too similar to another business of the same type.* Having a name too similar can cause confusion and create legal issues.
- *Check to see if the same domain name is available for your website.*
- *Avoid using words that have alternate meanings.* As an example, if you are located in Los Angeles or New York and you use the word "productions" in your name, many people will assume you are a television, film, or event producer of some sort.

In most states, fictitious or assumed business names like Food Fanatics need to be registered by filing a fictitious-name statement, referred to as a DBA (Doing Business As). You'll need to do a business name search to make sure there aren't any other businesses with the same name and then publish a statement in a general circulation newspaper that says you are intending to do business under that name. This information is then submitted to your local County Recorder's office. There are many businesses online that will happily do this for you for a fee.

Filing a DBA does not protect your use of that name worldwide. For that extensive protection, you will need to register your name as a trademark. Speak to an intellectual property attorney for additional information.

After filing a DBA you will be able to open a bank account in your company name.

Your Logo

You don't have to have a logo, but doing so helps to establish a professional image. If you can't design one yourself, try contacting your local art or design school about hiring a student. Having a student work with you to bring your logo to life will also give them the opportunity to showcase their talents. Collect literature with logos printed on them and study the ones you like the most. What do they have in common? Are they colorful? Are they simple? What attracts you to them? The more information you give a designer, the more quickly you will get the logo you desire.

Logos should be simple enough to grab people's attention and give them an idea about what type of service you offer. A logo with a chef's hat might give the impression that you are a personal chef, whereas one that pictures a paintbrush and a heat gun might give the impression that you renovate houses. Your logo in combination with your company name should make it clear to anyone what is it that you do.

Dressing the Part

As with all aspects of your business, it is important that you convey professionalism. Wearing proper clothing helps with this and is safer. (Sandals in the kitchen? We've seen it!) Clothing with your business name and logo printed on it becomes a great source of advertising.

Chef Jackets and T-Shirts

While they will make you instantly recognizable as a culinary professional, we find that traditional chef jackets actually make our clients uncomfortable and in some cases defensive. This is never good. We reserve wearing chef jackets to teaching classes and other appearances. We have lovely, no-wrinkle

Marketing Food Fanatics

Food Fanatics was the name of my catering company in the 1980s. The name was clearly established and, besides, I liked it. When I stopped catering full time and knew I could support myself by food styling and writing celebrity cookbooks and my own cookbooks, I added the tagline "Media Food Styling by Classically Trained Chefs" to all marketing materials.

Printed on the back of our business cards is "If you are a food show, or food segment producer, food photographer, prop master or art director, or a cookbook author or publisher, and you need food stylists, prop food, or prep staff, Food Fanatics is here to help!" We then go on to say, "What we do: Food styling for photography * Food styling for TV and movies * Segment blocking for cooking demos and TV shows * Prop food for TV shows, infomercials, and movies * Write entertaining and catering books * Develop, test and edit recipes * Teach classes and give food demonstrations." Make it easy for the new or existing client to know exactly what you do.

chef jackets with our company name and our first names printed on them for special occasions.

We have T-shirts with Food Fanatics printed on them that we wear to shoots and on locations. We give a T-shirt to everyone that assists us. In a crew of 50 people, none of whom know each other, anyone can find the styling team in our matching T-shirts. You can wear whatever you like as long as you appear neat and clean and are comfortable in what you are wearing.

Chef Pants

Chef pants are designed to be loose in fit and are made of substantial material to allow for air movement, which makes them cooler; plus, if you spill hot liquid on yourself, you can pull the material away from your skin to prevent burns. Try spilling boiling water down your leg when you are wearing jeans and you will see how just how much they don't protect you! Patterned chef pants hide stains very well, and you *are* going to get dirty styling. We always wear chef pants while working. And we have had prop masters tell us, their producers requested those fun girls "wearing those wacky chef pants." Any distinction to a client is good.

Aprons

We also wear aprons printed with our company name. Whether it's a full bib apron or a waist apron with lots of pockets, we need them to avoid getting our clothes grubby and smelly. We order an extra twenty aprons when having them made, and we send them as holiday gifts to favorite clients.

Shoes

Chef clogs offer support and slip-resistant soles and are the traditional choice, but not everyone can wear them. Others prefer leather athletic shoes or even lightweight hiking boots—whatever works best for you. But there are three things to remember:

- They need to be slip resistant.
- They need to offer sufficient support so that you can wear them all day on cement floors and not come away with aching feet.
- They need to be cleanable. Fabric and suede shoes will absorb spills and odors and get grungy very quickly.

Designing Promotional Pieces

By this time you've established your business name and logo. You've got your clientele targeted. It's time to start promoting your business and services.

Remember to be consistent with your designs. You want your materials to look like they all came from your company, not from six different companies. This is called "branding." Make everything you send out to be instantly recognizable as yours.

All your promotional pieces should drive people to your website, where they can find more information about your services.

Business Cards

Your business card might be the only promotional piece a potential client sees, so make the most of it: print on both sides! Use the back to describe what you do, any special skills or knowledge you want to advertise, or maybe include a short bio with your credentials. Make your contact information, including your website address, easy to see.

You can find online printers that charge very reasonable rates for color business cards printed on both sides. Companies like Overnight Prints (www.overnightprints.com) will even walk you through designing a simple card.

Business Card Alternatives

An alternative leave-behind that has proven most successful, even among non-smokers, is a matchbook with your information printed on it. Anything that someone is apt to hang onto rather than throw out will work: refrigerator magnets, pens, tote bags, sports bottles, hand sanitizers, Band-aids (so appropriate!), or even aprons, hats or T-shirts. Our T-shirts have become very popular!

Always make your website address obvious on any promo products. Even on the back of our T-shirts we print www.foodfanatics.net.

Postcards

A postcard with a stunning image on one side and your contact info on the other is a cost-effective marketing tool. There's more room for information than on your business card and they are relatively inexpensive to print and mail.

A postcard can double as a recipe card. If the photo on the front is appetizing and the recipe on the back looks easy, then recipients will most likely hang onto it. Anything you can send that has perceived value works: like our tips for working green: we tell everybody that we recycle every bit of waste that we can, that we use our own shopping bags for every trip to the store, that we travel and commute together to economize on gas. We also have all kinds of tips for re-purposing things like tin cans and paper towel rolls. Sometimes we send questions and answers on fun food trivia, or great food moments in history . . . use your imagination!

Brochures

A brochure isn't a necessary advertising piece for a food styling business; having a business card, a postcard, and a portfolio disc that drives people to your website is more than enough to get started with. But if you have your heart set on a brochure, create one that can fit inside a standard business envelope; this makes it convenient and inexpensive for you to mail out. Include your name, address, phone number, logo, and a description of your services, skills, and knowledge, as well as some quotes from satisfied customers and past clients. Specialty paper manufacturers sell brochure paper pre-printed with color and designs that can be created right on your computer using a template. If you are a savvy computer user, you can use one of many overnight printing companies, such as Overnight Prints, that will print double-sided 4 x 6- or 8.5 x 11.5-inch postcards from your design and UPS them to you for very reasonable rates.

Getting Good Press

Conduct a publicity stunt, like organizing the world's largest stack of pancakes, to collect money for a local charity or promote their pancake breakfast. Look for upcoming events to contribute your talents to. Don't be shy: inform local media so they can cover the story.

Write a press release of special or interesting things that you think the public would like to know about you or your services and snail mail or email it to food magazines, past clients, potential clients, and other media sources that can publicize you.

When mailing out anything to the press, always include a promotional kit that gives more information to those who might be writing about you or interviewing you. If emailing the information, include a brief biography of yourself and your business. We have up-to-date bios and company information in PDF format that is handy to send, plus downloadable pieces on our website.

Putting Together a Promotional Kit

Promotional kits are handy for two reasons: they can help you land new clients, and you can use them as press kits to gain free publicity for your services from food editors, magazines, and radio shows.

Typically, promotional kits consist of a resume, biography with photo of you (a small black-and-white photo will do), client list, articles written about you, and photos (either printed or on a CD) you've styled. Also include your business card and any other printed material you have,

Below is advice from someone who has had years of experience writing press releases: Martha Hopkins of Terrace Partners (www.terracepartners.com). Here she shares what she has learned.

Written correctly, a press release will catch the attention of the media and generate more coverage for your business than an advertisement ever would—and at a substantially cheaper cost. Editors and producers like to receive releases in a standard format so that they don't have to hunt for the pertinent information. You can organize your release differently, but you run the risk of having editors throw it out unread. Following these guidelines will give your information the best chance of being read:

1. Have something newsworthy to say. You don't want to waste someone's time with information they don't care about. Send them news they can use that's pertinent to their market.

2. Audience, Audience, Audience. Watch the tone and style of your writing to make sure it works for your audience. Journalists want to see factual information. Save your opinions for the editorial page.

3. Indicate the release date. If the release is applicable starting immediately, write "For Immediate Release." If the release should not be used until a later date, write "Hold Until xx/xx/xx" or "For Release on Halloween."

4. Include your contact information flush right on the same line as the release date. It should include your name, phone number, and email. Use a bold typeface for the word "Contact" to make it easy to find on the page.

WRITING A PRESS RELEASE

5. Write a catchy, to-the-point headline. Center and bold the text for a standardized format. Sometimes the title is the only thing an editor will read. If you don't get her attention here, your release may go straight to the trash.

6. List the city, state, and current date in bold at the beginning of the first sentence of the release.

7. Paragraph One: Get straight to the point and answer those five important journalistic questions: who, what, where, why, and when. It needs to have timely, immediate information.

8. Paragraph Two: Go into more detail about your business, your new offer, your event, or whatever you're announcing. To add credibility, quote a client or other reliable source.

9. In the final paragraph, provide general information about your business, such as, "Terrace Partners is a boutique packaging and publishing firm specializing in cookbooks. They are based in Texas." You can also repeat contact information here as well as important deadlines.

10. The end. Indicate the end of your release with three number (pound) signs below the last paragraph: ###.

11. Format the entire press release in Times New Roman (or another easy-to-read font) in 12-point type. Make sure to double space the text for easy reading.

12. Spell check and proofread! Nothing will catch the eye of an editor faster than a typo. Take the time to read your work carefully, rewrite anything that's confusing, and correct any errors.

Local Food Stylists Featured on TV Food Network

September 13, 2009
FOR IMMEDIATE RELEASE:
Contact: Denise Vivaldo, 310-836-3520, dvivaldo@earthlink.net

LOS ANGELES, CALIFORNIA—Local stylists Denise Vivaldo and Cindie Flannigan of Food Fanatics, a media food styling company, will be featured on an upcoming episode of "Will Work for Food" with Adam Gertner on TV Food Network. The segments will air on September 20, 2009, at 4:30 ET/PT and again on September 23, 2009, at 9:30 ET/PT.

Filmed recently at the Monrovia studio of photographer Jon Edwards, the styling pair showed Adam the tricks of the trade to beautiful food styling for cookbook photography. The food looks mouthwatering, but the secrets hidden beneath will shock viewers.

Denise and Cindie have been styling food for over 25 years in Los Angeles and handle jobs as diverse as cookbooks, packaging, billboards, menus, infomercials, commercials, and television prop food. They also teach food styling around the globe and in their spare time write cooking and entertaining books.

For more information, visit their website at www.FoodFanatics.net or follow their blog at www.FoodFanatics Unwashed.com.

Please contact Denise Vivaldo at 310-367-7102 for interview requests and information.###

Denise Vivaldo, Owner
Food Fanatics: Media Food Styling by Classically Trained Chefs
PO Box 351088
Los Angeles, CA 90035
310-367-7102
dvivaldo@earthlink.net

like a recipe postcard. Use anything about you and your services that will sell you to potential clients. Send your promotional kit to radio stations, local television news programs, newspapers, or magazines for potential appearances, interviews, and story ideas; this can get you valuable publicity. Organize the whole thing in a nice-looking folder, like the laminated color ones available at office supply stores.

Real-World Marketing Ideas

Other than your website, which we'll discuss later in this chapter, here are some marketing ideas to try; these have worked well for other food stylists, personal chefs and caterers:

- Teach a cooking class at local kitchen store.
- Use your car as mobile advertising with signage. Check with your accountant about any additional business deductions, and also check with your insurance agent to make sure this does not change your insurance rates.
- Speak at church groups, events, local career academies, chef groups, anyplace that will have you.
- Network within neighborhood groups, support groups, church or school groups, women's groups, business groups, Facebook and other social networking sites, friends or your children's soccer teams. Who knows—they might need a cookbook!
- Become friends with local caterers, as they may be contacted about food styling services but don't have the foggiest idea where to find a food stylist or even what a food stylist is.
- Join the local chamber of commerce, Business Networking International, Toastmasters International, or any other group where you come into contact with business owners.
- Get your local newspaper to write a story about

your services. Offer to write an article yourself with photos included. Always have a current head shot.
- Offer to style food for a local magazine or newspaper for free or for the cost of the groceries; create jobs for yourself.
- Donate services to charity auctions or city functions.
- Offer to build a beautiful buffet for a local film festival or movie theatre. Mimic food in the movie; pass out your cards.

The Internet as a Marketing Tool

These days, the first place someone will go to search for a food stylist is the Web. That's why you need an attractive site that clearly describes your services and experience. Potential clients will most likely be looking for someone to make their food beautiful, so be sure the photos on your site are gorgeous. Pretty photos will sell themselves, so don't handicap them by displaying them on busy backgrounds or with distracting graphics. Keep it clean, simple, and easy to navigate.

Having a well-designed and professional-looking website with keywords searchable in a variety of search engines is an excellent use of your advertising budget. Google (see www. google.com/adwords) and Yahoo (www.search-marketing.yahoo.com) also have sponsored ads that search your keywords and show your ad in the results—and you only pay for it if they are clicked on, called a "click through."

Your website should answer questions that potential clients may have. Be sure to include some biographical information and a photo of yourself. People are more likely to hire you if they feel they know a bit about you.

When I speak to networking groups it's usually about sales tips for the small food business owner. Sales are what drive every business. (I love to get paid to talk about something I think is incredibly fun. It's a double whammy.) You can be the most talented food stylist, chef or caterer in the world, but if you can't sell your services, you will not be able to support yourself. I love sales! I think of every sale as a game that I intend to win.

If you are not good at sales, take some entrepreneur courses. There are programs you can buy, or look online for free lessons. The easiest thing I can tell you about sales is to read *How to Win Friends and Influence People* by Dale Carnegie. It's the original self-help book, first published in 1937. It has been in print since then and has sold over 15 million copies. It never goes out of style and the information will stay with you. The premise is about understanding your own power. I used to give students a long bibliography of sales books, but having read them all, I am back to Dale Carnegie. I can tell you this, everything you need to think and learn about successful sales is in the Carnegie book. I reread it often to energize myself.

Successful selling in your business is the business of selling yourself. I take advantage of the fact that potential clients love hearing about my life in food, my career in food, and even my travels involving food. Many of my clients are celebrities. In our celebrity-obsessed culture, people love hearing about my experiences. I'm not sure why; the stories never change: I'm always the person sweating and the celebrity is usually watching. How fascinating can it be? I believe the message is that if I've helped celebrities with cookbooks that have sold millions, then I can help other potential clients too.

I set goals for myself involving sales. I try to email at least three or four new potential clients each week. I ask them if I can follow up by sending them a cookbook I just worked on or a new portfolio disc.

Last but not least, one of the easiest sales tools today is having a blog. Cindie and I found a wonderful young woman, Mandy, who has become our blog mistress. We send her bits of stuff on a day-to-day basis and she spins it into a blog. We have fun with it. The idea behind the blog is to give real insight into our business. What it does is generate sales of our food styling classes. So, by being our authentic selves and telling it how it is, we are filling classes that we love to teach. How's that for winning friends and influencing people?

FAQs
ABOUT
FOOD
STYLING

Inform potential clients of your experience as well as any other culinary services you offer. Below are some points to keep in mind when designing your website:

- Don't make people search all over your site for your email address and phone number. Make sure it shows up on every page.
- Have a clear and simple website so visitors will not get confused. If they cannot easily find your information, they might give up and look elsewhere.
- Pretty pictures sell, so include them on your site. Get help organizing them so your portfolio isn't confusing. Don't include any pictures that require an explanation.

Website Content

Your website need not be complicated. It is better to be clear and simple than to rattle on and on and confuse potential clients. Start with a very simple home page that includes your name, your contact info, a very brief description of what you do, and links to the other pages on your website. More links can be added later, but to start you should include a brief bio page, a list of clients, and samples of your work on a portfolio page.

Once you've established a website address and put up the first pages, you can add more information as you go along, including links to your clients' websites where your work is displayed.

FOOD FANATICS

food stylists

Portfolio   Clients   About

Food styling for photography • Segment blocking for cooking demos and TV shows • Prop food for TV shows, informercials, and movies • Food styling for TV and movies • Write entertaining and catering books • Develop, test and edit recipes • Teach classes and give food demonstrations

310-836-3520
dvivaldo@earthlink.net
Los Angeles, California

Blogs

People are generating interest through their blogs. A blog (short for Web-log) is an online journal that other people read and post comments to. We have our own blog called Food Fanatics Unwashed (www.FoodFanaticsUnwashed.com) that chronicles our adventures on a weekly basis. We get to show the silly, strange, and downright stinky side of food styling. A blog could be part of your existing website or a separate one. If you make it part of your business website, make sure all the content is appropriate for your potential clients to see.

The next step in the growth of our blog is to have an online forum for food stylists to share tips, tricks and techniques, to post resources and suppliers for tools and equipment, and to ask sticky food styling questions.

Getting Referrals and Repeat Business

When a client hires you again or passes your name on to someone else, its proof you're doing a great job. This is why you stay in touch with former clients, as you never know when they or someone they know will need your services. You might send attractively packaged cookies, brownies or other treats to clients based locally. We recently got a job writing and styling a celebrity cookbook that came from our having left a card and some cookies with them three years earlier. Sending out promotional pieces (mentioned earlier in this chapter) with a short note is another idea. Don't be pushy but do let people know you are available if they have a need for your services. And always thank clients who have referred you to others.

Keep track of where potential clients found your info. If it wasn't a referral, what was it? A mailing? An ad? Your website? Your portfolio CD? Your blog? Keep track of the success of your promotional ideas and stick with those that pay off.

Effective Client Communications

Communication begins the first time you interact with a potential client and doesn't end until you stop breathing. We get calls from clients we haven't heard from in years. Sometimes we get a director calling us for a shoot who remembers being on a set with us ten years ago, when he/she was a production assistant. This is why you need to be nice to everyone. We are on our third generation of production assistants.

Good communication skills will prevent misunderstandings, make your life much easier, and make it easy for clients to send you new business. Clients will not refer you if they have been disappointed in your services or behavior. We have gotten many wonderful new clients as a result of the bad work or behavior of other stylists. We are frequently complimented on our promptness and professionalism. A frequent complaint we hear is that clients were afraid to ask their previous stylist to change something because the stylist would "get really mad." This either shows really bad communication skills or really inappropriate work behavior or both.

Effectively conveying exactly what your service consists of is greatly important. As is giving your clients permission to tell you when they are unhappy with something or want to change anything. Changing the presentation on the plate is not about you. The job is to do the best job you can.

As an example, say a client wants to hire you for a one-day shoot and can only afford to pay for a half-day of shopping and prep. The client asks you to style a table of goodies so that it looks like a kids' birthday party. Then he mumbles something about wanting a separate photograph of each item on the table. On the table will be a two-layer decorated birthday cake, a dozen decorated cupcakes, a platter of three kinds of cookies, and a plate of brownies. Now you are up to five photos. If he decides he wants a separate photo of each kind of cookie, photos six, seven, and eight just showed up.

Here's the question: Do you think you can shop and bake enough cakes, cupcakes, three types of cookies and brownies in half a day? Tell him now if you will need more time to prep, or explain that you can work within his budget if you buy good-looking bakery product already finished. Your client needs to know what the time and cost differences are between making everything and buying it already made. These are the communications that have to take place when accepting a job. If the client decides he wants you to bake all the goodies, then he can either pay for more prep or drop some of the shots from his list. Give him the information to make an educated choice. Don't make promises you can't keep. If you can't get ten shots done in a day, tell him upfront how many you *can* get done.

Trust Your Gut

Sometimes in an initial meeting, a new client tells you they hate food stylists. They start with, "We hired a stupid girl last year who made awful-looking food and didn't clean up after herself." There are better ways to say the last stylist didn't live up to their expectations, but this does give you an opportunity to find out what your client's quirks are. Ask questions. Maybe the awful-looking food was their awful-looking product or their messed-up recipe, and they like blaming others. Maybe she was working in horrible conditions and couldn't have done any better. Maybe

the stylist was inexperienced or going through a bad time. Ask who the stylist was. Sometimes we find out their previous stylist is pretty darn great, which makes us wonder about the client and their expectations.

Now is the time to consider whether this would be a good client to take on. They are already annoyed. Are they going to think you are perfect in comparison to their last stylist? Or will you be just another stupid stylist they hired? My husband is an attorney and when I tell him these stories, he tells me that the client has just told you exactly what they are like. Or, as he likes to say, the evidence is in. You decide if this client is worth your time and trouble. Trust your gut instinct. Is it worth your time and trouble trying to re-educate this client?

When Things Go Wrong

When something does go very wrong at a job, try to remain calm. Try seeing issues from your client's point of view. Did the shot schedule fall behind because you forgot to bring the garnishes and had to run to the store twice? Or you needed a second cupcake pan? Or you didn't hire an assistant because you wanted to keep more of the profits? Don't beat yourself up about it, but also try to be honest about your part in a bad situation. Learn and move on.

Anything and everything can go wrong. How it impacts your business depends on how you choose to respond to it. We've styled for the cheap, the picky, the loaded, and the freaky. We rely on our intuition to assess people we are dealing with and how to make them happy while also taking care of ourselves and our sanity. We've found the best way to operate is to be straightforward with our clients. In return, we hope they do the same for us. It doesn't always work, but it always makes for a good story over a glass (or bottle) of post-job wine.

MAKING MONEY AND SELLING YOUR SERVICES

We have gathered as much information as we could (promising to respect privacy) so we can share with you what we have learned about stylist pricing in different parts of North America and around the world. We get dozens of emails every week from people we don't know, asking how much to charge for this job or that job, and here we offer our best advice.

One question that we asked stylists was if they supported themselves with other jobs in addition to food styling. The answer was a resounding "yes." The work they did fell into several catego-  ries: recipe development and testing, food writing and editing, culinary producing, assisting at cooking demos, teaching cooking classes, and working as (or with) a personal chef, caterer or even assisting an event planner.

This is important information if you are just starting out or thinking you'd like to become a food stylist. Chances are you are going to have to do more than one job in order to support yourself. It takes time to learn your craft, which is why we suggest assisting an established stylist. Assisting gives you income to

In the beginning of my career, I apprenticed with a great food stylist named Alan. A cable TV hostess introduced me to him. She knew I wanted to become a food stylist and got us together for a meeting. I worked for him as an assistant on and off for two years. Watching him taught me many valuable lessons.

When you are assisting, you have the opportunity to observe the dynamics of working with a photographer, client, art director, or cameraman without being the one responsible. Or, as I say, it's not your butt on the griddle. On a shoot, the lead stylist is the point person that deals with the photographer, client, art director, or cameraman for all the ideas, changes, or input. Sometimes there are also company owners, producers, investors, and hairdressers on the shoot that will voice opinions about the food.

A LESSON IN CLIENT RELATIONS

The assistant is there to assist the lead stylist. As an assistant, you can wait to be told what to do, as it is not your job to solve the problems until the lead stylist asks for your help. With that said, how the lead stylist handles changes and problems on the shoot will set the tone and energy for the entire day. It can be a great day, an okay day, or a really bad and very long day.

Alan taught me not to fight with clients. Not because he said, "Denise, don't fight with the clients." Oh, no. Because Alan couldn't control himself, he constantly fought with clients. He made himself and everyone on the set crazy. Instead of a united creative team, it was a war zone. He would become defensive and angry instead of just moving the lemon wedge. The huffier he got, the more the client would ask me to change something. This becomes a problem because food styling is like any other kitchen work in that there is a chain of command. And that means the assistant is not supposed to make changes without the lead stylist's approval or direction.

After I had worked for Alan for a while, I said to him, "Why don't you style the plates, and I'll work with the crazy client and get your plates approved so we can move a little faster." The client was a frozen Mexican TV dinner company whose people drove Alan crazy. For the next couple of shoots, I was the one putting the plate on the set. When the client said, "Move the lemon," I said, "Happy to!"

This worked for a few months, until the client wanted to hire me without Alan—and told Alan that. I never worked for Alan again. It was never my intention to undermine his relationship with his client; I was just trying to create less stress and make the client happy while making the shoot go as smoothly as possible.

Not long after that, I heard Alan got out of the business. He worked his way out of a career by being difficult. Years later we talked and he thanked me for doing him a favor. He was a great food stylist, just not a happy one.

Successful business careers are built on rewarding relationships. When we receive phone calls from the same clients over and over again, I know we are doing something right.

build your kit and portfolio, and it helps you to come in contact with a network of people that could hire or refer you. I have had some of the same clients for my entire career as a chef and stylist. They like me. They trust me. They know I do the best job I can. And now that Cindie has been with me for ten years; they like and trust her, too. These clients schedule their shoots to accommodate our availability.

Successful business careers are built on rewarding relationships. When we receive phone calls from the same clients over and over again, I know we are doing something right. Do all clients and jobs work out? No, unfortunately not. We've had some difficult clients, and we were happy to never work with them again. We will turn down jobs with past clients who were particularly troublesome. We have to weigh the issues: what we are really selling our clients along with our skills is our time. If we don't enjoy the time we spend working and running our business (or make enough money to be happy) we wouldn't be able to do this for very long. What's the point of staying in a business that doesn't make you happy?

Sometimes we make mistakes and a client doesn't call us back. It's not the end of the world. Life goes on. Mistakes are learning lessons. My philosophy is to try not to make the same mistake twice.

How to Charge for Your Services

Those weekly emails with money questions are from new or aspiring writers, food stylists, and cooking teachers asking us what they should charge for their services; many of them are our former students. They need help and direction because there are no set standards or fees; this is not a union job or a regulated industry. Clients will often try to tell you what you should charge. That's not right! Your fees depend on where you live, how much styling experience you have (your portfolio, website and client list are evidence of your experience), and how well can you sell and close a deal.

In Southern California (Los Angeles, San Diego and Santa Barbara), there might be thirty or forty food stylists that work consistently. This means they have a client list, a portfolio, and significant experience in the various areas (print, television and film) of food styling. Some stylists work in all areas; others do not. Los Angeles, New York, Chicago and San Francisco have very similar food styling markets and pay rates. I know this because I travel a lot in my work with clients, often styling in these cities. Also, as an author, I have hired stylists in other cities to help me when I am on a book tour. And, last but not least, when publicists or publishers call with a job (they hire stylists across the country for promotional or book tours), they tell me what other stylists are charging. Many times this information is given accidentally, meaning, when I quote my rate, they gasp and say something like, "Wow, that's as high as New York," or "Really? That's more than I paid in Chicago." Or "Your rate is comparable with the last stylist we hired."

Most clients are going to ask you to negotiate your rate. They are going to tell you they have no money, or are on a tight budget, or have already budgeted the amount for a food stylist, or they can't afford you, or they know someone who will do it for half of your rate, or their dog ate their accountant. I've heard every story. You'll have to decide from job offer to job offer if the project is worth your time, skill and energy.

I have no problem talking about money. I think it's important to share this information. If stylists are straightforward with each other, maybe we can upgrade our industry and develop some industry standards.

Food Styling Rates in Your Marketplace

How do you find out what the going rate is for food styling in your area? As I mentioned before, prospective clients will often tell you, but I suggest being brave and calling stylists in your marketplace to ask what they charge. Established stylists call me and ask me what I'm charging for specific types of work all the time. I am happy to answer their questions, and I ask them questions back. We need to help each other. Besides, I have nothing to hide. I want success for myself and others in my industry.

I've become good friends with one of my local competitors, and we tell each other when we decide to raise our rates so the other can do the same. Instead of a client's decision being based on money, they can choose who they like the best or feel is the best fit for their project.

Let me tell you what I know about food styling rates in the big cities I mentioned above, starting with myself. As an experienced food stylist in L.A. with a client base going back twenty years,

I can command as much as $1,200 to $1,400 a day for print work. That's packaging, cookbooks, billboards, etc. Stylists in New York, Chicago, and San Francisco also charge that day rate.

Will every client that calls me pay that? Absolutely not! But that is my starting point when negotiating my rate. On average, I bill $1,100 for myself and $600 to $750 for an assistant. If there is a lot of prep work involved, I may ask for a second assistant, who shops, preps, props, washes dishes, cleans up, and packs out. A second assistant's pay spread is between $350 and $500. If the client will go for that, I often bundle the three of us together for a total day rate of $2,000 to $2,300 (for a 10-hour day). Some stylists charge a kit fee for their food styling kits. Remember all the equipment we told you that you'd have to collect, take care of, and cart around? Well, you own all that. Think of a kit fee as renting the use of your kit to your clients. You can charge them a kit fee (between $150 and $350 per job, depending upon the job and the scope of your kit) or include it in your fee. Use it as a negotiating tool. Successful sales are about believing in your product. I am my own product.

I have found that by having clients going to my website, then speaking with them on the phone, and finally writing them an email stating my terms (always following up with a phone call or email), that I can usually close a deal. Do I take jobs for less than my day rate? Sure, you betcha, but I do seriously consider if it is worth it for me to take the job. It might be better to refer this job to someone else and ask for a referral fee from the stylist I hand it to. A normal referral is 10% to 15% of the styling fee the stylist collects, not including overtime. Always discuss this up front. If you are the recipient of a referred job, you should always ask the referrer what they want as a referral fee. Sometimes a fee isn't required or expected, but it is imperative that you ask.

This is all about sales; every successful business is about sales. I should explain that I sold real estate for years before I went to culinary school. Selling real estate is about making and accepting offers. Sometimes you have to throw in a free chandelier if you want to make the deal, but you have to keep looking at the big picture and find a way to make the deal. I often find myself selling my services a dozen times a day. It's a good thing I like doing it.

Different Fees, Different Jobs

For work on a television series, my day rate may only be $500, but I've signed a deal memo for twenty days of work. Taking into consideration that I'm making $10,000 and getting to work with a celebrity chef or on a cooking show I admire, if I have no other work lined up, this is a great twenty days of working with food and props. Instead of a day rate, I think of it as a project fee. My business is incorporated, so I take care of my own taxes. I'm constantly aware of how much money I am taking in, how much I need to live on, and how much it takes to run my business. You have to make choices as a self-employed person because you are creating your own income every day. And paying your own taxes (take 30% right off the top for estimated income taxes). And paying insurance. And covering all other business-related fees. It is so important to understand and appreciate how much your net profit is and what your time is truly worth.

No Guts, No Glory

Television does not require the same preciseness or experience that print and advertising work requires. When the camera is in motion, no one is able to look all that closely. Television and film are the easiest ways for new stylists to enter the market.

I was very lucky at the beginning of my catering career in Los Angeles. Several television production companies called my kitchen and asked me if I could build a buffet for their TV show just like the pictures they'd seen of my party buffets. I said sure. Why not? No guts, no glory. What I found out was planning a television segment was just like planning a party. I had the vision. I made the lists. I organized, prepared, and executed my buffets (all with a positive attitude and smiling face). I believed I would succeed (producers can smell fear; show business is where the saying "Never let them see you sweat" came from). What I needed to know about actual food styling I learned as I looked into the monitor and saw what the camera saw. Food looks different through the camera's eye. I loved the magic and manipulation. (It's easy to practice in your own kitchen with any camera. Teach yourself. I loved developing and perfecting tricks. Wait until you get to the "Tricks of the Trade" chapter!)

The first few television shows I worked on, I didn't even know what to charge. It was a producer that said to me, "Sweetie, you need to give me an invoice for $400 and turn in the food receipts." And that's what I did.

Rates in Other Parts of the World

We frequently work with international clients. We get calls because of the shortage of experienced food stylists in different parts of the world. China is a new frontier with tons of food and equipment manufacturing. Asia is buzzing with work. We get phone calls monthly for jobs in Hong Kong, but I keep telling them that's more of a commute than we're used to and we probably can't get there by tomorrow. Since we started teaching our food styling workshops, we've had students from Egypt, Canada, Mexico, Austria, Singapore, Shanghai, Uruguay, Brazil, Costa Rica, Columbia, Dubai, United Arab Emirates, Jamaica, Thailand, and the Philippines. All of these students came to study and further their education because they understood that there is a market in their local area for food stylists. We love meeting them. From what we have researched, the rates most of these stylists are charging are comparable to an assistant rate in the States. Unfortunately, many countries other than the United States seem to have no limit on the workday. If it takes twenty hours to shoot the pizza, there is no overtime. They get their day rate however long that day turns out to be. Labor is cheaper in many parts of the world, and the concept of worker protection is unknown.

We have worked with several food companies from Europe and have found that rates for food stylists in major European cities are comparable to those in New York or Los Angeles.

How the Worldwide Economy Affects Your Day Rate and Your Business

I am writing this after having lived through the economic turmoil of 2009. A day doesn't go by where old, new, or returning clients don't call and ask for a deal, discount, or favor.

The economy in the United States was slow. Business was slow. The rates food stylists charge depend not only on their experience, but also on what the market will bear at any given time. I watched the work in marketing and sales slow down. I had decisions to make. Is it better to take more work for less money? Or is this the time to thin the herd and lose those difficult clients? I wasn't ready to quit the business, something many others in this business had done. At the end of the day, I love this work. So I did a little of both and rode out the slow time.

Explaining How You Conduct Your Business

Every sale begins with an inquiry call. I've found that the easiest and quickest way to do business in today's market is to tell people up front how you do business—right on your website. Let them get to know you by reading about you. By the time potential clients call me, they have read through our website. They know a lot about us! Now, do clients read quotes and references from other clients? Yes. And are they impressed? Sure! Is it easier to sell with success under your belt? Absolutely!

Tell potential clients in your own words how you do business and put a picture of yourself on your site. Make the new client comfortable. Let them know you!

Tell potential clients in your own words how you do business and put a picture of yourself on your site. Make the new client comfortable. Let them know you!

Writing a Deal Memo

In this age of the Internet, deal memos can simply be the email between you and a client where the client describes a specific job and, in reply, you describe what that job will take and how much money it will cost to accomplish. Be specific about what you are providing. Include information about:

- Your day rate, including assistants.
- When you go into time-and-a-half overtime, double-time overtime.
- Your start time.
- Your estimate of the food (and props, if any).
- What equipment you are bringing with you.
- What the client is responsible for bringing.
- Deposits required.
- When balance of invoice is due.
- Your cancellation policy.

Ask your client:
- Who is paying the invoice?
- What is the company address?
- Do I need a purchase order (PO) number?

It's also a good idea to restate the job as you understand it. For example, "Photo shoot in Monrovia, 6 shots of chicken dinners, 1 serving each shot with sides, garnishes, and minimal background (wine, bread). Photos to be used for The Funky Chicken packaging for frozen dinners."

Being as clear as you can will prevent problems in the long run.

Food Shopping Estimate

Food estimates can sometimes be difficult for new stylists, but, like anything, practice makes perfect. I have a couple of tips to share that should help, but you must stay current with food prices (they can go crazy with inflation, the weather, or the seasons), and adjust your mental calculations. One of our assistants says I have a gift for guessing what the food total will be while the groceries are still in the cart. This is what comes with years and years (and years) of experience. I use the shopping cart as a walker!

You will need to give your clients accurate estimates of food costs and supplies. Many large grocery store chains have websites where you can find out the cost of specific items. If your shoot is for five different recipes of rack of lamb with side dishes and garnishes, your client might think it'll cost you about $200 to shop. You need to find out how much a rack will cost, multiply that by ten, add the cost of a bottle of red wine, a couple different types of artisan bread, six or eight types of fresh herbs, and enough vegetables, rice, potatoes, etc., to have side dishes for all five plates. Don't forget a couple of lemons, limes, green onions, tomatoes in various

We always get deposits from new clients. How much for a deposit depends upon the type and scope of the job and the track record of the company.

sizes, a variety of lettuces, yellow and red onion, cucumber—and oh, yes, paper towels, cooking oil spray, plastic wrap, Karo syrup, and prepared shelf-stable gravy and Alfredo sauce. Find out if these photos are showing a single serving or the whole rack with sides for a number of people. This all affects the food costs, which, on a job like the one described above, could be anywhere from $300 to $500.

There isn't always time to shop at a discount store like Costco, and you could end up spending more money (and your time) if you have to go to more than one store. Sometimes your best bet is the higher-end grocery store because you can be reasonably certain they will have rack of lamb and good-quality produce. The few dollars more you pay will be more than offset by not having to drive and shop at another store.

Dos and Don'ts of Food Estimating

- Go to one grocery store almost every day. Read price flyers from every store that comes in your mail. Be aware of the prices of every item.
- Get good at shopping; know where you can get exotic or odd items, where the ethnic specialty stores are located, and what's in season and what's not.
- It is standard practice in food styling for you to be reimbursed for all your purchases, but somewhere there is someone who is going to look at your receipts before writing out your check. Know that your clients are depending on you to be as frugal and honest as you can be with their money. Don't put personal items

on client receipts; buy your magazines and dog food separately.

Prep Rates

Often your client will ask for a prep rate. A prep rate can apply to shopping, picking up a table-cloth, preparing some food in advance, or doing some research on the food you are going to shoot (especially helpful if you are using a new piece of equipment supplied by your client). Much of the time an assistant can handle all of the work for the prep rate, leaving you to work on something else. I charge my clients an assistant's regular fee for prep days. This is fine with me, since I know I have a day or several days of paid work scheduled.

Deposit Money and Cancellation Fees

Many food stylists are timid about asking for a deposit from new clients, especially someone they feel they connected with through phone or email conversations. Don't fall into this trap. You can't trust people until they have proved they are trustworthy. We always get deposits from new clients. Honest clients don't have a problem with deposits. How much for a deposit depends upon the type and scope of the job and the track record of the company. We always request deposits for large jobs.

Here are some common scenarios:

- For a 1-day photo shoot with someone we've never heard of, we estimate the amount we'll be spending out of pocket on product and 50% to 60% of our estimated labor and use that as the deposit amount. Then the client pays us with a check for the remainder and our time at the end of the shoot.

- For a 1-day photo shoot with a well-known company we've never worked with, we'll ask for a deposit to cover the amount for food, and we bill them for the labor and any remainder.
- For a 7-day infomercial with two lead stylists and four assistant stylists, we require petty cash from the production company to cover all food and supply expenses. We also ask for a deposit of 50% to 60% percent of the estimated labor. This is true for production companies we know and for those we've never heard of. On large jobs like these with five people on your team, you can end up being owed $10,000 to $20,000. That's a lot of money out of your pocket if the production company doesn't pay you quickly.

So what do you do when someone cancels on you? You need to have your cancellation policy in writing somewhere on your deal memo or stated in an email to the client if you want to charge a cancellation fee. Cancellation fees are usually your normal day rate.

We rarely charge a fee, as we keep busy enough for it not to be a problem, but there are certain clients who cancel frequently and at the last minute. After this happens twice, we tell them that the next time there will be a cancellation fee. We need to charge a cancellation fee if we've turned down work and lost income because of the cancellation. Once they pay a cancellation fee, it cuts way down on their cancellations.

Cancellation fees are tricky. They must be explained upfront and in writing. Clients really hate being charged for work they didn't get. With that said, you may not get that client to call you again. Or maybe you don't want them to.

Budgeting Your Time

When clients want to know how much you charge, remember that you are selling not only your labor, but your expertise and experience. We keep a very close watch on the time spent on any given project, be it styling, teaching, or developing recipes. We don't want to end up working for free because we've miscalculated the time. We also don't want to quote day rates until we have enough information from the client to make an educated guess on what a particular job entails.

On the next page is a worksheet to fill out after speaking with clients about potential jobs. The answers will help you in budgeting your time and giving a more accurate job estimate to your clients. The more accurate you are in estimating time, the easier it is to get paid. Clients feel cheated if they pay more than they expected to pay.

Accounting for the Food Stylist

Keeping accurate account of your income and expenses is crucial to your success. Microsoft Money Plus Home and Business software is the one that works for us. There are easier programs and more complicated programs out there, but this covers everything we need. You can generate cash flow reports, income statement, and balance sheets, plus write checks and keep track of estimated taxes.

Fill out the blanks in hours (or fractions of hours) to get a time estimate for a job. The questions below relate to a satellite media tour or an author's live television appearance but can be used or changed to fit any type of styling job.

1. After reading the recipes you have been sent, how much time do you estimate it will take to:

• Make a shopping list? _____
• Shop:
  one store? _____
  two stores? _____
  three stores? _____
• Prepare recipes and sub recipes? _____

Note: We estimate every recipe will take at least 1.5 hours to shop and make. Baked items take longer. Your level of cooking experience should be taken into account. For television demos and satellite media tours, everything has to be prepared ahead of time. While on photo shoots there is often time to make the food during the shoot, unless there are complicated or time-consuming recipes.

2. Do the recipes call for any specialty items or equipment? An example would be expensive caviar or Madeline pans. Is the client aware of these extra costs and are they willing to pay for them? How much time do you estimate it will take to locate and order or shop for specialty equipment or items? _____

Note: Point out any issues regarding extra expenses or difficulty finding certain items to clients so they can decide if this is something important to the shoot or something they don't really need. If we tell a client that we foresee spending $200, we try to keep as close to that as possible. If we find that $200 won't cover it, we alert the client as soon as possible before spending any more.

Note: Point out to your client that each recipe averages between $40 and $50 dollars, including garnishes. If they want flowers, new tea towels, dishes, or table linens, that's more money.

3. Is there a prop person or art department for this shoot? If not, are you expected to bring the props? Is there a kitchen or do you need to bring all of the equipment? Are there linens, prep bowls, and utensils for the set or are you bringing them? How long will it take you to:

• Shop for any props or linens? _____
• Pack props? _____
• Pack any kitchen equipment? _____
• Pack any set equipment? _____

Note: If you can accommodate your clients by also acting as a prop stylist, and it's something you want to do, then by all means do it. But you should charge them an additional fee for this service. Find out how much prop stylists make in your area. You could be saving the client as much as $1,500 an appearance. Make sure they know this!

4. Does the client have a specific product they need to be seen on camera? Do they know beyond a shadow of a doubt that it is available in local stores? Or do they need to send you the product beforehand? How long will it take you to:

• Shop for specifically requested product? _____

Note: This seems like a no-brainer. Ha! We don't have the space for all of the horror stories about trying to find a product that didn't exist in our area. Sometimes the product is seasonal or local to a specific part of the country. Sometimes the person you are dealing with has incorrect information and you spend hours looking for something that doesn't exist because they gave you the wrong name. Sometimes it's a new product and not yet available. The person you are dealing with is not necessarily the one who knows the correct information.

5. The client should know that your work starts before the actual shoot and doesn't end until everything is cleaned and put away. How long will it take you to:

• Put all food and equipment in your car? _____
• Unpack all food and equipment when you get to the location? _____
• Set up your workspace? _____
• Set up the demos/set table? _____
• Get any last minute prep ready? _____
• Clean up your workspace? _____
• Clean up the demo/set table? _____
• Pack out everything? _____
• Unpack everything? _____
• Clean any dirty items? _____
• Put it all away? _____

To avoid tax problems, hire a bookkeeper or accountant, or purchase a small business accounting program that you understand and will use.

Taxes

Because you are now in business for yourself, you are responsible for your income taxes. This means paying quarterly estimated income taxes and your own social security taxes. Since taxes vary from city to city and state to state, you must find out what your specific tax responsibilities are. Many stylists get into trouble by not keeping up with their income and expenses on a timely basis. If you wait until the end of the year to figure out what you owe, you can be assessed interest and penalties beyond what you would have owed had you paid estimated taxes on time. A small business can quickly be buried under tax liabilities like these.

To avoid tax problems, hire a bookkeeper or accountant, or purchase a small business accounting program that you understand and will use.

Accounting programs will require you to enter your income and expenses or deductions so you can keep a running total of what taxes you owe. As a food stylist, you will have many business deductions, among them:

- Accounting fees.
- Advertising expenses.
- Assistant pay.
- Attorney fees.
- Automobile use, repair, gas, registration fees.
- Business gifts.
- Conventions and trade shows.
- Depreciation expenses on equipment and computers.
- Home office equipment and supply expenses.
- Insurance.
- Portfolio materials.
- Magazine subscriptions for industry-related subjects.
- Membership dues.
- Styling equipment and supplies.

Invoicing

The two rules of thumb for invoices are write them clearly and get them out quickly. There are many software programs out there to help you. Microsoft Word, Money, and Excel all have templates you can use. Or you can create your own invoices. On the next page are sample invoices for a food stylist and an assistant that include all of the necessary information.

Creating Additional Income Streams

As we've said before, most food stylists work on other food-related (or non-food-related, as the case may be) jobs to generate enough income to support themselves. As a food stylist, you are in a position to offer recipe development and testing services to your existing clients. Depending upon your talents, you can also work as a food writer, culinary instructor, culinary producer, personal chef, or caterer. Existing clients are the best source of additional work, but, as when marketing yourself, leave no stone unturned!

Recipe Development and Testing

Anytime a client gives you recipes to style from, mention that you also create and test recipes. We've gotten a significant amount of work this way. If you like creating recipes, this work is the

Sample Invoice for a Food Stylist

Invoice date:	January 15, 2010
Billed to:	Henry Vert, Chicken Express, 1234 Main Street, Anytown 90000
Payable to:	Food Fanatics, PO Box 351088, Los Angeles, CA 90035
Invoice number:	009-2010
Fed. Tax ID number:	12-3456789
Job date:	January 12, 2010
Job description:	Food styling for product packaging photos
Job location:	Jon Edwards Photography, Monrovia, CA
1 stylist, 1 assistant:	$1,400.00 (day rate based on a 10-hour day)
2 hrs OT at $210/hr:	$420.00 (first two hours of OT are billed at time and a half)
1 hr OT at $280/hr:	$280.00 (hours 13 and over are billed at double time)
Total labor:	$2,100.00
Food purchased:	$598.32* (Keep copies of all receipts for reference)
	*Receipts attached to hard copy of invoice
BALANCE DUE:	$2,698.32
	Payment is due 15 days after date of invoice.

Thank you.

Sample Invoice for an Assistant Food Stylist

Invoice date:	January 14, 2010
Billed to:	Food Fanatics, PO Box 351088, Los Angeles, CA 90035
Payable to:	Gina Papetti, 1234 Nice Street, Los Angeles, CA 90066
Invoice number:	2010-FF02 (number assigned by you, for your reference)
EIN, SSN or Tax ID:	555-555-5555
Job date:	January 12, 2010
Job description:	Chicken Express photo shoot for product packaging
Day rate at $400.00:	$400.00 (day rate based on a 10-hour day)
2 hrs OT at $60/hr:	$120.00 (first two hours of OT are billed at time and a half)
1 hr OT at $80/hr:	$80.00 (hours 13 and over are billed at double time)
TOTAL:	$600.00
Payment due:	February 15, 2010 (usually 30 days after date of invoice)

If you have any questions, please don't hesitate to contact me.
Thank you!
Gina Papetti
1234 Nice Street
Los Angeles, CA 90066
310-555-1234
ginapapetti@email.com

best. If you know a lot about food and can make a recipe work the first time out, you can make money. Since you are paid per recipe, every time you have to go back and retest a recipe, it's costing you money.

This is work you can do in your own kitchen on your own schedule. We charge a flat fee per recipe, plus the cost of groceries. Figure out how long it takes you to think up, shop, test, snap a picture, and write up a recipe when determining your fee. Don't forget to add in your overhead or you'll short-change yourself.

The amount charged per recipe varies by market, location, and client. Recipes with high exposure written for large companies can demand more than recipes written for a small local publication. The more experience you have and the better your recipes are written, the more you can charge. A recipe for the Anytown Gazette Weekly could get you $75, whereas a recipe for the Giant National Canned Goods Company could pay $375.

We use the billing worksheet to keep track of recipe testing work.

Food Writing

Like recipe testing, food writing jobs can come by way of your existing clients. If you enjoy writing you can pick up jobs just by letting clients know you are available. You can also generate independent writing jobs. You'll need some samples of work, which you can get by submitting articles to be used for free in local newspapers and magazines or on websites. If you have the time and inclination, you should have a blog to showcase your work. Many people get hired directly from someone seeing their blog or website.

Recipe Testing Billing Worksheet

Date	Recipes
1/26/2010	4
1/27/2010	6
Total Recipes:	10
10 recipes @ $300 per recipe = $3,000.00	

Receipts and expenses (receipts attached):

Date		
1/26/2010	Whole Foods	100.52
1/26/2010	Vons	70.08
Total Receipts and Expenses:		170.60

Total Billed to Client:	$3,170.60

Picking up a few personal chef gigs can provide you with bread-and-butter income.

Culinary Instruction

Whether you are teaching the occasional class out of your home or teaching at a local cooking store, culinary school, or adult educational institution, teaching can not only bring in some extra income, it can also expose you to potential clients. Pick a subject that you are passionate and know a lot about. Write up an outline for your class and use it as a proposal to present to different teaching venues, or use the outline to sell your class.

We teach food styling classes, but you could teach any kind of culinary class that would sell. Maybe a 3-hour hands-on class in making your own pasta or a 1-hour talk about cutting the fat in your diet. On the next page is an outline of one of our classes.

Culinary Producer

TV cooking shows need someone to coordinate the food that gets seen on the set. If you have experience on cooking shows, you can offer your services as a culinary producer. You'll need to know what a particular show needs in the way of set and backstage equipment and food. You'll be in charge of making sure the demos and segments get set up ahead of time, with duplicate (or triplicate or quad) prep in case something goes wrong; having heros and twins ready on time; diplomatically telling the talent they are mispronouncing a culinary term; telling the producers how long and/or how expensive it will be to get what they want. You'll be pulled in eighteen different directions at once. But it can be rewarding when the show is all done and you can sit back and watch it on TV. Having experience planning large events or catering large parties will give you a good idea about what it's like to work the plate-spinning job of culinary producer.

Personal Chef and Caterer

As a food stylist you'll be repeatedly asked if you ever do any catering or personal cheffing. Your clients see how pretty your food is and want to hire you for actual, edible food. There are laws and regulations you have to follow when providing food that people will eat. Food must be cooked in your client's kitchen or a commercial kitchen, as it is not legal to cook food in your own home and transport it. That being said, there is a market for people willing to cater small parties (under thirty guests). Larger, established catering companies don't like handling smaller or last-minute jobs, but for small parties, two days notice is often plenty. Hire an extra pair of hands to help you with setting up, keeping food refreshed, and cleaning. Until you know how much you can handle by yourself, it's a great comfort to have help. For more information on running a catering business, see my book *How to Start a Home-Based Catering Business.*

Picking up a few personal chef gigs can provide you with bread-and-butter income. As a personal chef, you will shop and cook food (typically four servings each of five meals) at your client's home one day a week or every other week. You charge a fee for the cooking day plus the cost of groceries. If you can pick up enough clients for two days a week, that will leave you the rest of the week for food styling. For more information on running a personal chef business see *How to Start a Home-Based Personal Chef Business.*

Food Styling Master Class

Day 1 - Saturday

8:30	Arrive and check in. Students pick up name tags.
9:00	Introduction to food styling
10:00	Meats: Poultry shaping, trussing, grill marks, browning, slicing, fixing mistakes
	Instructor demo: whole chicken, steak, hamburger
	Student hands-on: whole chicken and burger
12:15	Lunch break—Students on their own
1:15	Sandwiches: Layering lunchmeat, cutting, using condiments
	Instructor demo: sandwich
	Student hands-on: sandwich
2:15	Sauces: Consistency, how to keep from breaking, coloring and application
	Methods: squeeze bottles, spoons, droppers, cream and cheese sauces
	Pasta: Cooking, plating, and saucing. Less is more, creating movement
	Instructor demo: pasta, building height, applying sauce
	Student hands-on: pasta and sauces
3:30	Question & answer session
4:00	Class ends.

Day 2 - Sunday

8:30	Coffee, tea, water, and nibbles provided.
9:00	Photo shoot demonstration: TBD
10:00	Desserts: Ice cream, pie, layer cake, dessert sauces, brownies, whipped cream, and the use of dessert condiments
	Instructor demo: pie, cake, fake ice cream
	Student hands-on: ice cream & cake
12:15	Lunch break—Students on their own
1:15	Beverages: Instructors demo beverage special effects, discuss creating steam
1:45	Salads: Creating movement, different cuts for visual effects, how to use dressings, extending the life of greens, how to make it look stunning
	Instructor demo: salads
	Student hands-on: salads
3:00	Cheese: The different stages of melting, good fakes, pizza pulls
	Instructor demo: cheese pulls and melts
3:30	Question & answer session.
4:00	Class ends.

PREPARING FOR MAGIC TIME

The actual job of styling any plate of food is the end result of a lot of preparation. When you put that plate of beautiful food in front of the camera, it's "magic time." Magic time is a term used when the HD video camera starts rolling or the photographer begins shooting.

What You Need to Know Before You Begin

Let's walk through the steps it takes to get to you to the point where you actually style a plate. The process of a food styling job begins with a call from a prospective client. And that client has something they want to sell. Every element of your shoot will depend upon who that client is and what they are selling. Let's say you get a call to style a hamburger shot. There are three questions to ask. The first question is: *Who is the client?* Are they a:

- fast food chain?
- upscale restaurant?
- ground beef supplier?
- lifestyle magazine?
- grocery store?
- cookbook author?

Now that you know who they are, the second question is: *What are they*

NEWSPAPER "INSERTS" We style the food and often write the text for our clients. Writing text or recipe development creates another income stream.

selling? Here are some potential scenarios:

- A fast food chain is selling their specific burger. They will want you to make a hamburger exactly to their specifications. There will be little room for creativity. Your job here is to make each ingredient in the burger look as fresh as possible and to make the finished product represent the client's product as closely as possible. They should provide exact measurements; you will need product from their purveyors. As serving size is critical, you should have a scale with you to weigh product. Request a product "spec sheet" (listing of product specifications) to work from.

- An upscale restaurant is also selling a burger, but there is usually more leeway in how to present it. It may not be necessary to show in the photo exactly how much of each ingredient is on this burger. They may want you to shoot at their restaurant, in which case their kitchen or chef might produce the food in pieces and you will assemble it from these pieces to make it camera ready. If you are shooting a restaurant hamburger in a studio, it's best to find out what their hamburger looks like before the shoot. Not all restaurants have photos, but most of them do have plate description cards used by the kitchen staff specifying everything on that hamburger and in what amounts. There is

more creativity here since it isn't a giant corporation overseeing the placement of every tiny sesame seed. We will often go eat in the restaurant on our own dime (once we've been hired for the job) to check out their style. Or the client invites us—even better.

- A ground beef supplier is selling meat. They aren't selling buns or lettuce or condiments. Everything in that photo is secondary to the meat. They will provide you with their product and you'll probably be expected to shop for everything else. The burger patty is the star. The top of the bun should be tilted or on the side so the meat can be seen in all its glory. Ask whether they want grill marks or not. How cooked should it appear—rare, medium or well-done? How many pounds of hamburger will the manufacturer be bringing? In order to make the burgers as identical as possible, you will need to have a hamburger press or create a form. We often use a large biscuit cutter to keep the size consistent.

- A lifestyle magazine is usually selling a lifestyle idea. The image or artwork will accompany an article, also known as *editorial*. Whether it's a single recipe or an entire article, you will have more input into the final look of this food. An art director from the magazine might tell you that the burgers should look "homemade." Or the author wants it to look like Mom made them in the backyard. Chances are you will be expected to shop for all the ingredients in this shoot. Find out what the idea or theme of the article is. Is there a prop person? How many hamburgers do they want to see? Color of plates? What size plates? An entire table of food? Models? Grill? Sponsors? Are there burgers still cooking on the grill? Find out everything you can about the image being shot.

- A grocery store could be selling everything it takes to make that burger. They may or may not supply you with product. They may be selling buns, ground beef, onions, tomatoes or lettuce and want you to shop for it. They might be selling charcoal briquettes. How creative you can be depends upon the art director. You'll have to find out what they are going to do with the image and what their style is.
- A cookbook author is selling that recipe and, in a larger sense, the entire cookbook (most people buy cookbooks because they are attracted to the photos; on average, fewer than 10 percent of recipes in any given cookbook are ever cooked by the reader). Ask the author what look they are going for. They could want anything from extreme close-ups to elaborately styled tables.

Okay, so you know who the client is and what they want to sell. The third question on your list is: How are they going to use the image?

- A fast food chain might be using the photo for a menu board, for point-of-sale pieces, on a menu or a billboard, on their website, or all of the above. Typically, there is a single burger in a photograph, but there could also be fries, onion rings, or a beverage in the shot. These photos are usually shot at a studio.
- An upscale restaurant might use the photos for their menus, their website, in promotional pieces or even as art on their walls. A burger will usually be shot in context with sides and possibly a drink. These shoots are often at the restaurant but are sometimes done in a studio.
- A ground beef supplier could be using photos for packaging, ads, brochures or their website. Since the point of the photo is the meat, the photo will be up close and personal, probably with no background or a background that is out of focus. Manufacturing clients will usually shoot at a studio but will sometimes request that the photos be shot at their facility.
- For a lifestyle magazine, the subject of the article will influence how you style the burger. It could be an article on backyard grilling, healthy burgers, burgers for kids, gourmet burgers, unusual burgers, burgers that can kill you, etc. Your hamburger could be a generic, perfect burger on a plain white background or a picnic table full of burgers with all the party fixings (including the party guests) or anything in between. These can be shot at a studio or on location. Shooting on location is a whole other can of worms and you can read about it on page 148, "Location, Location, Location" section.
- A grocery store could use the photographs on billboards, the sides of trucks, a website, a newspaper insert, or in weekly sales sheets. This could be anything from a single hamburger on a plain white background to a tabletop with additional food and props or even a live model or two. A shot like this will usually be shot at a photo studio.
- Cookbook photos could be used inside a cookbook or on the cover. Frequently, an author will be paying for the shoot out of their advance (unless the author is a big name with a lot of publishing money behind him/her). Because of this, authors will be very concerned about money. Many authors we've worked with recently have called us to find out how to save on the cost, and we tell them what prep to do

the day before and what to shop for. Authors who pay for their own photos are very motivated to get as many images as possible from a day of shooting. This being the case, the more simple the food and the props, the more images can be shot in a day.

Once you know who your client is, what they are selling, and how they want to use the image, you are well on your way to knowing what you need to prepare for the shoot. You can move on to contacting the other people you'll be working with.

When you find out where you will be shooting, you will need to coordinate with the photographer or studio manager about what time you can get into the studio. If you are shooting in a restaurant, ask the restaurant manager about providing you a work space and table. Speak to the chef about how much product you'll need prepared for your use on the shoot (usually two to three times whatever amount is in a single dish).

If you are working with a new client or with a large budget, call the accountant from the client's company to get him/her to issue you petty cash to cover the amount you will be spending on product.

Contact the prop stylist or prop master (if there is one) to find out what props they are bringing. Ask about plate sizes, as this will affect the amount of food you need to prepare.

If shooting a photo to accompany an article, find out if you can get a copy of the article when it's published.

On some bigger jobs there will be a production coordinator to help you with all this; most of the time, though, you will be on your own. If you want to arrive at a shoot prepared, don't count on someone else supplying the information. Sometimes you will get paid for all the time this takes, sometimes not. This will depend upon how you sell yourself and charge for your time.

The previous chapter is all about money, go back and read it again if you need to.

Shopping and Protecting Product

Purchasing the best product you can without having to visit nine different stores is the key to spending your time wisely when buying product. Trust us on this: clients don't want to pay you for an entire day of shopping for a one-day photo shoot, even when the shoot involves ten recipes. Clients hire you without having any idea how long it takes to shop, prepare, or prop a shoot. It is your job to educate them. Once you've acquired the food, you'll also need to handle it properly so that it lasts until you no longer need it.

Shopping

Clients may ask you to shop in a half day (five hours), meaning they only want to pay you for half a day. You have to decide if that works for you. On shoots that don't require extensive shopping, we often shop on the way to the studio, adding that time to our total day. This means that when we get to a shoot we have already worked an hour of our budgeted time. Make sure your client understands this, as it effects your wrap time.

Your job when shopping is to buy the best-looking product you can. It truly helps to know all the stores in your neighborhood so you can build your shopping list according to which store or stores will suit your project best. It doesn't do the shoot any good to spend money on inferior product that you can't use. We often have problems when sending new interns shopping. They'll grab the first chicken or roast they see without really looking at it. Product must start out as perfect as possible or you are putting obstacles in your way before you even begin.

If your client asks for a specialty or out-of-season item and you can't find it, tell the client

immediately. Make them aware of the time and trouble you have gone through looking for it. They might not really need this item, or they might have a source for it.

For bigger and longer shoots with numerous shopping lists, you (or your assistants) might be shopping the day before, two days before and, possibly, every day of the shoot. Whatever you buy, and however much of it there is, if you don't handle it properly you will have wasted the time and money it took to get it.

Handling Product So It Lasts

Let's talk now about how to handle food so that it lasts, whether that means protecting it until the end of the day or for many days. As a food stylist, it is highly unlikely that you will ever have enough refrigeration. Learn to let that go. Many food items do not have to be refrigerated for them to stay looking good.

Frozen items that you are going to thaw can be placed in plastic bags (to prevent leaking) and left at room temperature. Items like pizza,

waffles, pancakes, fruit or vegetables can all be handled this way. Frozen items that need to stay frozen, like ice cream, can be put in a cooler with cold packs and will stay frozen overnight. If the weather is warm or you need to keep the product frozen hard, you can purchase dry ice at many grocery stores. Never touch dry ice directly, as it can result in frostbite. Freezer space is often very tight on shoots, and, unless your budget allows for renting a freezer, having a cooler or two available is a workable alternative.

Any leafy greens, herbs, green onions, or anything else that can wilt should be wrapped in damp paper towels and put in plastic bags. If kept cool, these foods will last overnight. If the weather is warm, you'll need to refrigerate or put in a cooler. Any cut vegetables (raw or cooked) should also be stored this way. Use a black marker to label them, as it's hard to find things when you're in a hurry and everything in the refrigerator is wrapped the same.

Product like fruit (with the exception of berries), potatoes, peppers, onions, avocados, firm

tomatoes, and squash can be left out, as is, for a couple of days. Keep in a cool place away from anything that could damage them. We usually keep these products in bus tubs under worktables if we are inside, and on sheet pans in a speed rack if we are outside. If it's hot or we are worried about critters, we try wedging whatever we can into a refrigerator or cooler (even a cooler without ice packs will protect product somewhat) overnight.

Raw poultry, meats, and dairy should be kept in a refrigerator to keep them looking their best—unless it's a cold evening, in which case your car is probably as cold as a refrigerator. There will be times when you have so much to lug and schlep that you'll have to leave groceries in your car. You might want to invest in a few coolers (or get your clients to pay for them) so you can protect product that is left in your car. If you have room in your trunk, keep a mid-sized cooler with you all the time.

In extremely hot weather (or on an unbearably hot sound stage) even with refrigeration, herbs, berries and leafy greens will expire. Make sure it is in the budget to replace these items every day or two of the shoot.

Writing a Trouble-Free Shopping List

More often than not, we find it a financial necessity to send an assistant to do the shopping. You can pay an assistant less than you would yourself. Assistants by their very nature don't have the experience that you do, so you need to be very specific when making shopping lists. If you put "apples" on your list, you could end up with 2 red or 18 green apples. Or maybe even a bag of pre-cut apple wedges. Be specific: 6 each red apples and green apples, medium size, 4 inches in diameter. Never assume that an assistant knows what is on your mind. We tell our assistants to always buy enough ingredients to build a recipe or a plate presentation at least 3 to 4 times. And even with this equation, we're often washing sauce off pasta or making a quick trip to the closest store to buy more.

Look at the recipes your client sent you; is there something that makes sense to get as a garnish? Will you need another type of food on that plate? What color is it? Buy side dishes that will make the main product stand out. Side dishes are often not mentioned on a shot list but the client will expect you to bring them anyway: green beans, salad, baguette, rice pilaf. These are cheap accessories that can save your butt and your sanity on shoot day.

Estimating How Much Food You Need to Buy

As stated above, our rule of thumb for photo shoots is to buy enough product or ingredients to make the hero plate or recipe (depending upon whether the shot is of a single serving or an entire platter of four, six, eight or more servings) at least three times. As you get to know your clients, you'll better be able to judge if you will be fine with just the bare minimum or if you'll need to bring a lot more for each job. It depends on your client and whether or not they change their mind a lot or really know what it is they want.

It's an entirely different rule of thumb for a television demo or food segment. You will need enough to make a hero, a twin (if necessary), a demo prepped out, and extra in case something awful happens. So that's four times the standard four-to-eight-serving recipe. We usually pick up a little extra of everything that goes into the recipe to decorate the set. We'll use baskets of garlic, bell peppers, onions, avocados or whatever is in the recipe, maybe scattering a few around the table to fill any empty spaces. They make inexpensive decorations and are pertinent to the recipe. Also, the talent might decide they want to be chopping a pepper during the program tease, so it's always good to have extra ingredients.

If you are buying product for a commercial or infomercial, it's critical to know how the director works and how many takes he thinks it will take to get the shot the client finally approves. It's

A Day in the Life of an Assistant Food Stylist

A typical day for an assistant usually begins with a grocery trip for the items needed for the shoot. Depending on the length or complexity of the particular job, the list of items could involve several hours in multiple stores. Remember to look over the list the night before you shop so you know if there are any difficult-to-find items that would require trips to specialty markets. You might have to do some shopping the night before.

Also, be prepared to leave the shoot during the day to pick up last-minute items at the store. This could happen several times throughout the day. When the shopping is done, the organization and prep begins. The lead stylist will usually guide you through the necessary steps to get started on the preparation of each needed recipe or dish.

Throughout the day it is important to be at least one step ahead on your prep and tasks (you never want the client, stylist, or photographer to be waiting on you). There will be many fast and slow periods throughout the day, but it is important to keep yourself busy. If you feel there is nothing to do, it's always a good idea to clean, including but not limited to washing and putting away the dishes and organizing the messes that are made throughout the day. The lead stylist will be occupied with his/her own responsibilities, putting finishing touches on the dishes as well as the set and working with the photographer and client. Assume that the cleaning is solely your responsibility; it's a good idea to clean as you go.

At the day's end, it is the assistant's responsibility to have the kitchen area clean, with all of the extra materials and tools packed and ready for loading. If the team will return to the same location for additional days of shooting, then you are responsible for clearly marking and packing away all of the unused product and essential prep for later use, in addition to cleaning and organizing the kitchen area.

When buying food for a commercial or infomercial remember that the more the food is involved in an action, the more of that food you'll need.

so hard to generalize about how much you will need, as it will depend upon the actual shot and whether the food can be used again or not. As an example, your client is a chicken farm and their commercial shows a roasted chicken being sliced in order to show how juicy it is. This means you'll only be able to use each chicken once. We've had directors that tried using the other side of a chicken so they could get two takes, but then the chicken is pointing in different directions, which means the continuity has been lost.

The talent will slice into the chicken, pressing against the meat with the knife to bring the moisture to the surface, making it look juicy. If they slip or get the words wrong or somebody on the crew sneezes, they'll need a new chicken. Whether you bring eight or twenty chickens depends upon your communications with your client, the director and your budget. The production will want you to buy as few chickens as possible, but you have no way of knowing how many you'll actually need. Nobody does. However many chickens are in your budget to buy, make sure the director and the talent know exactly how many are available to use. You never, ever want them to be asking for one more that you don't have.

We realize this isn't much help. When buying food for a commercial or infomercial, remember that the more the food is involved in an action, the more of that food you'll need. It's kind of like one of those math problems: If you have talent with X experience slicing into Y chickens, a director with Z amount of artistic pretensions, a client with a high uncertainty ratio, and an unknown

amount of refrigeration—how many hero chickens will you need to get the scene on tape?

Our attempt at humor is simply to get you thinking about all possible things that could come up and be prepared for every one of them.

How Seasonality Affects Product Availability

Sometimes a photo shoot will be scheduled way out of season: think a Christmas shoot in August. We keep some candy canes and whole cranberries in the freezer because we find them to be two items we can easily store. Other seasonal ingredients aren't so easy to store. What if your client wants Indian corn or pomegranates in May? You can sometimes find items from importers like Melissa's Specialty Produce and have it shipped to you. But you will need a few days lead time and the client will have pay the overnight shipping fee. Make sure your client knows about any seasonally difficult items. In most cases, it's not that the item can't be found; its how much it is worth to them. We've paid $500.00 for a case of pomegranates that arrived old and shriveled, but we shot them in spectacular light and they looked pretty good. Sometimes you won't be able to locate an item because it simply doesn't exist. The worst thing you can do is show up on shot day with empty hands. As soon as you run into problems, let your client know so they can decide what they want to do. They may change the shot or change the shoot date. They may decide to do some Photoshop magic. Whatever they decide to do, give them a heads-up as soon as possible.

Food Safety: Are You Kidding?

Food safety and food styling are two terms that don't really belong together. Don't get us wrong; food safety is an important issue when making food for consumption. We harp on it in every entertaining cookbook we write. But, as a food stylist, your main job is to style camera-ready food, not to cook edible food.

Let's be clear on what your job is: you are being paid to make beautiful food that stays beautiful until it gets its picture taken. That's what all the tricks in the "Tricks of the Trade" chapter are for. The food has to last under hot lights and still look fresh. Seldom, as a food stylist, are you being paid to feed people. These are two completely different jobs. There isn't a studio kitchen in existence that would pass a health department inspection. You may be cooking in a high-tech photo studio kitchen, or you might be working on a rickety folding table in an alleyway next to overflowing trashcans. One time we were the first to arrive at the location, a large park. We parked next to a few other cars and waited for the rest of the crew to arrive. That's when we noticed that the man in the car next to ours was naked. We decided to sharpen our largest knives. He drove away.

Photo studio kitchens often look nice, but, to be honest, you'll have no idea when it was last scrubbed down or if the pots were washed with hot water, or if the dishes were wiped with Windex instead of being washed. Which is why, when we are asked by talent or crew for a taste of something, we have to tell them nothing has been refrigerated properly and we just aren't willing to risk someone's health. It helps to think of your styled food as a prop, like a plate or a vase.

We very often work and cook in areas that lack power or running water. We "clean" with Windex or Lysol, neither of which is edible the last time we checked. Not only do we not have time to scrub those cutting boards with bleach after cutting raw chicken, we also don't have a sink to scrub them in. Without a sink, we have no place to wash our hands or our tools. Food styling is often one emergency after another, with hardly time to keep our work area clean, let alone sanitized. You will drive home smelling like something unidentifiable and vaguely disgusting.

If cooking outside, it's amazing how quickly those flies and yellow jackets find protein. And speaking of insects, always carry bug repellent. If you need to scare bees away from your food, a spray of Windex discourages them. Of course, this means that your work area and any food on it has been sprayed with Windex.

If clients or crew try to eat your food, it is your job to educate them. If that doesn't work, then warn them. If they are adamant (we've had it happen) and they simply take the food off your prep area, then they deserve what they get. We only hope the stomach cramps don't hit the greedy eaters until after the shoot has wrapped.

The Art of Food Suspension

After making your beautiful food, you will need to keep it looking as good as possible until you are ready to plate, style, and shoot it. Some foods last longer than others. Pancakes will stay nicely at room temperature all day, even two days, if wrapped well. But eventually pancakes will crack. Cooked chicken, fish, and meat (if you do not need to see pink inside) will hold at room temperature for two days if properly protected and stored in resealable plastic bags. No doubt about it, old food is going to stink when you open one of those bags. If you have room to refrigerate cooked proteins, then by all means do so, but remember the camera only "sees"; it doesn't smell. If the chicken breast still looks good, you might need to use it again to save money and time. On the other hand, refrigerated proteins shrink, so sometimes they are not useable if refrigerated.

How Long Will It Last?

Most of the time, you will make food the day you plan on shooting it, so you only need to suspend it

When the Food Has to Be Edible

At some time in your career, you'll have a project where your client insists the food you style also has to be edible. We've had this happen when we've worked on cooking shows and television dramas where there is a party scene or actors are eating together. Of course, we can cook tasty food, make sure it is uncontaminated, arrange it on clean platters, and deliver it, but if the food sits out for hours under hot lights it's no longer edible. If your food has to be edible you'll need:

• enough food for several takes.

• enough food to replace any that stays out too long.

• to have refrigeration available to hold food until the scene is ready to be filmed.

• a way to heat or cook any food that needs it.

• a way (and work space) to get the food ready when taping begins.

If you look at television shows and commercials with food, you'll notice that people aren't actually eating much of it; it's just filmed to give that impression. What is actually happening is the plated hero food is never touched and a few bites of chicken or vegetable that are edible are placed behind the hero food where it won't be seen on camera. This saves a lot of money, as the hero food doesn't have to be switched out, only edible bits added when necessary. Also, keeping small amounts of food hot or cold near the set is immensely easier than keeping many plates of food safe to eat. Simply stated, it costs more money to prepare food that is being eaten. Make sure your clients understand this. People are much more inclined to change their specifications when they know they'll save money.

Food Suspension

Suspension, also called "holding" is keeping food for a period of time in "hero" condition, maintaining its color and keeping it from drying out and/or oxidizing (darkening). Here are the ways foods are most often suspended:

• Paint oil on meat and poultry to bring back the look of freshness.

• Paint a solution of vinegar and water on meat to keep it from changing color.

• Paint an antioxidant on fruits to keep them from turning brown.

• Spray water on some fruits and vegetables to bring back color, life and texture.

• Keep cooked foods at room temperature so they do not shrink during refrigeration or expand due to heat.

for that one day. Some styled food has a very limited lifespan. Other food will last for days. The general rule is to keep as much as possible at room temperature, sprayed with oil or water, covered with damp paper towels, and placed in resealable plastic bags or covered with plastic wrap. All the food listed on the next page is cooked and styled food that, unless otherwise stated, is covered with damp paper towels then wrapped in plastic wrap or placed in resealable plastic bags.

By learning about food suspension and how to refresh and hold food, you save a production a lot of money in food cost and save yourself hours in labor. Hours that you don't have, by the way. As long as nobody has to eat it, it doesn't matter how old it is. The camera won't know and we're certainly not telling.

Organizing Your Time

Completing any job successfully begins with organization and planning. What you don't know will come back to bite you in the ass. Get as much information as possible from the client, the photographer, the producer, and anyone else you're working with. Don't assume anything. As an example, we had a producer ask us to decorate a demo cooking table so it looked like Thanksgiving. We brought a dozen different-sized pumpkins and red and yellow leaves. He was very upset. His exact words: "What do pumpkins have to do with Thanksgiving?!" Okaaay. We could have avoided that problem if we had thought to ask what his idea of Thanksgiving was. He wanted gourds, lots of gourds. The kind that look like they have a horrible case of acne. So we sent a PA (production assistant) to the store to buy gourds. Luckily we had time.

We include an assistant in the budget for every shoot possible, unless it is very clear that the job doesn't require one. Depending upon how your business is structured, the assistant will invoice

HOW LONG CAN FOOD BE SUSPENDED?

FOOD	METHOD	TIME
Egg, sunny-side up	held immersed in oil	2 days
Egg, sunny-side up, held on a plate	sprayed with oil	1 hour
Egg, scrambled	sprayed with water	4 hours
Egg, omelet	sprayed with oil	2 days
Chicken, whole	sprayed with oil	2 days
Chicken, breast/thigh/leg/wing	sprayed with oil	2 days
Chicken, sliced/diced/shredded	sprayed with oil	2 days
Turkey, whole	sprayed with oil	3 days
Steak	sprayed with oil	1 day
Hamburger patty	sprayed with oil	1 day
Beef, whole roast	sprayed with oil	2 days
Beef, sliced roast	sprayed with oil	1–2 hours
Beef, shredded	sprayed with oil	1 day
Pork, whole roast	sprayed with oil	2 days
Pork, roast sliced	sprayed with oil	2–3 hours
Pork, shredded	sprayed with oil	1–2 days
Lamb, whole roast	sprayed with oil	2 days
Lamb, roast sliced	sprayed with oil	2–3 hours
Lamb, rack	sprayed with oil	2 days
Lamb, chops	sprayed with oil	1 day
Pork, chops	sprayed with oil	1 day
Fish, filets or sides	sprayed with oil	2 days
Shrimp	sprayed with oil	1 day
Salad greens, undressed	sprayed with water	1–3 hours
Vegetables, most	sprayed with oil	2 days
Pancakes and waffles	not sprayed	1–2 days
Pasta, plain	tossed with oil	2 days
Pasta, sauced with additions	sprayed with oil	2 days
Cakes and pies	no covering, no spraying	2–3 days
Cookies, brownies	in resealable bags	4 days or more
Fake ice cream	no covering, no spraying	forever

Denise's Food Suspension Epiphany

Early in my career I worked at KQED in San Francisco. Several big PBS cooking shows were shot there. It wasn't filmed in a big fancy studio; it was more like camping. We had to bring in every piece of equipment, every glass and dish we needed. We washed the props and pots in a grungy prop sink. The sink didn't have a disposal, so we engineered a nylon stocking over the trap to catch any wayward food in the hopes of not clogging the drain. We changed the food sock when it got full. We called it "the haggis."

The oven was set up on a loading dock where we cooked in the San Francisco fog, wind and rain. It was on a union job, which meant when the AD (assistant director) called "wrap" we literally had to drop everything and walk away, as the producers had forbidden any overtime. If we stopped in the middle of a scene, then we had to pick up the same scene the next morning, meaning the set remained a "hot set" and nothing could be moved. The food remained where it was.

The first time this happened to me, I had to leave food out on a buffet. I was only able to cover it with damp paper towels. When I got in the next morning, I was amazed to find out that most of it looked pretty good. I sprayed oil and water all over it, refreshed what I could and left the rest. And you know what? It looked great on camera.

either you or the client. Sometimes we will pay an assistant out of our own fee because it's worth it to us to make our day easier.

Planning a Job

Time management and organization are the keys to running a profitable food styling business. Make sure you know what your client is hiring you to accomplish. It's the nature of the business for the actual job to change several times before you even get there. Be sure to communicate to your client at the beginning that adding or changing things along the way may result in additional charges for your time or otherwise increase their costs.

We discuss this in the "Different Niches of Food Styling" chapter, but it is so important that it bears repeating. Here's what to consider when planning a job:

- How long will the shopping take? Can it be taken care of in one trip? Are there specialty items that will require visiting more than one store?
- If there are specialty items, do they need to be ordered? How many days in advance?
- How long will prep take? Are there any labor-intensive items that need to be prepared the day before?
- How involved is the job? How many pairs of hands will it require to get done in the budgeted time?
- Does the job require a backstage kitchen or main prep area and a separate satellite prep area nearer the set? This means you'll need another pair of hands, preferably two, since it eats up a lot of time running between the two prep areas. We like to have a third pair of hands (or legs, as it may be) just to float between the two

Always purchase the best-looking product possible; it will save you time and stress later on.

areas, helping out where necessary or making grocery store runs.

☙ Are there any rentals involved? Will the rental company be charging the production for the rentals or do they require a check or deposit upon delivery? Who is interfacing with the rental company?

☙ What is the start time? When is the first shot scheduled? Does this give you enough time to prepare or do you need to arrive earlier? How early can you arrive?

☙ Does the job require that you attend a pre-pro (pre-production) meeting or a visit to the location before the shoot? Most clients won't want to pay for your time for meetings. Rarely a necessity, the meeting is more for your client's comfort and is usually a waste of your time. Insist on being paid if you think the meeting is unnecessary; usually they will decide a telephone call is sufficient.

☙ What does unloading and setting up involve? Do you have to set up an entire kitchen or do you simply walk in with your kit in hand?

☙ What does breaking down involve? Is there extensive cleaning? Will you have extra hands to be cleaning up and packing out towards the end of the day so that when you are on your last shot it is just a matter of minutes before you're out the door?

Shopping

After you get the shoot information, your next step is to make a comprehensive shopping list. Always purchase the best-looking product possible. Do not try to save your client's money by buying cheaper product unless you know for a fact

that the cheaper product isn't going to be clearly seen in the photo. Starting with the best possible product will save you time and stress later on. If an assistant is shopping, make your list very clear. Specify exact amounts and brands. Go over the list to avoid any confusion. Make sure your assistants know they can call you with any questions.

Prepping

Questions to ask yourself when figuring out how much prep time you will need:

☙ Is a prep day (or half day) in the client's budget? It is your job to give your client a realistic idea of how much can be accomplished in the time given. If you have a client with an ambitious number of shots, they might be happier to pay for some prep time than to risk having to pay for overtime. For example, say your client wants 12 simple shots in 10 hours, including shopping time. After shopping, unpacking, prepping and styling your first shot, you'll be 3 hours into your time; figure in a half hour for lunch (on photo shoots lunch is provided by the photographer, paid for by the client, and the half-hour is included in the 10-hour day. On video and film productions, lunch is provided by the production company and the half-hour or hour, the director or producer decides, depending upon the shoot schedule, is deducted from the 10-hour day, making your day 10-1/2 to 11 hours) and a half hour to clean and pack out and you're at hour 4, leaving 30 minutes for each shot. You and your assistant together are charging.

—$100 an hour for a 10-hour day
Hours 11 and 12 are at time-and-a-half = $150
All hours after that are at double-time = $200

Precise, Perfect Prep

When you make beautiful food for the camera, you are creating something that is going to be frozen in that moment of perfection. It'll go up on a billboard, on a magazine cover, menu board or product packaging. You won't get a second chance, so it is vital that your food be as perfect as possible. Be precise in your prep. Make sure finely cut herbs are just that. Discard any blemished product. Brush off crumbs and smooth any unsightly jagged edges. Rinse off any excess bits and pieces, as they look distracting to the camera. An ugly image will come back to haunt you.

You end up working 15 hours, costing the client a total of $1,900.

If a prep day had been approved, you could have charged for your assistant to shop and prep at a lower rate, allowing you to bring enough prepared food with you so that the first shot is up a half-hour after you arrive; and, as all food has been prepped, the time needed to finish and style it is significantly reduced. You get the shots done in 10 hours and your client's cost was:

—$1,000 for the shoot day

—$500 for the prep and shopping day

—Total cost = $1,500, a savings of $400 from the scenario above.

- How many shots will there be?
- How many dishes in each shot?
- How much of it do you have to prepare from scratch?
- Are there any items that can be purchased already made or partially made?
- Are there any recipes that must be made the day before, like cheesecake or crème brûlée, gelatin, pudding, baked goods, etc.?
- If the client will pay for a prep day, what else can you prepare ahead of time? We generally prep everything we possibly can in the time allotted to us. This frees up time on the shoot day to handle client changes that inevitably come up.

When shopping, buy as many prepped or ready-to-use items as you possibly can. A large part of using your time wisely is knowing what products are available. If your client wants everything made from scratch, be sure they know what it's costing them. Assure them that, in many cases, you can start with something pre-made and alter it so that it will work for them.

Location, Location, Location

Your jobs will take you everywhere. You can never assume that because you've worked in twenty different studios you know what to expect

The Good, the Bad and the Ugly

Photography studios can be beautiful places equipped with everything you'd ever need, or they can be dingy rentals with not even a trashcan or sink. We've worked them all. Sound stages and television studios are the most surprising because the expectation is that they are very nice. Well, yes, the part the camera sees is nice. The part the camera doesn't see is another story. Take one of our local morning news shows as an example: they rarely have food on the show, so they don't have the facilities to support it. That means we set up in the parking lot, the hallway, or huddled in a dark corner of the studio trying not to make noise while the show goes out live.

On sound stages, as well as all other sets, you get used to walking over a mine field of cables, power boxes, C-stands, apple boxes, sandbags, tripods, boom cameras, random pieces of plywood, and crew members. They will usually have a table for you to prep on and a prop table for the set. That's it. You'll need to bring everything else, including all props that go on the set table. You'll pack up everything and take it home with you to wash it. The upside of television studios is that you are in and out of there in a couple of hours.

with the twenty-first. Get as much information as you can from your client, then ask for the studio manager's info so you can contact him/her yourself. Your client may think they know what your needs are but, believe us, they don't. Always double-check. Be as prepared as you can. You can't be shy about getting what you need to do your job.

Working where it's convenient isn't always comfortable. Walking back and forth from the kitchen gets really old after nine hours of standing or bending. Ask for a small set table to help you stay organized.

Every location has specific requirements. Many locations, especially photo studios experienced in shooting food, will have all the appliances you'll need, and you will only need to bring your kit. Other locations will have little or nothing. Still, a one-day shoot might require only your kit and a portable burner. But what if you are hired for a multi-day shoot at an unequipped location? Be sure you know what equipment you need to make the food you are being hired to produce. Following are descriptions of some of the locations where you'll find yourself working, with suggestions for the equipment you may need.

Working With and Without a Kitchen

Most shoots will be one or more days long. The type of equipment you'll need will vary, depending upon the shoot particulars. If you are on location (more often for filming, not photography) you will most likely be prepping outside. You may need to have a truck (called a "cube truck") outfitted with the equipment secured inside it or in an area on the property, like the garage or back patio, where you can set up a temporary kitchen. If you are in a studio, you may have an actual kitchen with a stove, refrigerator and sink, but the stove might not work, the refrigerator could be filled with crew food, and there might be one square foot of counter space on which to work.

Rental Equipment for Outdoor Kitchens

Find out what foods you'll be preparing before ordering equipment. If a couple of portable burners will suffice, you won't have to rent an oven. Or there may be a sink nearby that you can use so you don't need to rent one.

You will need some or all of the following:

- Speed racks, 2 to 4.
- Sheet pans, 20 to 40.
- Stove and/or oven.
- Propane with extra canister.
- Refrigerator, more than one if necessary.
- Freezer, if necessary.
- Sink (with water tanks if no water is available).
- Tables with risers, 2 to 6, depending upon shoot.
- Pop-up tents for sun/rain protection.
- Chairs or stools.
- Garbage cans with liners, at least 2.

Rental Equipment for a Cube Truck

Cube trucks are big, empty trucks that can be outfitted with all kinds of equipment. Since space is at

a premium, find out what equipment will be necessary. Don't rent an oven if your portable burners will do. Don't rent a freezer if you don't need one. Any space not taken up by equipment is better used as work space. The trucks have waist-high counters with secure shelves above and below for storage. The stylist gives the production coordinator a list of needed equipment and the production coordinator arranges and pays for the rental.

We often cook out of trucks when shoots are at private homes or other outdoor locations.

We've cooked in trucks at the beach, in the mountains, on the shoulder of the Pacific Coast Highway, in the parking lot of the Los Angeles Coliseum, even in the parking lots of studios that have no kitchen facilities. The back end opens up and there is usually a side door we leave open for airflow. Depending upon the weather, you will want to ask the production company for a heater or an air conditioner. The truck will be parked with the other production trucks, usually some distance from the set. This will necessitate renting equipment for a smaller satellite prep area nearer the set.

Cube trucks need to be connected to a generator or other power source. Residential power isn't sufficient. An electrician on the production will connect the power to the truck. If the truck needs to be moved, then a driver from the production will move it. To outfit the inside of the cube truck, you will likely need:

- Speed racks, 2 to 4 (1 or 2 for the satellite kitchen).
- Sheet pans, 20 to 40 (half for the satellite kitchen).
- Stove and/or oven.
- Propane with extra canister.
- Refrigerator (second refrigerator for the satellite kitchen, if necessary).
- Freezer, if necessary.
- Microwave for satellite kitchen, if necessary.
- Sink (with water tanks if no water is available).
- Tables with risers, at least 4.
- Pop-up tents for sun and rain protection.
- Chairs or stools.
- Garbage, 2 to 3 cans with liners (1 for the satellite kitchen).
- Fans and air conditioner or heater.

If the weather permits, some tables can be placed outside the truck (under a pop-up for shade) for extra workspace.

Rental Equipment for Private Homes

You will usually be set up in a garage, patio, backyard, or cube truck. If the production company isn't used to dealing with food, they will tell you that you can use the kitchen in the home. Ask if they are filming in or near the kitchen. If yes, then you can't cook in it because the house kitchen is part of the "hot set." This has happened to us so many times it's not funny anymore. You can't prep and cook in a kitchen where the crew can hear or see you cooking. The soundman will go mad. Rental equipment needed is the same as for Outdoor Kitchens and Cube Truck above. If you are working outside, make sure to ask the production company to supply you with pop-up shade or rain protection.

Rental Equipment for Backstage Kitchens

Visit the studio to see what facilities are available to you, or get the studio manager's number so you can call and find out what they already have. Many studios now have descriptions of their facilities online. If your client is filming or videotaping (rather than taking photos), you will need to set up your kitchen area far enough away so as not to interfere with the sound or create smoke. You will need:

- Speed racks, 2.
- Sheet pans, 20.
- Stove and/or oven if location doesn't have one.
- Refrigerators, even if location has one you may need an additional reach-in.
- Sink, usually available at the location but you always need to check.
- Tables with risers, at least 4.
- Chairs or stools.
- Garbage cans with liners.

Satellite Kitchens

When we are in studios or on sound stages, we usually prep in a different room or a kitchen down the hall. This necessitates having a small satellite prep area near the set. This also necessitates having another pair of hands at that satellite prep area. Which necessitates having one more person to be a runner between the kitchen and the satellite. For a satellite kitchen you'll need:

- Work tables, 1 to 2.
- Speed racks, 1 to 2.
- Sheet trays, 10 to 20.
- Refrigerator, if necessary.
- Microwave, if necessary.
- Garbage can with liners.

Whenever rentals are involved, make sure they will be delivered to your location when it's convenient for you. Find out from the studio or location manager what the earliest time is that someone will be there to take delivery. Find out if they can be delivered the evening before so you can plug in the refrigerator and/or freezer.

The Art of Packing: The Whole Kit and Kaboodle

Our kits fit into the trunks of our cars. This is important because shopping for most jobs fills our back seats. For larger jobs we often shop for dry goods and supplies the day before and, if we can, drop everything at the location. Sometimes it's necessary to rent a cargo van to hold everything; the van should be billed to your client or come out of your petty cash budget. Usually we only have one or two cars full of stuff. We make an effort to pack everything so that we can easily carry it. For food and supplies we use tote bags or have them bagged in a paper bag inside a plastic bag. The reason for this is that the amount in a standard bag is easy to carry, and if you put the bag in the refrigerator, the plastic bag will keep the paper bag from tearing. Also, the shape of paper bags makes them easier to stack into a car. We create a stable base of un-squishable items for the bottom layer and place more delicate items on top.

We also use bus tubs (plastic tubs of the kind busboys use to carry dirty dishes to the kitchen) to pack dry goods, props, and any extra kitchenware. This way we can pack a layer of sturdy items in our cars, putting more delicate groceries in bags on top. When on set we use the bus tubs to hold our dry goods and dirty dishes and sometimes turn one into a sink.

Who Knew There Were This Many Stairs?

We don't use wheeled cases or carriers because they take up a lot of room and are useless when faced with dozens of stairs (or yards of mud or acres of sand). Unless you are very strong, get used to making many trips and only carrying a comfortable amount. The alternative is to seriously hurt your back or legs.

Figuring Out What You Need

Take a look at the sample client worksheet for a photo shoot on page 74. Not only does it keep track of everything you need to remember, but it gives you a script for selling your services and closing deals.

Getting the most information from your clients before arriving at any set or studio will make your job easier and the whole day go more smoothly, with as few "oh no" moments as possible. After nailing down all this information, you will be able to determine if one or more assistants are necessary and if there is need for a day of prep beforehand.

Everything you have to plan for on a project translates into a cost or charge to your client. Sometimes I'm charging for a day of prep and the prep is simply renting a van, calling assistants, finding that special cake, driving to the florist, or going to the mall for a certain color tablecloth.

You need to write down every detail and keep track of your time. It will impress your clients. When I spell out for my clients all it takes to make a successful shoot, they realize it's not as easy as we make it look.

To help you with organizing your time right from the beginning, use the sample form shown on page 57, in the "Different Niches of Food Styling" chapter.

When providing food for television, it is best to get as much information as possible since TV people are extremely difficult to get in contact with. You may only be interacting with one person on the production, probably the producer but maybe the prop department, depending upon the specific show.

Now you are aware of all the myriad details that go into every shoot. In the next chapter we give you the tricks, tips and techniques for making beautiful styled food.

1. **THE SINK IS NEVER** hooked up to water pipes. There is a hose to supply water to the faucet, but the drainage water goes into a bucket that the art department has to empty after every taping. It's a stinky mess.

2. **EITHER THE BACKSTAGE** kitchen manager or food stylist shops for and prepares every piece of food. The talent or chef is responsible for their performance in front of the camera, not for the food. Some television chefs provide recipes and ideas; some don't.

3. **THE CLOSE-UP** of a hero plate is called the "beauty shot." If it's used for a segment tease after a commercial break it's called a bumper. You bump the audience so they know what you are going to show them.

4. **MOST APPLIANCES,** pots and pans, and knife sets that appear on camera are sent free to the show. This is known as product placement. Sometimes the companies that supply product are show sponsors. That means they've also kicked in money. Prep equipment and set equipment are two different things. You don't cook in set equipment. Any equipment appearing on the set is set equipment, and is considered a prop. You should ask what is available for on-set equipment. If the props and set equipment are not product placement, then the prop master or art director provides it.

WHAT PEOPLE DON'T TELL YOU...

5. **SOME PRODUCTION** companies will not want to give any products free advertising, so they will "greek" out all labels that might be seen on camera (by blacking out with a marker or obscuring with electrician's tape), or they will insist on getting paid by any company that might benefit from their products being shown on television.

6. **THE FOOD IN THE SET** refrigerator is usually empty packaging. Refrigerators are too loud to be plugged in during taping.

7. **SETS ARE USUALLY** not stored once a season is over. It's cheaper to build a new one than it is to store an old one, so old sets are taken apart or destroyed.

8. **THE STOVE IS NOT** hooked up to a gas line; it runs off a propane tank.

9. **IF IT IS A UNION SHOW** (meaning the crew members belong to a union or the show is being shot on a union lot) you will never touch anything relating to the set. You won't light the stove, you won't move the table, you won't touch anything. That is somebody else's job. You prepare the food and a union member puts it on the set.

10. ON THE OTHER HAND, on a non-union job you will be completely responsible for all of the food and equipment. It is nobody's job to help you with your stuff; so, if you need help you'd better bring it with you.

11. CAMERA LEFT OR RIGHT is the opposite of the talent's left or right, everything is oriented from the camera's viewpoint.

12. THE FOOD BUDGET for a TV show can be $15,000 to $20,000-plus dollars a season, usually thirteen shows.

13. MOST FOOD segments for national shows are rehearsed or blocked (walked through) for the camera. This helps the director of photography and the cameraman to follow the action of the food. Blocking a recipe is also called "stepping out."

...ABOUT TELEVISION COOKING SHOWS

14. WHEN A CHEF OR TALENT is baking a cake and they open the oven to find one already done, the baked caked is called a "twin." If it has to be shown frosted at any point in the show, the stylist may have a second finished cake, called a "triplet."

15. EQUIPMENT FOR THE SET is not used in the backstage kitchen. Set equipment needs to be kept set-ready. There are often two, three or more pieces of each item so that there is always a clean one available.

16. IF IT'S A SHOOT TAPED ON LOCATION in a private home, the kitchen is the set and an additional kitchen is installed with rented equipment and used as the backstage kitchen. This kitchen is often located in a garage (if you're lucky), backyard (inside a tent if you're lucky), or in a rental cube truck outfitted with kitchen equipment.

17. WHEN COOKING is done on camera, one of the most important things is "sizzle." That means when the chef or talent puts food in a sauté pan, that pan had better be hot enough to sizzle and smoke. It is the stylist's job to manage the temperature of the set stove, either by turning it on and monitoring the heat or making sure the right crewmember gets it done. Ultimately, it is the stylist's responsibility.

18. STYLED FOOD for the camera is often embellished. Food appearing on camera may not be edible or even cooked all the way. When the audience is eating samples, these have often come directly from the backstage kitchen and cooked to real time. This is where knowledge of food safety and sanitation is important.

TRICKS OF THE TRADE

Now you are ready to do some actual food styling! Don't get frustrated if you don't get the effect you want the first time; it takes practice. And with practice, you become familiar with how food (and the products used to style food) behave over time and under lights, how far you can go when manipulating it, and what to do to fix problems. We alter these techniques to suit the particular job at hand and whatever we have available at that moment. It's like being an artist only using (mostly) food products instead of canvas and paint. As you get more experience, you will learn how food acts and reacts and what you can do to control it. In the end, it's playing with your food!

Poultry

Nearly all styling jobs involving poultry will involve chicken or turkey. Styling a duck or goose is similar to styling other birds, but they need to be cooked longer to look done since they have a thick fat layer just under the skin.

Styling any type of product begins with selecting and purchasing it. Start with the best-looking ingredients you can find, with as few flaws as possible. For example, we typically buy organic chickens because

When styling poultry, the flesh should look succulent and moist, with no raw pink meat showing. Any skin should look golden brown and tight.

the skin has fewer flaws and it will take enhanced color better.

When styling poultry, the flesh should look succulent and moist, with no raw pink meat showing. Any skin should look golden brown and tight. The shape of your poultry should be plump, with no depressions, dings or dips. Food stylists inevitably develop their own preferred techniques and materials for making beautiful roasted birds: we are masters of invention! We've heard of stylists who paint turkeys with wood stain and shoe polish. Whatever makes the bird look good is kosher; we all use what we have available to us at the time. This job is about solving problems as quickly as you can with the materials at hand.

To get you started, here is a list of items you will find useful when styling poultry:

- Coloring Spray for Poultry.
- Paprika or Coloring Paste for Poultry, recipe on page 160.
- Cooking oil spray.
- Kitchen twine.
- Butane torch top and fuel.
- Toothpicks or T-pins.
- Dishwashing soap.
- Shallow baking dish or sheet pan with 1-inch sides.

Coloring Spray for Poultry

This makes a yellow-brown color suitable for use on poultry, fish, breads, pies, pastries, and any other golden-brown products. Use a small spray bottle with a 2- to 4-ounce capacity and a fine spray nozzle. Most pharmacies carry small 2-ounce sprayers that work well. The recipe can be doubled for larger sprayers. This recipe is for a 2-ounce sprayer.

Instructions:

1. Fill sprayer three-fourths full with water.

2. Add 1 tablespoon Kitchen Bouquet or other browning liquid, like Gravy Master or Savoie's.

3. Add 8 drops of standard yellow food coloring, not gel coloring, as it is much more concentrated.

4. Shake well.

5. To test the color, spray onto white paper towels. Add more Kitchen Bouquet or yellow food coloring if needed.

6. Keep coloring sprayers in a leak-proof container or a resealable plastic bag.

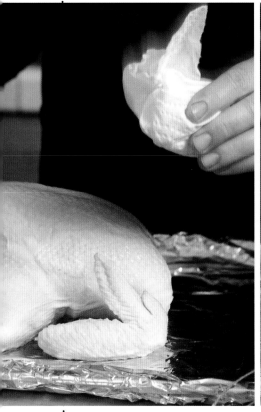
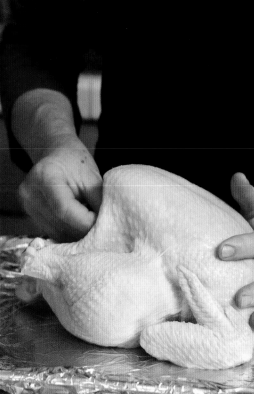
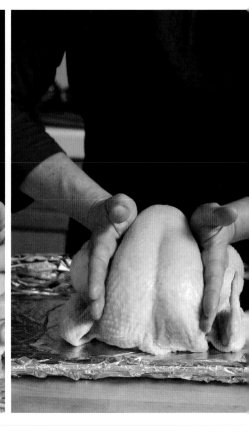

Coloring Paste for Poultry

This makes a dark reddish-orange color. Use it to rub into the skin of poultry or thin it with vegetable oil and apply with a brush or sponge. This is excellent for daubing on too-light areas of skin.

Instructions:

    1. Place 1/2 cup paprika in a small bowl.

    2. Add 2 tablespoons vegetable oil.

    3. Add 2 tablespoons Kitchen Bouquet.

    4. Add 2 teaspoons Angostura Bitters.

    5. Stir all ingredients together and store in a small, airtight container at room temperature.

Roasted Whole Chicken and Turkey

These instructions are for product that will be used whole, not sliced or cut into. Color the bird a bit lighter than you think you'll need. You can always darken it after you have looked at it through the camera.

Preparing poultry for cooking:

1. Select a bird with as nice a shape as possible. Always try to use fresh, not frozen, turkeys when possible, and one without a pop-up gauge. Wash the skin of the bird with diluted dishwashing soap and blot it dry with paper towels.

    2. Stuff the cavity with onion wedges, wads of paper towels, or whatever is handy, pushing

up the breast from the inside to give it a plump look.

3. If your bird is lopsided you can massage it into better shape. Being careful not to tear the skin, push the sides of your hands down and inward, between the breast and legs, so that the breast meat is pushed up to create a plump heart shape. Pushing the skin down between the breast and leg will give your bird more definition.

4. French truss the wings by bending the wings back behind the bird to keep them in place during cooking. If you would rather have the wings in an upright position, wrap the last joint loosely in foil to prevent burning.

5. Tie the drumstick ends together close to body so they don't spread open during cooking.

Cooking and coloring poultry:

1. Line a shallow baking dish or sheet pan with foil and spray it with cooking oil. Place the bird on the prepared pan and spray it lightly with oil. Bake in a preheated 350 degree F oven for 15 to 20 minutes for a whole chicken, 30 to 45 minutes for a turkey.

2. The skin will begin to tighten and the meat underneath will become opaque. (All meat should be *undercooked* unless it is being prepared for cutting. Meat that is cooked through will shrink from loss of moisture and can develop wrinkles in the skin.) Remove bird from the oven.

3. Begin spraying the skin lightly with coloring spray to build up the desired color. Let it dry a few minutes between coats so the color doesn't run.

4. If you do get runs or drips, don't panic: simply rub color into the skin with a cosmetic sponge or your hands. If the color goes too dark, blot the skin with a damp cosmetic sponge.

Finishing and garnishing poultry:

1. Lightly apply heat from a butane torch to tighten any areas of the skin that appear loose or undercooked. Also use the torch to heat any areas that look raw or pink and on the bony ends of the drumsticks. Keep the torch moving, as too much heat can cause the skin to tear open.

2. Sprinkle paprika or dab some coloring paste for poultry on top of the breast and drumsticks where the bird would get the most heat in the oven. Cover any tears, marks, or too-light spots with paprika or coloring paste.

3. Spray lightly with cooking oil spray so that the bird looks moist. If you sprinkled paprika on your poultry, then spraying with oil will make it

looks less red and will even out the color.

4. Garnish with a sprinkling of cracked pepper or chopped herbs if desired.

5. Fill cavity with stuffing, herbs or whatever else is appropriate for the photo.

Roasted Chicken or Turkey Legs

When a leg is called for, always start with a leg and thigh attached so that you have extra skin to work with.

Instructions:

1. Wash the skin of the bird with diluted dishwashing soap and blot dry with paper towels.

2. Pull back the skin just enough to expose the joint where the leg and thigh connect.

3. Separate the leg at that point, cutting the skin back but leaving enough skin to pull under the leg.

4. Secure the skin under the leg with a T-pin or toothpick.

5. Cook, color and style the same as for poultry, above.

Chicken or Turkey Breast or Thighs

When a breast or thigh is called for, get a piece with extra skin to wrap around and tuck under, or buy a second piece so you'll have extra skin.

Instructions:

1. Wash the skin of the bird with diluted dishwashing soap. Blot dry with paper towels.

2. Secure the skin with T-pins or toothpicks, placed where they won't be seen.

3. Cook, color and style the same as for poultry, above.

Sautéed or Seared Chicken

Whether removing the skin or leaving it on, the cooking method for sautéed or seared poultry is the same.

Instructions:

1. Poultry should be cooked over medium-high heat in a preheated, lightly oiled skillet, preferably nonstick. Place top (or best-looking) side down and cook until desired color is reached.

2. Turn and cook just until the poultry no longer has any raw meat showing. (It will still be very raw inside.) Alternatively, after turning the poultry, place a few tablespoons of water into a hot pan to create steam, then cover the pan and turn off heat; let sit for about 2 minutes, or until all surfaces look cooked.

3. Remove poultry from the pan and spray it with cooking oil spray to keep it moist and to prevent oxidation. Cover with damp paper towels. If you need to hold the poultry longer than an hour or two, it should be placed in a resealable plastic bag.

A cast-iron grill pan is a useful addition to your kit. It is the easiest way to put grill marks on ground meat, steaks, chicken, chops, fish, vegetables, or even fruit.

Refreshing Poultry

Sometimes poultry that has been holding for a couple of hours only needs a light spray of cooking oil to refresh it. If your bird is looking a bit worse for wear, or if it's been sitting around all day (or longer) then briefly reheating it will give it back some life. You can do this by going over it lightly with a kitchen torch or heat gun. Or you can put it in a low oven for a few minutes. The downside of warming it in an oven is that if it's been sitting around long enough to get a little stinky, then the heat will make it worse.

Getting Good Grill Marks

There are numerous ways to add grill marks to food. The obvious way is to cook food on a grill, but usually this option isn't available in studio kitchens. Also, grilling doesn't allow you as much control as the options below.

Grill Pan

A cast-iron grill pan is a useful addition to your kit. It is the easiest way to put grill marks on ground meat, steaks, chicken, chops, fish, vegetables, or even fruit. Your grill lines will be evenly spaced and can be touched up with a charcoal starter or a heated metal skewer; or they can be painted in with a tiny brush dipped in straight Kitchen Bouquet or drawn in with dark brown or black eyeliner pencil. We keep an inexpensive Lodge cast-iron grill pan in our kit. Yes, it is heavy, but it is also indestructible.

Instructions:

1. Heat the grill pan over high heat. Blot the meat dry with paper towels. Decide which side is the better-looking side. Spray the hot grill pan with cooking oil spray and carefully place the meat in the skillet, best side down.

2. Let the meat cook without shifting it until the desired grill marks are achieved.

3. Thicker cuts of meat can be turned and cooked on the other side. Thinner cuts of meat and most fish can get overcooked this way. Instead of turning it to make the second side look cooked, add a tablespoon or two of water to the hot pan, then cover the pan and turn off the heat. Let the meat sit until steam causes the surface of the meat to look cooked.

4. Use a kitchen torch to touch up any places on the meat that don't look cooked enough.

To further enhance grill marks, see "Charcoal Starter" or "Metal Skewer" below.

Charcoal Starter

Grill marks can also be added or enhanced with an electric charcoal starter. This handy tool consists of a plastic handle and thick metal rod bent into a loop. This device gets extremely hot, so

unplug it as soon as you are done using it to avoid accidental burns.

Instructions:

1. Place the product on a foil-lined baking sheet. Plug in the charcoal starter in a secure and nonflammable area. We like to have a heavy-duty, upside-down sheet pan to rest it on to protect the surface underneath. Charcoal starters get super hot; just because they are on a sheet pan

doesn't mean the surface under the sheet pan is heat-proof. You could still damage it.

2. Using the marks from the grill pan as your guide, press the charcoal starter into the product, rocking it slightly to mark the ends. Remember that any natural dips or dents in the meat will be more lightly marked than bits that stick out, which should have a darker grill mark.

3. If necessary, darken with coloring spray for poultry or meat.

4. Spray with cooking oil spray to keep it looking moist and to prevent oxidation.

Metal Skewer

If an outlet isn't available, you'll need an alternative to the charcoal starter. We always carry metal skewers in our kits for just such occasions. You will need a portable burner, kitchen torch or other flame source.

Instructions:

1. Heat a metal skewer over a flame until it's very hot. You might need to hold the skewer with a potholder while it heats up.

2. Press the hot skewer into the meat to make dark marks.

3. Repeat until the desired look is reached. It may take several applications to make one grill mark, as the skewer cools down quickly.

Meats

We've said it before but it bears repeating: styling any type of product begins with selecting and purchasing the product. As with chicken, start with the best-looking meat product you can find, with as few flaws as possible. Organic meats have whiter fat but conventionally grown varieties can be larger. Consider what is best for your specific job.

All meats, with the exception of those being cut into, should be undercooked. When meats are cooked all the way through they quickly dry out, which causes them to shrivel and shrink. Undercooking meat will keep it plump and moist longer.

By using proper holding techniques, you can cook meats for the camera hours in advance. Spray it liberally with cooking oil spray, cover it with damp paper towels, and either wrap it with plastic wrap or place it in resealable plastic bags.

There are a variety of ways to refresh cooked meats. You can spray with a fine water mister or cooking oil spray (the oil lasts longer; blot it with a cosmetic sponge before photographing if you overdo it). Be aware that some brands of oil sprays leave foamy bubbles that disappear when you blow on them or spray them with water. You can daub a little dark Karo syrup onto the surface of red meats for moisture and a darker color.

It's better to use a light hand when browning meat, building up the color gradually rather than trying to achieve the desired color right from the get-go. You can always make it darker but you can't make it lighter.

Here's a short list of items you'll find handy when on any meat-styling job:

- Coloring Spray for Meat.
- Paprika or Coloring Paste for Meat.
- Cooking oil spray.
- Denture cream (white) or Vaseline.
- Kitchen twine.
- Butane torch top and fuel.
- Toothpicks or T-pins.
- Shallow baking dish or sheet pan with 1-inch sides.

Coloring Spray for Meat

This makes a red-brown color suitable for use on the cooked surface of red meats. This recipe will fill a 2-ounce sprayer. You can multiply it by as many times as you like.

Instructions:

1. Fill a sprayer three-fourths full with water.
2. Add 1-1/2 tablespoons of Kitchen Bouquet.
3. Add 4 drops of yellow food coloring.
4. Add 3 drops of red food coloring.
5. Shake it well.
6. To test the color, spray it onto white paper towels. Add a little more Kitchen Bouquet or red food coloring to adjust color if necessary.
7. Keep coloring sprays in a leak-proof container or a resealable plastic bag.

Coloring Paste for Meat

This makes a dark red-brown color suitable for use on the cooked surface of red meats.

Instructions:

1. Place 1/4 cup paprika in a small bowl.
2. Add 1 tablespoon Angostura Bitters.
3. Add 2 tablespoons Kitchen Bouquet.
4. Add 1 tablespoon vegetable oil.
5. Stir together thoroughly to mix.
6. Store in an airtight container at room temperature.

Coloring Gel for Meat

This concoction needs to be made at the time you are using it, as it does not last more than a day or two. Apply to cooked meats with a small paintbrush to cover any parts that look raw. This mixture is especially effective in disguising fat.

Instructions:

1. Place 1 tablespoon clear piping gel in a cup.
2. Add 1/2 teaspoon Kitchen Bouquet.
3. Add 1/4 teaspoon Angostura Bitters.
4. Stir together thoroughly to mix. To prevent drying out, cover the mixture with plastic wrap when not using. Recipe can be multiplied.

Roasts

Selecting a roast is as important as cooking it. A roast should be more than 3 inches thick and should have a nice white layer of fat around it. Choose a roast that is deep red.

Cooking roasts:

1. Place the roast on a lightly oiled baking sheet, fat side up. Sprinkle it lightly with paprika. Spray it with water or oil and rub paprika into the surface of the roast.

2. Roast in a 350-degree F oven for 20 to 30 minutes, or until the meat looks cooked on the outside, or, if roast is being sliced into, until the desired doneness is reached.

3. Remove the roast from the oven and let it cool for at least 10 minutes before handling.

Coloring and finishing roasts:

1. Spray with Coloring Spray for Meat or rub with Coloring Paste for Meat until the desired color is reached.

2. Add extra color and a browned look by applying heat with a kitchen torch.

3. Spray the roast with cooking oil spray.

4. Garnish it with cracked pepper or chopped herbs if desired.

Cover with damp paper towels to hold it until ready to use. If you need to hold a roast longer than an hour or two, it should be placed in a resealable plastic bag or covered loosely in plastic wrap.

Steaks

Purchase the nicest-looking steaks you can find. Avoid any large areas of fat running through the meat as they will cause the steak to alter shape during cooking. Buy steaks about 1-1/2 inches thick unless your job requires filet mignon, in which case the size can be 1-1/2 to 2-1/2 inches thick. A steak less than 1 inch thick tends to look more like a piece of sliced beef than a steak.

Gristle doesn't shrink like the rest of the meat does during cooking; it will stick out and become very obvious. If gristle is on the edge of your meat, simply cut it off. If the gristle is in the interior of the meat, cut out about a third of the gristle from the non-hero side before cooking.

Prepare the steak for cooking:

1. Trim excess fat and gristle from the steak.

2. Determine which is the better-looking side.

3. Rub all surfaces of the steak with dark Karo syrup. Blot well with paper towels.

Cook and color steaks:

1. Heat a skillet or grill pan over medium-high heat. Spray steak with cooking oil spray and then place steak, pretty side down, in the pan. Cook it until the desired color is reached.

2. While the steak is cooking on the good side, use a kitchen torch to brown the sides of it and get rid of any undesired redness. Flip the steak over and cook a minute or two, then turn off the heat.

3. Remove the steak from the skillet and place it on a plate. Fill any cracks using a Coloring Gel for Meat (see recipe on page 170).

4. To keep steak moist and fresh looking, rub lightly with a little dark Karo syrup.

5. Spray steak with cooking oil spray and cover with damp paper towels until ready to shoot.

Ham

Sliced or diced ham is given color by searing it in a skillet over high heat and then spraying with cooking oil spray and covering with damp paper towels. Here's our method for a traditional-looking whole ham that is not sliced into, with or without the bone. Specialty hams like Serrano or pancetta aren't usually cooked, and they're typically shown all or partially sliced.

SPECIALTY HAMS
Serrano or pancetta aren't
usually cooked, and they're
typically shown sliced.

Instructions:

1. Use a paring knife or a razor blade to score the top of the ham about 1/4 inch deep (or more if you need to go through the fat layer), making a diamond pattern on top.

2. To decorate, push a whole clove into the center of each diamond or into each intersecting cut, depending upon the look you want. For an old-fashioned ham, first place pineapple rings over the entire top of the ham and add a maraschino cherry in the center of each ring.

3. Brush the surface of the ham with honey or Karo syrup.

4. Bake ham at 325 degrees F until the ham just starts to brown.

5. For additional browning use a kitchen torch.

6. To hold, spray ham with a cooking oil spray and cover with damp paper towels.

Spiral-Cut Ham

Spiral-cut hams usually come with a glaze already applied. The trick is to keep the cooked glaze and the thin surface layer of fat from peeling off of the slices.

Instructions:

1. Heat the ham in a 325-degree F oven until nicely browned on top.

2. Use a kitchen torch to brown any areas of fat that are too noticeably pale.

3. Spray the ham with cooking oil spray and cover it with damp paper towels until you're ready to style.

4. Fold and curl down the first 4-6 slices of ham, using cotton balls and toothpicks to reinforce the slices from underneath.

5. Before shooting, make sure the ham has not turned dark. A good test is to look at a piece that has not been exposed to air. If the ham has

Sausages need to be cooked just enough so that they don't look raw but not so much that the skin tears, while at the same time getting a nice seared or grilled look.

darkened, fold down the next slice.

6. Patch any holes in the ham with Vaseline or white denture cream. If you have any bits of hardened glaze and fat that are peeling off, glue these with Vaseline or denture cream. If the surface is too shiny, blot it with paper towels. If it's still shiny, spray it with matte spray (Krylon Matte Spray or Blair Matte Spray Fixative). This technique works on poultry as well.

Sausage

The problem with sausages is that if they are too cooked, the surface quickly develops wrinkles. And with raw sausages, the skin is prone to splitting. They need to be cooked just enough so that they don't look raw but not so much that the skin tears, while at the same time getting a nice seared or grilled look. Find out what the cooked sausages are supposed to look like when finished: straight like some breakfast sausages or curved? Can you purchase sausages or do you need to use your client's product? Following is our method for solving the sausage conundrum. It works well on both raw and cooked sausages.

Instructions:

1. Blot the sausages dry with paper towels.

2. Spray them with a coloring spray (either the one for Poultry or the one for Meats, depending upon which works best with the type of sausage you are styling) and massage the coloring spray into the sausage skin so the coloring is even.

3. Spray lightly with cooking oil spray and place the sausages in a nonstick skillet over medium-high heat. Turn sausages constantly for even coloring and so that they don't overcook.

4. Grill marks can be added (see instructions under Getting Good Grill Marks on page 164). Use a very light touch, as too much heat will cause the skin to split.

Bacon

Whenever possible use thick-sliced bacon, unless your client dictates otherwise.

There are three ways to cook bacon. The method you choose will depend upon the equipment available to you.

METHOD 1

Place the bacon on a wire rack inside a shallow baking sheet, pressing the bacon into the spaces between the wires so that the bacon will bake "wavy." Bake in a 325-degree F oven for about 30 minutes. Alternatively, make your own rack by twisting pieces of foil for the bacon (called "curlers") to lie on. Place foil in a shallow baking sheet and bake as specified above.

METHOD 2

Fry bacon in a skillet over medium heat until done but still a bit wiggly, adjusting the waves in the bacon with tongs as it cooks. Blot with paper towels to absorb excess fat. Alternatively, thread the bacon onto a thin bamboo skewer, pushing meat together to make the bacon wavy. Fry it in a skillet over medium heat until just done. This method also works when baked in an oven.

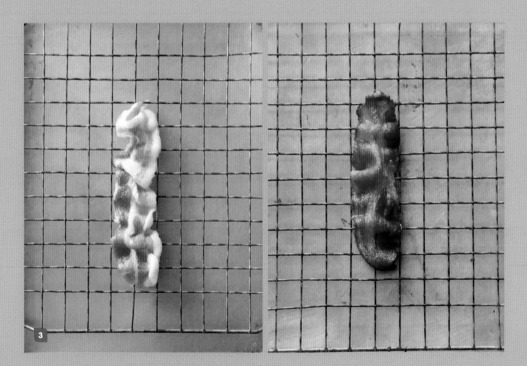

METHOD 3

Microwave on a non-metal grid rack, pressing it into ridges to give a curled look. Cook it on high until the desired doneness is reached. To refresh bacon, spray it with cooking oil spray or dip it in clean hot oil. Coloring Spray for Meat (page 170) can be used to darken bacon. Alternatively, bacon can be brushed with a little light or dark Karo syrup.

Burgers

Making a fast-food burger requires information from your client. If your client manufactures or sells burgers, then make sure they provide all product: the meat, the tomato, the bun, the pickles, etc. If they use a specific tomato-slicing machine, then they will need to provide you with sliced tomatoes or give you the exact thickness of the slices. They probably have a specific size tomato that their restaurants use. Ask for the dimensions. For any other type of burger shoot, you will most likely be responsible for purchasing the product yourself.

Use the leanest ground meat possible to avoid shrinkage. A hamburger press can be used for uniform burgers. Or make patties by hand. Make them a tiny bit bigger across than the buns you are using. The higher the fat content of the ground meat, the more the patties will shrink during cooking.

Instructions:

1. Make patties slightly larger than the hero bun.

2. Place a patty hero-side down in a hot skillet or grill pan until a nice brown color is reached.

3. While the first side is cooking, apply heat to the sides of the patty using a kitchen torch.

4. Turn and cook it for a few minutes more, until the bottom is no longer raw and the patty is cooked enough to hold its shape. Use a kitchen torch to cook the sides, if necessary.

5. Remove the patty from the skillet and place on paper towels to absorb excess fat and blood.

6. Color with Coloring Spray for Meat (recipe on page 170) or apply straight Kitchen Bouquet with a small paintbrush wherever extra browning is desired.

7. Patch any holes with white denture cream or Vaseline that has been mixed with Kitchen Bouquet and/or small bits of cooked meat.

Buns

Buns are very important to burger building. It won't matter how beautifully you arrange the other ingredients if your bun is lopsided or wrinkly. Purchase buns that have smooth, even-looking tops. A common problem with prepared buns is that they are packed in plastic bags while still warm, which causes them to steam, wrinkle and squish. Which type of bun you use depends upon your client. If they leave the type of bun up to you, then get a bun with personality—like a Kaiser roll or a whole wheat bun with a little texture.

Finding a white-bread bun with a smooth top in a grocery store is nearly impossible. Typically, if we know we are using generic buns from a supermarket for a shoot, we'll buy 3 to 4 dozen, knowing that only 2 or 3 buns will be perfect. The other option is to order buns from a bakery (if you have the time), usually two days before the shoot. Order buns unsliced and packed in a single layer in rigid boxes. This will protect them and keep them from steaming and getting wrinkly.

Before shooting, sort through the buns and select heroes. Slice the buns with a very sharp bread knife. Match the best tops with the best bottoms, then determine which part of the bun is best for using as the front.

To prepare buns for styling:

Instructions:

1. Trim bun tops and bottoms of any jagged edges with a small pair of sharp scissors.

2. If your hero burger is going to have the bun top on top (rather than off to the side or leaning against the burger), then pick out some bits of bread from the center inside surface. This makes the bun sit lower on the burger so that the burger won't look like it's wearing a hat (see Fluffing Buns on facing page).

3. Spray the inside cut surface of buns with Scotch Guard to keep them from soaking up condiments and meat juices. If you need hero buns to last longer than an hour or two, store them in resealable plastic bags to prevent them from drying out.

Fluffing

Fluffing originally referred to the job of a "fluffer" on adult movies, whose job it was to keep the actors clean and "ready" for the next scene. When a food stylist "fluffs" the food it means to refresh it a bit, i.e., spray it with a little water or oil, replace anything that has gone limp (pun intended) and just generally make it look all happy and new without replacing the whole thing. Fluffing is fluffing, whether it be buns or . . . whatever.

STACKING INGREDIENTS
A good example of stacking using lettuce on the bottom of a bun that sits too high in the upper left photo and one that sits just as seen in the upper right photo.

Fluffing Buns

When buns sit too high it makes the burger look like it's wearing a hat (photo above left). While cute, this look is not generally the look your client is going for. Removing a bit of bread from the top bun is also the first step to smoothing out shallow wrinkles in buns. Following is our method for fixing soft buns that are lightly wrinkled.

Instructions:

1. Remove a little bread from the inside of the top bun.

2. Dampen a paper towel with very hot water and form it into a smooth wad. Place the wad inside the top bun in the space where you've already removed a bit.

3. Place the bun, towel side down, on a wire rack sitting on a baking sheet.

4. Place it in a 350-degree F oven for about 3 minutes, until the top smoothes out.

5. Remove from heat and let cool a minute before handling. If necessary, or to make bun sit

Condiments are usually added
after the burger is on the set and
has been lit by the photographer.

flat on burger, remove the paper towel from the bun before styling.

Building Burgers

The goal in building a burger is to create the burger your client wants and needs. The directions below are for building a basic, standard, everyday hamburger suitable for most situations where the meat is on the top and all other ingredients are underneath it. Condiments like mustard and ketchup usually go on top of the meat.

Instructions:

1. Start with the hero bun base. Spray with Scotch Guard. Add lettuce evenly, like a skirt, so that it is clearly seen but not sticking out, obscuring the bun underneath. (Use curly leaf lettuce unless otherwise dictated by the specific shot.)

2. Add tomato, onion and pickle slices (or whatever product you are using).

3. If your tomato and onion are not level, the finished burger will look like it's leaning backward; prop up the back with bits of cosmetic sponges or cotton balls.

4. Add the cooked hamburger patty, propping up the back if necessary.

5. Add the top bun and look at your burger from the viewpoint of the camera. Prop it up where necessary to make the burger look straight and level.

6. Add "water" droplets to the tomato, lettuce, and onion either by spraying with water or by applying small drops of glycerin with a skewer or toothpick.

7. If using condiments, add with a medical syringe-type applicator, eyedropper or squeeze bottle. Condiments are usually added after the burger is on the set and has been lit by the photographer.

If you are adding cheese for a cheeseburger, place a slice of American cheese on the meat and melt it with a clothes steamer or heat gun before placing it on the bottom bun, lettuce, etc. Or place the burger in a warm oven until the cheese barely begins to melt. (American cheese will stay opaque longer than real cheddar cheese, which will turn transparent after it has been heated and begins cooling down.)

Sandwiches

As with everything else in food styling, the kind of sandwich you'll build will depend entirely on your client. If someone contacts you about shooting a sandwich, you'll want to ask these questions: What is the image selling? What is to be on the sandwich? What type of bread is to be used? Will the sandwich be cut? The answers will affect what you shop for and how you build and style the sandwich.

Sandwich Building

Generally speaking, the cheaper the sandwich meat, the easier it is to handle. If you are styling a generic sliced deli meat sandwich, then the goal is to create movement and interest with the arrangement of the meat. On the other hand, if you are asked to style a sandwich that illustrates what to do with leftover Thanksgiving turkey, then you will need to use thicker slices of roasted turkey. For a sandwich that is being cut into, you will need to build it with

flat layers of meat. After slicing, separate the layers of meat slightly with toothpicks to create some space and interest and break up the layers of meat.

As with the buns described above, spray inside surfaces of hero bread slices with Scotch Guard. Bread slices will look fine for about an hour but any longer and they will start curling a bit and drying out. To hold them longer, place them in resealable plastic bags until ready to style.

Instructions:

1. Build your sandwich with the top crust as the front. Place a layer of curly leaf lettuce on the bottom slice of bread, making sure not to have too much lettuce in the center where it will cause a hump. Contain the lettuce so that it sticks out from the bread just a bit here and there. If it sticks out in every direction, it looks like your sandwich is wearing a skirt. Remember: no one will see the inside of the sandwich; they only see the front and maybe one side.

2. Add the sliced meat in soft folds, making sure the front and sides look good. Cut excess meat from the interior of the sandwich to avoid a hump. Trim any broken ends with sharp scissors.

3. Make sure your sandwich is level. If the sandwich slopes down in the back, add meat, bits of cosmetic sponge or cotton balls to prop it up.

4. Add tomato and/or onion slices if using.

5. Stand back and look at your sandwich from the angle the camera will see it: Is it listing to one side? Is it sloping backwards? Prop it up with pieces of cosmetic sponges or cotton balls. If the back is too high, remove some product to lower it.

6. When the sandwich is on set, look through the camera and see where you want to add any condiments. Add condiments with a medical syringe-type applicator, squeeze bottle or eye dropper.

To hold sandwiches and to keep them from drying out, cover them with damp paper towels. Keep the hero top slice in a resealable plastic bag to keep it from drying out, as dry bread tends to curl up.

Before photographing, replace any lettuce that has wilted. Sometimes you will be able to push old lettuce into the sandwich where it won't be seen then add a "ribbon" of fresh lettuce off the end so as to disturb the finished sandwich as little as possible.

If you are using cheese slices, the cheese should be placed directly on top of the meat, placed so that the corners of the cheese can be seen by the camera, making it obvious that there is cheese on the sandwich. American cheese has a very plastic texture and will curve down a bit, making it an excellent way to hide a trouble spot.

NOTE what a difference a little pepper makes.

Breakfast Foods

Breakfast foods present their own unique set of issues. The single most difficult item is eggs sunny side up. The egg whites need to be cooked through, but the yolks can't take much heat or they will change color and the membrane surrounding them will become a cloudy white. You'll go through a lot of eggs to get one or two perfect ones. If we know we need two fried eggs for a photo, we'll buy at least two dozen eggs.

Eggs

Nothing says breakfast like eggs, but they are tricky little buggers. If yolks cook too long they change color, but if they are too raw they will tear and run when you breathe on them wrong. To complicate matters further, the factors that impact the way eggs look and how they respond to being cooked are so numerous it makes your head spin: the age of the eggs, temperature fluctuations, the chicken's diet, the chicken's breed, so many things you have no way of knowing. Depending upon the specific job (your client may specify exactly what kind and size of egg to use), we often buy two different sizes and brands to cover all bases. We've

bought jumbo eggs, using only the thick (or thin, depending on the look desired) part of the white, and medium eggs for the yolk.

Sunny Side Up

When cooking eggs sunny side up, the heat of the oil needs to be kept at an even, low temperature. The easiest way to do this is to use an electric griddle with the temperature set to low, with a nonstick pan placed on top of the griddle. Most griddles are long enough to fit two pans. To make fried eggs on a stovetop, use the heaviest-bottomed nonstick skillet you can find, or, better yet, place a small nonstick skillet on top of a larger cast-iron griddle or tortilla pan (something with sides low enough so that the nonstick pan sits flat) to evenly disperse the heat.

Pour oil (vegetable, canola, or corn) to a depth of about 3/4 inch into the pan. Heat the oil over low heat to the temperature of very warm water, about 120 degrees F (oil should be cool enough to stick your fingers into with no danger of burning). Separate the yolk from the white. Place each in a small cup or bowl. For a flatter white, use only the thin albumen (the thin part of the white); for

a thicker white use the thick albumen (the part of the white that stands higher and spreads less, immediately surrounding the yolk), discarding the thinner, runnier part. In lower grade and older eggs, the thick albumen becomes thinner, making it difficult to distinguish from the thin albumen. Remove the chalazae (the white cord-like thing attached to the yolk) carefully from the yolk using a medical syringe-type applicator. Raw yolks are very delicate and tear easily, so you'll need to be very careful. Some eggs have much weaker yolks than others. It's a good idea to have more than one brand of egg to work with. To cook, follow the instructions below:

Instructions:

1. Gently slide the white into the oil.

2. Let cook just until it has set.

3. While egg is still in pan, make a small hole (we use a large round pastry tip) in the white where the yolk is to be placed.

4. Gently place the yolk over the hole in the white. Yolk should be just submerged in oil.

5. Using a flat spatula, remove the egg.

To refresh eggs, spray them with oil. To hold eggs for up to 24 hours, immerse them in room-temperature oil.

To patch small holes caused by bubbles of air in the cooked whites, either daub a little plain yogurt into the holes with a small paintbrush or plug the holes with small bits of cooked white.

For yolks that sit higher on the white (the more they cook, the flatter they get):

1. Cook whites in warm oil until they are just cooked through, then remove from the pan with a flat spatula.

2. Cut a circle out of the white where the yolk is to be placed. Make the size of the hole just slightly smaller than the yolk itself. We use the larger end of a pastry tip.

3. Using a freshly cracked and separated yolk (yolks that have been sitting around, even for 20 minutes, will easily break), gently slide the yolk into the hole. Place the yolk on the white after the white is in position on the hero plate, as moving it will cause it to break.

Scrambled Eggs

Compared to sunny side up, scrambled eggs are a walk in the park. Scrambled eggs should look moist and golden yellow. Not all eggs are created equal; yolks come in a variety of colors. You can add a little yellow food coloring to the eggs when you beat them or add a few extra yolks if yours are too pale.

Instructions:

1. Cook eggs in butter (for a little golden brown color) or vegetable spray over medium-low heat in a nonstick pan.

2. When the eggs are almost done, cover and remove from heat; this allows any raw egg to

Omelets

are cooked like scrambled eggs except they are folded and stuffed with either food or cotton balls or both, depending on the style of the omelet and the type of photo.

1 Heat the pan over medium heat and sauté any ingredients that need to look cooked, such as onions and peppers.

2 Wipe out the pan, spray it with oil and place over heat. Pour in the beaten eggs. When the eggs begin to set, push the cooked part up with a small spatula, allowing raw eggs to run underneath. (This creates a thicker omelet with more surface texture that is less prone to tearing. Too-thin omelets tear easily and too flat omelets lack visual interest.)

3 When most of the eggs have set, place a cover over the pan and remove it from the heat. Let sit for 3 to 5 minutes. This allows any raw egg on top of the omelet to firm up.

Finished omelets will last all day and even into a second day if kept sprayed with water or oil, covered with a damp paper towel, and placed in a resealable plastic bag. Use a good nonstick omelet pan sprayed with oil. Use three large eggs for a standard 8-inch pan.

4 Look at the underside of the omelet to determine which side will be the top, or hero, side. Slightly pull apart several cotton balls (to loosen and soften the edges) and place over what will be the bottom side of the folded omelet, leaving an inch of space between cotton balls and the edge of the omelet.

7 Plate the omelet on the hero plate and finish filling it. Repair any tears in the egg with denture cream or Vaseline.

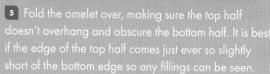

5 Fold the omelet over, making sure the top half doesn't overhang and obscure the bottom half. It is best if the edge of the top half comes just ever so slightly short of the bottom edge so any fillings can be seen.

6 Add ingredients to the open edge of the omelet.

Refresh omelets by spraying with water or oil spray. Keep them covered with damp paper towels until ready to shoot. To refresh the cheese, add a little more on top of the old and melt it with a heat gun.

8 If using cheese, melt it with a heat gun when the omelet is on set. Refresh omelets by spraying with water or oil spray. Keep them covered with damp paper towels until ready to shoot. To refresh the cheese, add a little more on top of the old and melt it with a heat gun.

Add a little baking powder to increase the height of the pancakes if necessary. The hero side of the pancake is the side that cooks first.

finish cooking without the eggs becoming too dry.

3. Spray finished eggs with water to moisten and give the eggs the look of freshly cooked eggs.

4. Transfer eggs to a plate that has been coated with a little oil (this keeps the eggs from sticking when you have to transfer them). Keep them covered with damp paper towels until ready to use. If kept moist, scrambled eggs will last half a day.

Pancakes

Pancakes are made according to the instructions on the packaged mix. Add a little baking powder to increase the height of the pancakes if necessary. The hero side of the pancake is the side that cooks first.

Use a pancake mix to make the desired amount of batter. Finished batter will keep for a couple of hours if covered and refrigerated. Thin it with water to the desired consistency when ready to use. Use a ladle or measuring cup to portion pancake batter so all pancakes are the same size. Use a nonstick skillet or griddle sprayed with oil over medium-high heat.

To make pancakes that are evenly browned, it is important to have your skillet at the right temperature. To control the heat, we lift the skillet and carefully wave it around to cool down the surface just a bit. If batter is placed in a too-hot pan, it will get dark brown in the middle, where the batter first comes in contact with the hot pan, and the pancake will get ring marks along the edges as the raw batter flows outward.

Making Perfect Pancakes
Instructions:

1. When the skillet is hot, spray it with oil, wipe off any excess with a paper towel (too much oil will make dark brown spots on pancakes), and hold the skillet away from the heat to allow it to cool down for about 10 seconds. Return skillet to heat and pour in the batter.

2. Tip or shake the pan briefly to make the pancake a perfect circle. This must be done as soon as the batter is poured into the pan or the pancake will not color evenly.

3. Let it cook until bubbles appear on surface.

4. Turn the pancake carefully with a heat-resistant spatula, pushing in any batter that seeps out around the edge so the edge is smooth.

5. Cook until pancake is cooked through.

6. Remove pancakes from heat and place them in a single layer on an oiled surface like a sheet pan or baking sheet. Don't stack pancakes on top of each other until they have cooled to room temperature or they will steam and get wrinkly.

Before stacking, trim any ragged edges with small sharp scissors.

If the hero side of a pancake is too light, you can brown it in a hot skillet or spray it lightly with Poultry Coloring Spray (recipe on page 158).

Stacking and Topping

Before placing toppings on pancakes, make sure they are at room temperature. If topping with syrup, use cheap syrup full of sugar, as real maple syrup is too thin. Brown Sugar Karo syrup or Pancake Karo syrup works very well. Place squeeze bottles of syrup or Karo in the freezer for at least an hour before using to get the syrup as thick as possible.

If adding butter, make scoops of margarine with a small portion scoop and freeze, or buy margarine in sticks and cut into pads, place on wax paper, and freeze.

Instructions:

1. Pick out the best hero pancake for the top and set aside. It's a good idea to have several hero top pancakes if syrup or butter is being used. This way, if you need to re-do the shot, you can just replace the top pancake.

2. Spray pancakes with Scotch Guard so the syrup or melted butter won't soak in as quickly as it would otherwise.

3. Pick out as many pancakes as you need to make your stack, minus the top one.

4. Arrange the pancakes so their best edges are facing front.

5. Place yourself at camera angle and look at your stack. Adjust pancakes by placing thin bits of cardboard, cosmetic sponges, or pieces of cotton balls between layers.

6. Place one of the hero pancakes on top.

7. If using powdered sugar or fruit, add it now. If using syrup or butter, wait and add it when the plate is on the set.

For syrup: after the pancake stack has been lit by the photographer, remove syrup from freezer and pour over the top. Start with a little syrup; you can always add more.

For melted butter: after the stack has been lighted correctly, add the frozen butter scoop or pat. Use a lighter, kitchen torch, clothes steamer or heat gun to melt the butter pat. Or have some extra butter already melted and drip it onto the frozen butter a little at a time.

Waffles

Waffles should be made and handled in the same way as pancakes. Cut off any rough edges with a pair of scissors before cooking. If using frozen waffles:

Instructions:

1. Place them on a nonstick baking sheet and cook in a 300-degree F oven until they just begin to brown.

2. Let them cool before covering with plastic wrap so they won't get wrinkly from the steam.

3. Darken waffles with Poultry Coloring Spray (recipe on page 158) if necessary.

4. Refresh them with a little cooking oil spray as needed.

5. If adding syrup or butter, see instructions for Pancakes on facing page.

Cereal

Sort cereal using a 1/8-inch wire screen to get rid of crumbs. Sorting is not necessary for all shots, only for those where cereal is being poured or where the camera is very close to the bowl.

If using fruit, be sure to use fresh, firm pieces. Frozen peaches are the exception, as good-quality frozen peaches look very close to fresh. Never wash strawberries, raspberries or blueberries. The moisture will make strawberries and raspberries get mushy quickly, and it will take the "bloom" off the blueberries.

Use shortening to make a false bottom in the hero cereal bowl. Make sure shortening fills 2/3 to 3/4 of the depth of the bowl, and smooth it out to the edges of the bowl so any liquid you pour in won't sink underneath. This creates a raised surface for the cereal to rest on. You can

also insert some pieces of cereal directly into the shortening to create definition between the pieces.

Milk is not generally used, since it soaks into the cereal and makes it soggy. Milk can also photograph as slightly bluish and thin. Depending upon the shot, we use white school glue or heavy cream.

In addition to a photo of cereal in a bowl, with or without milk and fruit, there are three other kinds of shots that are commonly done: the drop shot, the spoon shot, and the milk pour shot.

A drop shot, usually for television commercials, is when you see cereal being poured out of a box (and sometimes landing in a bowl). For this kind of shot, first remove dust and small broken bits of cereal by placing it over a 1/8-inch mesh screen and shaking it. Pick through the remaining cereal to remove broken and unsightly pieces. Coat the remaining hero pieces with hair spray (this reduces surface dust). Using a C-stand, position a hero cereal box (if the camera will be seeing the box) or a curved piece of thin cardboard (like a partial funnel) above the area to drop the cereal from, out of sight of the camera. Pour cereal onto the cardboard so that it slides down and "drops" into the target area.

A spoon shot is one in which a spoon is fixed in place near the hero bowl with a C-stand and filled with "milk" and cereal. Using white glue (or heavy cream) in place of the milk, place glue into the spoon and then carefully place hero cereal pieces into it.

A milk pour shot is where milk is seen being poured into a bowl of cereal. We use cream or half-and-half, whichever gives us the correct look for our pour, depending upon the lighting, the distance it's being poured, and the size of the spout it is being poured from. The pour is usually from a prop pitcher (if a pitcher is being seen in the photo) or a large Styrofoam cup (if it is not being seen), as it bends easily into a funnel.

Fruit

Not all fruits act the same when they're cut, as they sit under lights, or as they age. Start by purchasing the best-looking product you can find. Below are tips for handling and styling fruit.

Apples, peaches, pears, and nectarines will brown when cut. Sprinkle them with lemon juice or a solution of Fruit Fresh anti-browning powder and water. Use an apple-red-colored lipstick to fix any imperfections on red apples.

Avocados brown quickly when exposed to air. The more firm the avocado, the more slowly it will brown. Keep cut pieces immersed in vodka. When cut avocado is on the set, keep it moist by spraying it with vodka until ready to shoot. The vodka evaporates and leaves a natural finish on the surface of the avocado. Alternatively, spraying it with oil also works well but leaves a shiny surface not desired for all photographs. The oil spray lasts much longer and is excellent when using sliced avocados for television.

Bananas should be purchased with no brown or soft spots. Slightly green bananas work best if they will be peeled. Sprinkle exposed areas with lemon juice or a Fruit Fresh solution.

Blueberries should be left just as they are. If washed they loose their light-colored bloom, making them look like little black beads.

Lemons, limes and oranges will dry out after being cut. Keep cut pieces wrapped in damp paper towels or spray them with water to refresh.

Raspberries and blackberries should be kept cool but otherwise left alone, as they disintegrate faster when washed.

Strawberries, whole or cut, can be sprayed with water to freshen. To refresh the green tops of strawberries, rub them with a little oil right before using.

Tomatoes should be cut at the time you plan to use them, as they age quickly. Spray cut surfaces with water or keep the cut product wrapped in damp paper towels.

Vegetables

Like fruit, vegetables in their natural state are quite beautiful. Keeping them as beautiful as possible after cutting and cooking is the part we're concerned with in this book.

The vegetables listed below can be sautéed in a little oil (never butter, as it can solidify and leave a residue) or blanched in boiling water just long enough to bring out their color. Refresh by soaking briefly in icy water.

- Asparagus
- Broccoli
- Brussels sprouts
- Cabbage
- Carrots
- Cauliflower
- Celery
- Green beans
- Onions
- Peppers
- Potatoes
- Summer squash

Exception: Mushrooms need to be left dry. If you refrigerate them, wrap them in paper towels to prevent them from absorbing moisture and becoming slimy. To cook, sauté them in a little oil. If using them sliced, cook only on one side. Add a few drops of lemon juice at the end of cooking to keep mushrooms from browning.

Herbs

While some herbs are very hardy, most have a tendency to wilt at room temperature if not protected properly. Keep root ends of herbs in cold water, or keep bunches of herbs wrapped in damp paper towels. Refrigerate if you need them to last more than one day.

Some herbs will stay fresh looking for hours, like rosemary, some varieties of thyme, and oregano. Others, like cilantro, chervil, dill, and basil, will wilt in an instant. Bring back wilted herbs by soaking them in icy water.

If using relatively small amounts of herbs, consider buying live plants in small pots, available at stores like Whole Foods and Trader Joe's. You can keep them watered and fresh until the instant you need them. And any leftovers can be planted.

Salads

For beautiful salads, arrange the ingredients so there is separation, definition and movement of ingredients. Resist the urge to scatter ingredients evenly throughout the surface of the salad, as this will pull the eye in every direction at once, causing the overall effect to be confusing.

Wash lettuce and wrap it in damp paper towels. Place it in a resealable plastic bag and refrigerate so that it will stay as cold and as crisp as possible. If the greens get a little wilted they can be brought back to life by immersing them in a solution of icy water and Fruit Fresh anti-browning powder. Or just icy cold water.

Prepare all vegetables in advance and keep them wrapped in damp paper towels inside resealable plastic bags. Any vegetables that are cut into flowers or other decorative shapes should be prepared in advance and kept refrigerated in ice water.

When styling salads in glass hero bowls, be aware of any unwanted water on the inside surface of the bowl. Pay attention to the arrangement of colors and textures that you can see through the sides.

If the hero bowl is not clear, make a false bottom of paper towels dampened with icy water, moist cold mashed potatoes, or shortening. For larger bowls, wrap damp paper towels around an ice pack or two to preserve the crispness of the greens. Since greens wilt and flatten quickly, it is a good idea to start with a false bottom.

Use toothpicks, straight or T-pins to hold vegetables together as needed.

Always mist salad with water before shooting. Use a fine brush to put glycerin "water droplets" on vegetables with hard surfaces like carrots, the skin side of tomatoes, cucumbers, etc.

If using dressing, drizzle or paint it on when the salad is on the set. Dressings that come in mister bottles are a good choice, as they allow you to add dressing in a very controlled way.

Pizza

The first question to ask when you find out you are shooting pizza is, "Will there be a pull?" A "pull" is when a slice of pizza is being lifted away from the pizza, causing the cheese to stretch between the pulled slice and the rest of the pizza. You will want to know this because a cheese pull can take at least half a day to get right.

On a big pizza shoot, a portable pizza oven will probably be in your client's budget. Pizza ovens come on wheels and can be brought directly to a location. They are powered by propane and are about 5 feet wide, deep and tall. On most other pizza shoots you will be using whatever oven is at the location. Since pizzas are cooked at a high temperature, check to see that the oven is clean; otherwise it may smoke and set off the studio alarms. This has happened to us on more than one occasion.

Cheese should be stretchy to create a nice-looking pull. Use the mozzarella that comes in the string cheese snack packets. Peel apart the cheese in long, thin strands, 1/4 to 1/2 inch wide by about 1/16 inch thick. You want to end up with a bunch of string cheese ribbons. To construct a pizza for a cheese pull you will need:

- Pizza dough.
- Thick pizza sauce—we use tomato paste thinned with a little oil and darkened with a few drops of Kitchen Bouquet.
- String cheese.
- Shredded mozzarella cheese (not water-packed or fresh).
- Toppings as desired.
- Pizza pans—we use the pizza pans that have a perforated bottom so the underside of the crust hardens.

Preparing the Pizza
Instructions:

1. Roll out the dough to the desired size and bake it on a pizza stone or a pizza pan in a 400-degree F oven until firm and lightly golden. Remove from heat.

2. Decide what size your slice of pizza will be and make a template stiff enough to support the slice. Heavy-duty cardboard plates work well. Make it a little bit smaller than the actual slice all the way around so the camera won't see it.

3. Decide on the spatula that will be used to hold the pizza slice. (Before taking the photo, the photographer will need to secure this spatula

in place on the set with a C-stand, unless somebody with extremely steady hands is going to stand there with the spatula. *This cannot be you* as you will be busy working on the cheese.)

4. Have or make a stand-in pizza for the photographer to light. If you use the hero, the cheese will solidify by the time you are ready to pull the slice.

Preparing the Pull

Instructions:

1. Spread sauce over the crust (sauce for pizza should be thick to prevent it from soaking into the crust and making it soggy), coming to within 1/4-1/2 inch of the edge.

2. Cut the desired size slice into the crust using a large sharp knife or a pair of scissors. (Place the whole crust and the slice on the pizza pan.)

3. Place string cheese ribbons across the cuts, thicker in some areas, thinner or not at all in other areas. (If you cover the entire cut with string cheese, when you pull it up and away from the rest of the pizza you have a solid wall of melted cheese, not the stringy, holey look that is preferred.

4. Scatter torn bits of string cheese lightly over the rest of the pizza.

5. Sprinkle pizza with shredded mozzarella cheese, obscuring the string cheese pieces. Caution: too much cheese at the tip of your cut slice will make the slice weigh down, causing the tip of the cut slice to bend downward when pulled.

6. Add toppings. If using mushrooms, sauté them on one side for a golden brown color before adding them to the pizza. Don't place toppings over the cuts in the pizza, as they will interfere with the cheese pull. If you are adding pepperoni or using large ingredients, slice them where they straddle the cut so they won't inhibit the pull.

7. Place the pizza in a hot oven, about 400 degrees F, until the cheese melts.

8. Remove the pizza from the oven before the cheese starts to bubble and brown. Cover it loosely with foil until ready to use.

The Pull

Instructions:

1. Place the hot pizza on set. Put a cardboard template under the cut slice. If the pizza is very hot, let sit for a few minutes or the cheese will be too liquid and you won't get that stretchy pull.

2. Place a spatula under the cardboard template that holds the slice. The photographer will attach the spatula to a C-stand or somebody with very steady hands will hold the spatula.

3. The spatula needs to be moved up and away from the pizza in small increments while the photographer shoots.

4. If the cheese starts to harden, you can use a clothes steamer or heat gun to re-melt it.

If you are not showing a cheese pull, hold the cooked pizzas until ready to shoot by spraying them with cooking oil spray and covering with damp paper towels until ready to use. Pizzas can be refreshed so they look hot by applying heat to the surface with a heat gun or clothes steamer. Pizzas will last all day if treated this way. Extra cheese can always be applied to the top and melted to freshen the look of an old pizza.

Pasta

There are dozens of different pasta shapes and each one will be a different styling experience. Here are some general rules that apply to most varieties of pasta.

Dried pasta can be boiled up to a day in advance if slightly undercooked; drain it well, coat it lightly in oil, and store it in resealable plastic bags at room temperature. Fresh pasta cannot be made ahead; you will need to make it shortly before the shoot. Cook fresh pasta just until it looks cooked; drain and cool it immediately in an ice bath, drain it again and coat it lightly with oil. Cover it with damp paper towels until ready to shoot.

Cook any additions to the pasta separately by blanching briefly or lightly sautéing. Wrap them in damp paper towels until ready to use.

Pasta has a tendency to flatten out when placed on a plate. You can get around this by creating a support base underneath the pasta. Use mashed potatoes or shortening (never use warm ingredients when you have shortening underneath, only room temperature or cold!). In a pinch, damp paper towels, cotton balls, or even squished bread will work.

Instructions:

1. Have all ingredients for your pasta plate at hand.

2. Place a small mound of the support material of your choice in the center of your plate or bowl. (Use a smaller amount than you think you will need. If you use too much you will be able to see it underneath and between the pieces of pasta. You can always stick more in later if you need to.)

3. Add your first layer of pasta to cover the supporting material. If you are using large,

sturdy pasta like penne or bow tie, stick some directly into the sides of the support material—not straight up, that would look silly, but all around the sides like a balding porcupine. If the pasta is a strand type like spaghetti, linguini, or fettuccini, then you can stick a couple of broken toothpick pieces into the support material so that about 1/4 inch sticks out. Place pasta in a swirling pattern over and around the supporting material.

4. Figure out what your hero side is and add or move pasta so that there are no large gaping holes and there are not too many pieces all running in the same direction. If using a hollow pasta, make sure there aren't a lot of holes pointing straight at the camera. Look for negative spaces and shafts of pasta lying parallel to the edge of the plate or to other food. Basically, look for anything that draws your eye in a way that you don't intend.

5. Begin adding ingredients, placing them so they create interest and movement, cutting to fit if necessary.

6. Garnish on set.

Pasta can be refreshed by spraying it with oil. Keep un-sauced pasta covered with damp paper towels.

If using sauced pastas, toss pasta with a tiny bit of sauce, enough to give the pasta a light coloring, before styling. Add more sauce on pasta after the dish is styled and in front of the camera.

Soups and Stews

The trick with soups and stews is to put support on the bottom of the bowl so that any ingredients will be lifted to the top of the soup, where they will be seen. Clear marbles, fake ice, even chunks of raw potato make a good base to build on. For thicker stews, damp paper towels pressed into the bottom of the bowl will work as a support.

If you're styling already prepared soups, make sure you have 4 to 6 times the amount that will show on camera. Work with the product at room temperature for the best results. Fill hero bowls with the last bit of liquid when on the set, as the shifting it will do while you carry it from your prep area to the set will make a messy ring around the edge of the bowl that is impossible to clean.

Clear Soups

A clear soup is any soup whose liquid is clear enough to see the ingredients through. These soups need to be styled in such a way that the ingredients are close enough to the surface to been seen rather than resting on the bottom of the bowl.

Pour the soup into a strainer placed over a bowl to separate the liquid from the solids. Rinse the solids with warm water to remove any small broken bits or clinging fat. Pick through and discard any discolored or imperfect pieces. Determine if the strained soup liquid is usable. If there is too much fat or if the liquid is too cloudy, you will need to make a substitute. We find that using purchased chicken broth and coloring it with tomato sauce, yellow food coloring, and/or Kitchen Bouquet gives us reliable results.

Instructions:

1. Prepare the soup liquid.

2. Add supporting material to the bottom of your hero bowl. Depending upon how transparent the liquid is, fake ice, clear marbles, or large pieces of potato can be used. The potato is best,

as you can insert toothpicks into it to keep added ingredients in place. Place some of the hero ingredients in the bowl.

3. Pour in prepared liquid to about the half-way point.

4. Add and arrange the remaining ingredients. Add some more liquid if necessary to bring the level of the soup to about 1/2 inch under where you actually want it.

5. Pour the remaining liquid into the bowl when it is on the set.

6. Look through the camera before garnishing.

Cream Soups

Cream soups, by definition, are smooth and so not very interesting to the eye. You'll need to create something to draw attention, like swirls in the surface or a garnish of some kind.

Instructions:

1. Separate out and rinse any solid ingredients in the soup (unless the solid bits are so small as to make them more a part of the texture of the soup instead of added ingredients).

2. Adjust the consistency of soup, making it

thicker if necessary by adding a prepared white sauce (the Ragu or Classico brands of Alfredo sauce work very well for us) or making it thinner by adding water or cream.

3. Adjust the color, if necessary, with Kitchen Bouquet to darken, Alfredo sauce or cream to lighten, yellow mustard, tomato sauce, or food coloring to adjust color.

4. There is nothing but surface to shoot, so finish garnishing on the set. Make swirl marks with a spoon if the soup is thick enough to hold the shape, or garnish with a little cracked pepper or whatever your client will allow.

Stews

Instructions:

1. Place the product in a strainer or colander to separate the liquid ingredients from the solid ingredients.

2. If the liquid has any visible fat floating on the top, either spoon it off or re-create liquid using purchased chicken or turkey gravy, Karo syrup, and Kitchen Bouquet for coloring.

3. Rinse the solids under warm running water to remove any clinging fat or small messy bits.

4. Pick through to find the best pieces.

5. Place all the "second best" pieces in a prep bowl and combine with half of the liquid.

6. Add supporting material to the bottom of the hero bowl if using.

7. Pour the liquid-solid mixture into the hero bowl to fill about three-fourths full.

8. Place the rinsed solids on top.

9. Paint extra liquid over the solids.

10. Pour a little more liquid into the bowl when it is on set.

11. Garnish in front of the camera, looking through the camera for best placement.

Mexican Foods
Refried Beans

Good luck. They are going to look like cat food (or worse) no matter what you do. Expose as many whole beans or bean chunks as possible and spray them with water so they shine nicely.

Enchiladas

Dip tortillas in warm-to-hot oil before filling and rolling. Stuff them with filling, cotton balls, or paper towels. Straight pins will help hold a tortilla together if the fold is on the top. Dress the open ends of the enchiladas with the hero product. Top with sauce and cheese. Melt the cheese with a heat gun or torch. Shoot at once, as cheese does not last long before it starts to sweat and becomes transparent.

Garnishes

Olive slices, cilantro, chopped chives, chopped red, yellow or green onion, green onion brushes, radish slices, or diced peppers are all typical garnishes for Mexican foods. Keep cut garnishes wrapped in damp paper towels until ready to use.

Salsa

Make fresh or buy the fresh salsa found in the refrigerator section of most grocery stores. Strain off excess liquid and add freshly chopped tomatoes, onions, and cilantro if necessary.

Guacamole

Make it fresh. Spray it with water, vodka, oil or a Fruit Fresh solution. Or buy a prepared brand with the most chemical additives you can find and the best green color. These will stay stable the longest before turning brown. You can always dress it up by adding freshly chopped avocado and any other ingredients you like.

Tacos

Each company makes their tacos to their own specifications. All of the fast food tacos are primarily the same. Because the style of cheese used for most fast food tacos doesn't last long in front of the camera, you should keep the cheese nearly frozen and work the strands into the taco just before shooting. If using pre-made shells, look for a shell that is a little shorter on one side, as this will help show off the food.

Dairy

Most foods look better and are easier to handle when at room temperature. This is not so for most dairy products. Cheese and butter melt or can be too hard to work with if they're cold. Here are some tips to make working with dairy easier:

Butter and Margarine

Use a paring or utility knife to groom the sides and ends of sticks of butter or margarine. Make sure the product is very cold. If it gets too warm it is difficult to work on and is easily marked. Freeze the product after you get it looking the way you want it to keep it perfect until ready to use.

It is often desirable to have an uneven, rough and broken surface on hard and semi-hard cheeses.

To melt pats of butter or margarine use a lighter, kitchen torch, steamer, or heat gun. To give a pat of butter or margarine a melted look without heating or changing the shape of it, simply brush or drip some melted butter or margarine over it.

Cheese

Either a double-handled cheese knife or a large single-handled cheese knife is a must for breaking down large wheels or blocks of cheese. It is often desirable to have an uneven, rough and broken surface on hard and semi-hard cheeses. You can achieve this by partially cutting the cheese and then breaking it the rest of the way.

Melting cheese can be done in the course of the cooking process or by applying heat with a heat gun, steamer, or kitchen torch. Always melt cheese less than you think is necessary, as you can apply more heat once the cheese has been placed on the set and lit. If shredded melted cheese begins to sweat or turn transparent, you can add fresh cheese on top and melt as stated above. (See Pizza, page 205 and Burgers, page 179 for more information on melting cheese.)

Soft cheeses, like Brie, need to be at room temperature to show the ripe, gooey interior. If you get a soft cheese that isn't yet ripe, you can gently apply heat with a heat gun to get it looking gooey.

Whipped Cream

Whipped cream will deflate quickly at room temperature, especially under hot lights. It can be stabilized by whisking in confectioners' sugar. The type of whipped cream that comes in aerosol cans is useless for food styling, as it only holds its shape for 10 seconds before melting.

Rich's Pastry Pride (available at restaurant and bakery supply stores) is a thick, creamlike liquid that can be whipped to any desired consistency and will never break down or melt. It works better and lasts longer than whipped cream. It can be whipped to the consistency of softly whipped cream or to the consistency of buttercream frosting, or anywhere in between. If over-whipped, it will loose its soft, silky quality.

Cool Whip works really well for dollops. To make a hero dollop, Stir thawed Cool Whip until it is smooth, then flatten the surface with the back of a soup or tea spoon. Drag the spoon across the surface of the Cool Whip, gathering enough product in the spoon to make a nice shape when dropped onto product. This takes a little practice but it works well. Sometimes you'll need to push the dollop off the spoon from the back with your finger. Cool whip makes a great substitute for sour cream, whipped cream and other dairy-related products.

All these options result in a very white product. If the photographer needs the white to be

toned down a bit, you can do this by adding Kitchen Bouquet and/or yellow food coloring (begin with tiny amounts).

Desserts
Real Ice Cream and Sorbet

- Chest freezers should be delivered one day in advance to allow freezers to come down to minimum temperature.
- Always get an extra freezer to work from. This will allow the rest of the product to stay at the proper temperature.
- Use only 3-gallon ice cream containers to work from.
- Working temperature of ice cream should be between 12 and 17 degrees.

Special Equipment for Working with Real Ice Cream

The problem with shooting real ice cream as well as other frozen products is that they melt!

We sometimes use fake ice cream (see facing page) as a stand-in, or wad up a damp paper towels (sometimes we even color the paper towels with coloring spray, mash it into a scoop shape, and plate it in something similar to the hero plate) so the photographer has something to light.

When you have to work with real ice cream because it's what your client is selling or is specifically asking for, you will need specific equipment not necessarily in your kit:

- Ice cream scoops—the best overall size is #16, but having a variety of sizes is good.
- Sieve or strainer for separating any additions to the ice cream. As an example, if you are using ice cream with chunks of cherries in it, you will need to place some of it in a sieve and rinse it under warm water to have the actual cherry bits to use when styling the ice cream.
- Wax paper to place hero scoops on before plating. We usually line a plastic tray with wax

paper, then place scoops on top and put the tray in the freezer.

❧ Dry ice in a cooler to move the hero ice cream from the prep area to the set, and to hold it near the set.

Fake Ice Cream

Fake ice cream is basically just powdered sugar and a solid fat of some sort. You can experiment with all types of combinations. Some stylists add purchased cake frosting to get the desired creaminess. Other people add a small package of instant vanilla pudding mix. Some stylists add a little corn syrup. Texture is the important thing when making fake ice cream. Your ice cream should have the texture of pastry dough or Play-Doh, yet not be too crumbly. To test its appearance, pack fake ice cream into an ice cream scoop and press it against a tabletop. Holding the scoop steady against tabletop, press the lever on the scoop once, then release the lever and lift scoop away from the fake ice cream. When the surface texture of the fake ice cream scoop looks like real ice cream, you have the proper consistency.

It takes a lot of practice to make a realistic-looking scoop of ice cream. The surface should have many fine ridges, also known as *barking*. Finer ridges look more like high-quality ice cream. Remember that you will only see half of any scoop of ice cream, so don't worry about it if half of your scoop is perfect and the other isn't; just place it so the pretty side is toward the camera.

We find that using a kitchen torch to heat the ice cream scooper before scooping creates a consistently fine-grained texture; but you should try getting beautiful scoops without heating the scoop first, as the heat causes the surface of the fake ice cream to harden.

When made up, this recipe looks just like real ice cream. To make it you will need:

- Traditional ice cream scoops, heavy-duty, in the size desired
- 1 cup vegetable shortening
- 2 pounds powdered (confectioners') sugar
- 2 teaspoons corn starch
- Food coloring

Making fake ice cream:

1. Use a stand mixer with a paddle attachment.

2. Beat together 1 cup shortening and 1 cup powdered (confectioners') sugar at low speed until combined. Add the rest of the powdered sugar very gradually at low speed until mixture has the texture of Play-Doh. Add corn starch and continue beating for at least 10 minutes on medium-low speed. During this time, add food coloring as necessary. Always add food coloring in a small amount and allow it to be completely mixed into the fake ice cream before adding more.

3. Place the mixture on a work surface and knead briefly. Make a few practice scoops and adjust consistency at this time. If the mixture doesn't come easily out of the scoop, knead in a teaspoon more of cornstarch. If the mixture is too dry, knead in a tablespoon of shortening. If it's too wet, knead in 2 tablespoons of powdered sugar.

Scooping fake ice cream:

1. Pack the ice cream into a scoop, leaving a little sticking out around the edges as a "skirt" or "apron," pressing the scoop down into the table and using the lever just once. If you push the lever more it will ruin the surface texture of your scoops. Clean the scoop between uses.

2. Alternate scooping method: Heat the inside of an ice cream scoop with a kitchen torch or over a stove burner for about 8 seconds. Be careful not to touch the metal part of the scoop with your hands because it will burn you. Also, if the scoop is too hot the sugar will burn.

Styling fake ice cream:

1. Make sure the bottom of your fake ice cream is flat or slightly concave so that it will sit flat when plated. Press a non-hero scoop into the bottom of the bowl to use as a base for the hero scoop.

3. Dribble a little melted real ice cream into the bottom of dessert bowl for a realistic touch.

4. Drizzle on fudge sauce warmed to desired consistency.

5. Add toppings and a few drops of melted real ice cream for realism.

Note: If the ice cream has additions such as fruit or nuts, mix these in when you knead the mixture by hand. Always reserve extra additions to dot on the surface of the hero scoop.

Fake Ice Cream Alternatives

Nothing about food styling is set in stone. Different stylists put their own spin on whatever they do, including making fake ice cream. Here are a few more methods we've had success with:

- Instant mashed potato flakes can be used as an ice cream alternative. Make them according to the package instructions but using less liquid.
- Prepared cake frosting combined with more powdered sugar is another option. Using colored or chocolate frosting will give you a head start on making colored or chocolate ice cream. Use a traditional ice cream scoop as previously directed and this recipe will come out looking just like real ice cream.
- Prepared cookie dough mixed with powdered sugar added to get the proper consistency is another option that's been used successfully.

Drips and Melts for Fake Ice Cream

For realistic looking drips, use white toothpaste colored with food coloring and thinned with water to the correct consistency. Or mix food coloring with cream and apply it with a paintbrush or an eye dropper, or daub it on with a paintbrush. A third alternative is to use actual melted ice cream. Pour a little of this mixture into the bottom of the dessert bowl after your fake ice cream has been put in place. Resist the urge to paint your scoops with this melt liquid, as it will make them look like plastic.

Toppings for Ice Cream
Chocolate Sauce

Some chocolate and fudge sauces are very thick and need to be thinned with chocolate syrup or dark Karo syrup to the desired consistency. Others simply need to be warmed in a microwave for a short while. If using on real ice cream, don't heat the sauce or it will immediately melt your ice cream. Instead, thin to a pouring consistency with Karo syrup or a mixture of Karo syrup and water. Sauce can be placed in a pastry bag fitted with a round tip, or

in a squeeze bottle, or it can be applied by drizzling from a spoon.

Nuts, Jimmies, and Other Additions

Use partially thawed ice cream to glue toppings to frozen ice cream. Stick fruit or other toppings in the partially thawed ice cream and then attach it to the frozen ice cream. When the two touch, the frozen ice cream will freeze the partially thawed ice cream to itself.

Additions can be inserted directly into fake ice cream. If you make a small hole with a toothpick before inserting any additions, they will stay just fine.

Fake Sorbet

After some experimenting with various ideas for making non-melting sorbet, we finally hit on one that works like a charm and looks totally real. After you scoop this mixture it will stay in place without melting for days.

Instructions:

1. Dissolve 16 packages unflavored gelatin in 4 cups water.

2. Thaw 1 pound of frozen fruit (whatever kind gives you the look you want) and puree it before stirring into gelatin mixture.

3. Refrigerate it and let it set until firm, at least 3 hours.

4. Use ice cream or portion scoops in desired sizes to make scoops.

5. Place scoops on a wax paper–lined baking sheet and freeze them to get an icy look, or use as is.

6. Plate and garnish as desired.

7. This will keep in an airtight container in the fridge for weeks or will freeze for years. Thaw to scooping consistency before using.

MUSEUM WAX
or modeling clay
is used to position
utensils on plates.

Cakes

Whether you make a whole cake or a single slice, the methods are still the same. Here we give instructions for baking whole cakes and for stabilizing and frosting a slice of layer cake.

We use insulating strips when baking, as they really do make cakes bake more evenly. Step 3 below details exactly how to make your own. Or you can buy insulating strips, sold under the name "Magi-Cake or "Bake Even Strips" and available at cake decorating supply stores.

We also use xantham gum to strengthen cakes. The fewer egg yolks in a cake the more delicate the cake itself will be. On a recent shoot, where we were required to make a cake from a specific packaged white cake mix, we watched in horror as our perfectly styled slice slowly compressed under the weight of the frosting. Luckily, it was a two-day shoot and we had time to make it again—the second time with a little xantham gum added to the mix.

The instructions below are for cakes made from boxed cake mixes. If you can order sheet cakes or round cakes from a good bakery to work with, these will be much sturdier and won't need the extra stabilizing methods described below.

Baking even cake layers:

1. Spray cake pans with oil and line with parchment paper. Spray the parchment paper with oil.

2. Add a half teaspoon of xantham gum to the packaged cake mix for stability (necessary for soft cakes like white and yellow, optional for chocolate or spice cakes) if making a two or more layer cake slice.

3. Wrap cake pans with an insulating layer. To make this, tear off a piece of aluminum foil a bit longer than your cake pans are round. (For example, you'll need a 29-inch piece of foil to go around a 9-inch cake pan.) Dampen several paper towels and fold into 1-1/2-inch strips. Place the damp towels down the length of foil, then fold the foil over the towels. Ring the outside of the cake pan with the foil and secure it with kitchen twine.

4. Bake cakes according to package directions, erring on the side of overdone rather than underdone. Let cake cool before handling.

1 Frost the top and sides of the cake. Add frosting to any areas between the layers that need it.

Frosting a Slice of Layered Cake

2 Clean excess or messy frosting off the cake layers with a brush dipped in rubbing alcohol.

3 To create a "sliced" look, drag a serrated knife down over the frosting, dragging a bit of it onto the layers below.

4 Finish frosting the top and sides. (A nice look for frosting is dragging the blunt end of a skewer through the frosting, drawing overlapping 8s. It looks both casual and a bit elegant.)

5 Decorate the sides as desired.

6 Decorate the top as desired.

Whole and cut, frosted and unfrosted: decorated and undecorated cakes can be frozen until ready to shoot. They loose that chilled look in a few minutes under the camera and lights.

Soufflés

Soufflés are so difficult to style. Real soufflés have a life span of a minute, and fake soufflés are difficult to make look good.

Fake Soufflés

Angel food cake method: Using a prepared angel food cake (the kind with the pretty cracked top surface, not the kind that is packaged upside-down so the flat bottom of the cake is on top), cut pieces of it to fit into the hero soufflé dish. Pinch, push, and arrange so that it has your desired look. Whip a couple of egg whites to a soft foam and brush some onto the surface of your angel food soufflé to disguise any obvious joined edges. Bake in a 350 degree F oven until the egg whites turn golden.

An alternative is to use an angel food cake mix and prepare according to package directions. Pour into soufflé dishes and bake as you would a real soufflé (with a collar of parchment paper wrapped around the dish). Soufflés made this way will hold their shape longer. Any additions (like cheese or raspberry puree) can be stirred into the cake mix right before baking.

Real Soufflés

The "flying by the seat of your pants" method is to make a series of soufflés and have them ready to come out of the oven and in front of the camera in 5- to 10-minute intervals. Make according to your recipe and have enough product and soufflé dishes to make it 10 or 12 times. Putting a bit of cream of tartar (about 1/4 teaspoon for every 4 egg whites) in with the egg whites as they are being beaten will help stabilize the soufflé a bit, giving it a few extra minutes of life.

An alternative that is stable (meaning it won't deflate) is to make your soufflé in a soufflé dish twice the size of your hero dish (steps are pictured on facing page). Bake it according to a standard soufflé recipe. After your soufflé deflates and completely cools, carefully remove it from the soufflé dish. Put a false bottom in your hero dish and place the deflated soufflé on top of that. The upside of this method is that you can alter the top surface of your soufflé by placing cotton balls underneath to puff it up. The downside is that it doesn't work for large soufflés, as the soufflé

dish you'd need would be bigger than would fit in your oven. And the physics involved . . .

Cheesecakes

Frozen cheesecakes are much easier to work on. Freeze before slicing and keep frozen after styling. You can place your frozen hero slice on the set so it can be lit. Don't take the final photo until all frost has melted from the surface and the cheesecake no longer looks frozen. This will only take 5 to 10 minutes. Don't freeze toppings.

We usually use pre-made cheesecakes available in the frozen section of grocery stores. Make sure you buy whole cheesecakes that have not been sliced. If we need to have cheesecakes baked

to specific sizes, we make them the day before. The Philadelphia Classic Cheesecake recipe off the Kraft Foods website is foolproof.

Pies

Because of their flaky crusts, pies are difficult to handle. We use the prepared pie dough available in the refrigerator case of most supermarkets. There are usually two crusts in a package, which we knead together, intentionally overworking to strengthen it. If ordering crusts pre-made from a bakery, specify that you want them hard, not flaky.

If styling a slice, make sure the pie is either at room temperature or colder and cut a piece to the desired size. Use a pie spatula as a template if it will be in the shot. Style the pie slice on the hero plate, as a slice of pie is very difficult to move without cracking the crust. Support the back side of the crust with cotton balls until the photographer is ready to take the photo.

If you are making your own filling, sprinkle some gelatin into the mixture to firm it up. If ordering from a bakery, specify that the filling be firm. Ask for a pie's worth of extra filling on the side. For styling pre-made pies, purchase similar extra filling and use it to style cut sides of the pie.

Pieces of cotton ball can be inserted into the filling to prop up the top crust (if you have one). Crusts that develop cracks can be spackled with a mixture of crust crumbs and denture cream or Vaseline.

Brush exposed nuts and chocolate in cookies and other desserts with a little oil to highlight them and create a bit of contrast to the doughy part.

Cookies, Pastries, Brownies, and Other Desserts

Re-dress the surface of pastries by removing excessive fondant or frosting and adding new raisins, nuts or jam. If pastries look a bit old, place them in a warm oven for 5 minutes to bring them back to life.

Brush exposed nuts and chocolate in cookies and other desserts with a little oil to highlight them and create a bit of contrast to the doughy part.

Brownies have the tendency to gum up and lose texture on the cut sides. If possible, freeze brownies before cutting. Or roughen up the sides with a toothpick. Mix brownie crumbs with denture cream or petroleum jelly to make a spackle to fill any holes.

Chocolate

When chocolate is too shiny, spraying it with a matte dulling spray (Krylon Matte Spray or Blair Matte Spray Fixative) will take the shine off. If the surface is too dull, brush or rub lightly with oil.

Melting chocolate in a double boiler: To melt large amounts of chocolate (more than 8 ounces), use a double boiler over very low heat. Do not let chocolate go over 90 degrees; when chocolate gets too hot it will burn and seize up. To rescue seized chocolate, remove any burned bits and mix a teaspoon or two of shortening into the remaining chocolate. As you stir it, the chocolate will cool down and smooth out.

Melting chocolate in a microwave oven: To melt small amounts (under 8 ounces) of chocolate in a microwave, break it into small pieces and place it in a microwave safe bowl. Microwave on high at 30-second intervals, stirring in between, until the chocolate has melted and is smooth.

Jell-O

The recipe below makes a very firm product that will last a long time under hot lights. Let this mixture sit in the refrigerator for two days uncovered. When working with Jell-O, keep a container of cool water handy to rinse your tools and fingers in. Keep your fingers wet at all times when working with gelatin or Jell-O.

Instructions:

1. Place 2 large (6-ounce) packages Jell-O of desired color in a large bowl.

2. Add 2 packets plain gelatin.

3. Stir in 3-1/2 cups slightly warm water until the crystals have dissolved.

4. Cover and refrigerate or pour into molds and refrigerate.

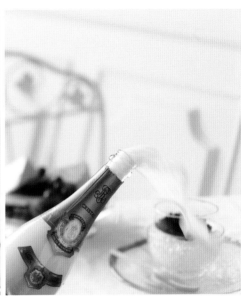

Beverages

Making room-temperature coffee look hot and warm beer look cold are techniques all food stylists should have in their repertoire. Here are the tricks we use to get beverages to look the way we want them to.

Sodas

Sprinkle a little salt or crushed bits of Alka Seltzer into sodas to bring back fizz if they go flat.

Champagne

Sprinkle in a little sugar for more bubbles. Blow compressed air into the bottle for a foam explosion.

Beer

Make sure to use clean glasses. Use cool, not cold, beer and replace when it begins to go flat. You can "re-foam" beer many times before it completely dies on you. Re-foam beer by vigorously stirring it with a long skewer or sprinkling in a little salt or crushed bits of Alka Seltzer (this should only be used as a last resort, as it builds up on the bottom of the glass where it can be visible

to the camera). An alternative is to carefully and very briefly spray some compressed air into the beer. This creates tons of foam. It can also cause the foam to overflow the glass if you blow too much air into the beer.

Red Wine

Dilute real red wine or use red food color, grape juice, or cranberry juice diluted with water. (If red wine is used full strength it usually shows up too dark in a photograph. If the photo is lit for the wine, the rest of the photo will come out too light.)

White Wine

Use real white wine or use yellow and the teeniest bit of red food coloring *very* diluted with water. Or use white grape juice diluted with water.

Cocktails

Liquor is thicker than water, so it's best to use real when you can for the right effect. Trengove Studio's Ice Power and Ice Crystals can be mixed with water to create an icy slush. Acrylic and glass ice cubes give a cold look to beverages without the inconvenient melting.

Coffee, Tea, and Hot Chocolate

Kitchen Bouquet or soy sauce diluted with water makes an acceptable fake coffee or tea. Bubbles are key to making coffee look freshly poured and hot chocolate frothy and rich. The same technique can be used to make bubbles for either. We like the way Dial Direct Foam soap in the pump bottle works and we use it for cappuccino foam.

As with everything you style, propping and lighting will greatly affect the final image. Here we have what are basically 4 cups of coffee but each with a totally different feel.

Instructions:

1. Make a mixture by adding a few drops of clear detergent to a quarter cup of the beverage (coffee, hot chocolate, etc.).

2. Stir vigorously to make foamy bubbles.

3. Spoon bubbles onto the surface of the hero when ready to shoot.

This is not recommended for extreme close-ups because soap bubbles create a rainbow effect on the surface of the bubbles.

Beverage Effects

Not all liquid effects are created equal. Condensation and water droplets are simple, whereas splashes are very difficult (and very messy) to get right.

Condensation and Water Droplets

All the methods below will also work on fruits, vegetables and any other non-porous surface. The best fine mist water sprayers we've found are Evian misters. They're not cheap but the large-size sprayer will last for months.

To make condensation you will need:

- Paper towels
- Tape
- Scotch Guard
- A ventilated area for spraying Scotch Guard
- A fine mister to spray water
- Glycerin or Aqua Gel
- Toothpick or skewer

To create condensation:

1. Determine your fluid level by estimating how far up you will be filling your glass. Cover this area with a collar of paper taped around the glass above the fluid level.

2. Spray the surface of a clean glass very lightly with Scotch Guard and let it dry a few minutes. If the glass is clean, it will dry completely clear.

3. Using a fine mist sprayer, mist the glass with water. The Scotch Guard holds the spray beaded on the surface of the glass, keeping it from running off. It will evaporate after awhile, so you'll need to reapply the water spray as necessary.

4. Holding the glass around the top where it's protected by the paper towel collar, place the glass on set and remove the collar.

5. Fill the glass to desired fluid level with liquid.

To create small droplets:

1. Mix a little glycerin in a spray bottle with water (about 1 part glycerin to 4 parts water) and spray it onto a Scotch Guard-treated glass (following directions 1 and 2 above).

2. Or mix a little Aqua Gel with water in a spray bottle (about 1 part Aqua Gel to 12 parts water) and spray it onto the glass (see page 250). Aqua Gel is very gummy, so if you use this mixed with water, you will need to shake the bottle very well *every time* before spraying.

To create large droplets:

1. Dip the end of a toothpick, skewer or tiny paintbrush into glycerin or Aqua Gel and apply directly to your surface.

To create really big drops:

1. Take a bit of Museum Gel (a clear, removable adhesive to help secure clear glass props in place, made by the makers of Museum Wax) and roll it into a ball slightly smaller than the size of your desired drop. Place it on whatever surface you are using and allow it to sit for a few minutes. It will smooth out as it flattens and become completely clear. We've made drops as big as half an inch this way. It's kind of freaky and cool at the same time.

Splashes and Pours

Splashes are more of a photography technique than a food styling technique. A food stylist would be used if there is any other food in the shot, like the cereal in a milk pour shot; or a stylist may be hired to help get the liquid to the proper consistency for the desired splash or to help the photographer with re-sets and cleaning the props and set between shots.

There is a talented young photographer in one of our favorite studios who is a natural at splashes, so we asked her about how one of these photos comes together. She tells us, "As far as shooting pours and splashes, it's more about the photographer making a huge mess, doing the splash over and over, shooting all the while to see what we get. Then compositing the bits and pieces we like in Photoshop to get just the right pour, just the right shapes for the splashes, so it looks like it all happened together naturally. I do all my own retouching, so I know what pieces I am looking for when I'm splashing over and over again."

Another way to get splashes and pours is to use acrylic ones made by Trengove Studios. You can have them specially made or rent them (rental fees are between $25 and $100 a day).

Other Effects: Steam and Smoke

Nothing says "hot" like steam, smoke and flames. There are a variety of ways to achieve these effects, described below.

Microwave Method

Place a wet paper towel or cotton ball under the food. Cover it with plastic wrap and microwave it until steam comes out when the plastic wrap

is removed. Timing on this technique will vary according to the type of food, plate, and microwave used. After removing the plastic wrap, the edge of the dish will need to be wiped off. This method is great for video and television, as those mediums won't necessarily see the moisture on the rim of the plate.

Clothes Steamer Method

This works well on pizza, pasta and other foods that have cheese or sauce in them. This technique works especially well on plated food where control is needed and where the microwave technique might overcook the food. For video and television, place a large tent of foil over the plate of food, leaving an opening to insert the end of the steamer. A minute before shooting starts, insert the steamer into the foil tent and let it steam. When the camera is ready to roll, remove the steamer and close the hole in foil. When the cameras are rolling, remove the foil and get out of camera range. For still photography, after the food is on set and lit, hold the steamer over the food, allowing steam to penetrate the food. Hold over food for at least 30 seconds. Remove the steamer from camera range. Steam will keep rising for about 10 seconds.

Chemical Methods

A-B Smoke is a compound made up of two different liquids that create a light smoky-steamy vapor when combined. To use, saturate two cotton balls, one with the A liquid and one with the B liquid. Insert both into or behind the food so they touch. The A liquid can also be applied to the food surface, then sprayed with the B liquid to produce the vapor. A-B Smoke cannot be legally shipped in some states, as it is considered a hazardous material. It is also a skin and lung irritant, so be careful when using, and use in ventilated areas.

Another chemical steam/smoke method is calcium chips, also know as steam chips or calcium turnings. They are tiny bits of calcium metal that react when combined with water to create steam. Both A-B Smoke and calcium chips are difficult to find outside of Southern California. Calcium chips are also considered a skin and lung irritant and a hazardous material.

Boiling Water Method

Place a cup behind the food where it won't be seen by the camera. Just before shooting, pour boiling water into the cup. This will create steam for up to a minute and it can be quickly and easily replaced with a new cup and boiling water to keep steam coming. The downside of this method is that the steam can look like it's coming from behind the food rather than from the food itself.

Real Heat Method

Place a skillet (or other pan or pot) over high heat. Place food inside and spray some water into skillet with a water mister right before shooting. This works great for still photography as well as video and television.

Here is a quick reference guide for the materials we use most commonly in food styling:

COLORING MATERIALS

• Kitchen Bouquet to darken.

• Soy sauce to darken and for faking coffee.

• Worcestershire sauce to darken.

• Angostura bitters to add a warm orange color.

• Food coloring for changing and enhancing color.

• Beet juice for adding a magenta-red color.

• Paprika for adding a red color and hiding imperfections.

FOOD GLUES

• Vaseline to hide cracks in fish and meats; not to be used with warm or hot foods; can be colored or mixed with other ingredients to make a food spackle.

• White glue to position dry foods.

• Shortening to false-bottom dishes and to use as a food support for cold or room-temperature foods.

• Polygrip denture cream, white, to glue foods together or to fill cracks; can be used with warm and cold food, wet and dry foods, and can be colored or mixed with other ingredients to make a food spackle.

• Clear pastry gel to hide cracks in fish and meats; not to be used with hot foods; can be colored or mixed with other ingredients to make a food spackle.

THICKENING MATERIALS

ADDITIVES USED FOR FOOD STYLING

• Xanthan gum sprinkled very sparingly into liquids to make thicker.

• Cornstarch stirred into liquids to thicken, but needs to be heated.

• Arrowroot stirred into liquids to make thicker.

• White glue used in place of milk in some cereal or oatmeal shots.

• Flour stirred into liquids to thicken but needs to be heated; will cloud clear liquids.

• Karo syrup stirred into thin liquids to add a bit of thickness and body; helps to keep mixtures from separating.

SMOOTHING MATERIALS

• Karo syrup stirred into liquids that are lumpy or dull will make these smoother and shinier. It will also thicken thin liquids and thin thick liquids. It's the great balancer.

Correcting or Changing Food Color

Food coloring is not always the best option when trying to alter the color of foods, as it is highly concentrated. If you use too much, there is no wiping it off. These are the products we use most often for coloring foods:

• Kitchen Bouquet, soy sauce, or Worcestershire sauce will darken food.

• Angostura bitters will brighten the surface of cooked foods, adding an orange color. Diluted with water and sprayed on.

• Karo syrup comes in light, golden, and dark varieties, so it can be used to correct the color of foods. Wipe the golden color onto cooked chicken or fish, and the dark color onto cooked meats to add a delicious-looking shine.

• To give cut meat a more rare appearance, paint with very diluted red food color or beet juice.

• Cream or half-and-half stirred into liquids will lighten the color of opaque liquids, as will a purchased, shelf-stable Alfredo sauce.

• Cooking juices from the bottom of your baking dish or skillet can be brushed straight onto food or mixed with a little Karo Syrup, Vaseline, denture cream, pastry gel, or even oil to darken areas of cooked meats.

Flame

The fluids below will burn with a nice flame while producing a minimum amount of smoke:

❧ Denatured alcohol.

❧ Lighter fluid.

❧ 150-proof alcohol.

❧ Rubber cement.

❧ Sterno, liquid.

❧ Nail polish remover.

A small cotton ball soaked with any of the liquids listed above will burn for a few minutes. Set on a heat-proof surface such as heavy-duty foil (regular foil will burn), a metal spoon or a small metal or heat-proof glass container, and place behind the desired food so that the camera sees only the flame. You can place rubber cement right on the food, but the food will burn. In addition, solid Sterno can be cut into small pieces and set alight. Make sure you place it on a heat-proof surface before lighting. The flames in the photo facing were from ignited rubber cement.

Faking Hot Coals

Normally, faking hot coals is the responsibility of the photographer, but it's good to know how it's done. Spray charcoal with Krylon red-orange florescent or neon paint. Coat with real charcoal ash or apply Arid Extra Dry antiperspirant directly to the charcoal for an ashy look. This gives the coals the very real appearance of being hot. Coals should be backlit through a yellow, orange, or red gel.

Appendix A
Glossary

Below is a short glossary of common culinary, food styling, photography, and television and movie production terms that you might come across in your work.

al dente: (culinary) Firm, not soft or mushy; to the bite (usually referring to vegetables and pastas).

ambient light: (photography) The available light completely surrounding the subject. Also known as available light.

angle of view: (photography) The area of a photograph that a lens covers or sees.

apple boxes: (photography) Strong wooden boxes used as supports to lift items like furniture.

art department: (photography, television, and film) Anyone connected with the look of the set. This may also include set decorators or prop people in charge of any dishes, glasses, linens, or anything else that appears on camera.

art director: (photography, television, film) Accountable for the creative development as well as the complete look of all advertising projects or product.

assistant director or AD: (television, film) Subordinate to director; responsible for set organization on behalf of the director to ensure an overall smooth production.

au sec: (culinary) To cook something, usually in a sauté pan, until all liquid has evaporated, or until dry.

B-roll: (television, film) Video that is shown with a voiceover, usually shot without the talent, like a close-up of a pair of hands chopping a tomato or pressing the button on a blender.

back lighting: (photography) Light coming from behind the subject toward the camera lens. At times this creates a silhouette effect.

bain marie: (culinary) Container of hot water used to keep foods hot.

basic lighting: (photography) Lighting developed on a photography set to be adjusted once the hero is set in place.

batonnet: (culinary) 1/4 x 1/4 x 2-inch strips.

beauty shot: (television) Close-up shot of a finished styled dish.

béchamel: (culinary) Sauce made by thickening milk with a roux.

best boy: (television, film) The assistant lighting technician or assistant to the key grip.

beurre manie: (culinary) Mixture of equal parts raw butter and flour mixed together into a smooth paste.

blanch: (culinary) To cook an item partially and briefly in boiling water or hot fat (usually a pre-preparation technique).

blocking: (television, film) Plotting and arranging the placement of talent, camera, and microphone, as well as the movement in a production.

bounce lighting: (photography) Indirect light source facing away from the subject in need of illumination and bouncing off of a reflective surface to indirectly light the subject.

bracketing: (photography) Taking several photographs of the same scene and setup under different exposure settings to ensure a properly exposed photograph.

braising: (culinary) To cook covered (2/3 of the way) in liquid, usually after preliminary browning.

brunoise: (culinary) 1/8 x 1/8 x 1/8-inch cubes; a very small dice.

bump or bumper: (television) Segment tease shown before a commercial break to inform viewers on what segment is coming up.

burning: (photography) Using additional light exposure during film progression to darken selected areas of a photograph, sometimes done digitally in Photoshop.

C-stand: (photography, television, film) A multipurpose grip stand.

call to action or CTA: (infomercials) B-roll with a voiceover telling people to "call to action," or buy now with this number.

call sheet: (photography, television, film) Form that outlines all of the scenes to be filmed and all of the personnel and equipment required for shooting on a specific day. This also includes start and finish times for the overall production on that day.

camera angle: (photography, television, film) The viewpoint of the camera in relation to the photo subject.

camera front: (photography, television, film) The area of a dish/food item that is fully styled and visible to the camera.

cameraman: (television, film) The person in charge of filming/taping during production on the correct angles and cues.

caramelization: (culinary) Browning of surface sugars caused by heat.

chiffonade: (culinary) Cut into fine shreds; long, thin slices.

chinois: (culinary) Very fine, cone-shaped sieve. Also a china cup.

client: (all) Person or group using the services of a professional stylist. They ultimately have the final call on a shot.

cookie: (photography, television, film) A perforated material used to break up light or create a shadowed pattern.

compositing: (photography) Taking bits and pieces from several different photos and combining them in one file, usually using Photoshop. Often used for flames and splashes.

confit: (culinary) To cook something in its own fat, usually duck.

deglaze: (culinary) Using a liquid to remove cooked-on residue (flavor) from a pan.

depth of field: (photography) The area of the photograph that is in focus.

diffused light: (photography) A softened light with fewer shadows and more even coverage overall.

director: (television, film) Considered the manager of the production; in charge of running the production by visualizing the scripts, controlling and adjusting the artistic aspects of a film while maintaining order and guiding the technical crew as well as actors.

director of photography (DP): (television, film) Person who supervises the filming of movies, commercials, television series, and any sort of filmed production.

dodging: (photography) A technique used during the printing process to manipulate the exposure of a selected area on the photograph; reduces the exposure for areas of the print that the photographer wishes to be lighter. Most often done digitally in Photoshop.

DPI: (photography) Dots per inch; the measurement of the resolution of display and printing systems.

emincer: (culinary) To cut very thin slices.

establishing shot: (television, film) Shot that sets up a scene's setting or its participants.

exposure: (photography) Amount of light received by a sensor or film.

extras: (television, film) Hired to provide background for television, movies, and photo shoots.

fill light: (photography, television, film) A source of illumination that lightens shadowed areas caused by the main light, reducing contrast within a photograph.

filter or gel: (photography, television, film) A thin piece of colored gelatin placed directly over the light source to create an alternate quality of light that is output to the set.

flash point: (culinary) The lowest temperature at which the vapor of a combustible liquid will ignite.

fluff: (food styling) To refresh different items on the set after they've been under hot lights for a significant amount of time to ensure they look their best.

food stylist: (all) One who develops, tests, and cooks recipes, and arranges and decorates food to be professionally photographed and filmed.

gaffer: (television, film) Chief lighting technician for a production; also in charge of the electrical department.

garnish: (culinary) Decorative, edible item used to ornament or enhance the eye appeal of the food or dish.

gluten: (culinary) Substance made of proteins present in wheat flour that gives structure and strength to baked goods.

greek: (television, film) To make the label illegible; usually done to brand names on products by obscuring with colored electrician's tape or blacking out with a marker so it can't be read or seen on camera.

hero: (photography, television, film) The best-looking food item; chosen by the food stylist to use as the item photographed or for close-ups.

hot set: (television, film) A set that is still being used and so needs to stay exactly as is. If anything is moved it must be replaced in exactly the same spot.

hot spot: (photography) A very bright, often overly lit area in a set caused by too much reflected light.

image resolution: (photography) Amount of detail a photograph holds, in dots per inch or DPI.

interpretation: (all) Distinctive personal vision.

julienne: (culinary) 1/8 x 1/8 x 2-inch strips.

key grip: (television, film) Chief grip who works directly with the gaffer to create shadow effects for set lighting and who also oversees camera cranes, dollies, and other platforms.

liaison: (culinary) A binding agent, often made of cream and egg yolk, used to thicken sauces and soups.

location: (television, film) Area other than a studio or soundstage chosen to film certain scenes that are unable to be filmed on a studio set.

location manager: (television, film) Person in charge of maintaining a good relationship between the production company and the owners of the location, as well as knowing all pertinent information about it, such as location of switches, outlets, fuse boxes, bathrooms, neighborhood regulations, etc.

main light: (photography) Primary source of light used in the lighting setup, usually the brightest.

martini shot: (television) Final shot of the day, because the next "shot" is one they drink from a glass.

mirepoix: (culinary) Classic mixture of vegetables used as a common flavoring in many foods; usually 50% onion, 25% carrot, 25% celery.

mise en place: (culinary) Ingredients prepared and ready to use in a recipe/dish.

pan: (television, film) A horizontal movement of a camera on a fixed axis.

panning: (television, film) Following the activity and motion of a moving object with the camera; this causes the object to look clear and sharp and the background blurred.

poach: (culinary) To cook gently in a liquid that is hot but not boiling, between the temperatures of 160 and 180 degrees F.

postproduction: (television, film) Usually the final stage of a production, occurring after all filming is complete. This is when special effects and soundtracks are added and the editing is done.

prep: (culinary) Preliminary preparation of individual food items and elements.

producer: (television, film) Person who supervises the sitcom, show, or film; also acts as the contact between the production company and the various personnel involved in the postproduction process.

production assistant or PA: (television, film) Assistant for the production whose job it is to do a multitude of tasks, from getting coffee to running to the store to washing up to assisting wherever help is needed.

production team: (television, film) Any person associated with the action of completing the assigned project.

prop master: (television, film) Person in charge of bringing the items (props) used to create a certain look.

prop stylist: (photography) Responsible for everything seen in a photo that is *not* food. This includes tableware, furniture, plants and flowers, candles, fabrics, and whatever else might be in the photo.

ragout: (culinary) Well-seasoned meat or fish stew, usually including vegetables.

ragu: (culinary) Thick and full-bodied meat sauce (staple of Bologna in northern Italy).

reduction: (culinary) Liquid concentrated by cooking to evaporate the water.

rehearsal: (television, film) A run-through held before the scheduled filming to work out any problems during the actual production.

reset: (television, film) Redo of a scene; everything needs to be put back exactly as it was to do again.

retouching: (photography) Changing a photograph, usually digitally, by altering highlights, shadows, and color, often to fix blemishes.

roasting: (culinary) To cook foods by surrounding them with hot, dry air, usually in an oven.

roux: (culinary) Cooked mixture of equal parts flour and fat; used as a thickening agent.

sauté: (culinary) To cook quickly in a small amount of fat.

scrim: (photography, television, film) A metal "window screen" that is placed in front of a light to cut down on the light intensity.

seamless: (photography) A roll of paper used as a surface and background for photography. It curves up from the tabletop or ground and hangs behind whatever is being photographed so that there is no visible join between the bottom surface and the back surface.

seasonings: (culinary) Different aromatics used to flavor dishes.

second unit: (television, film) Team that shoots scenes not involving the main cast.

set tray: (food styling) A small portable tray that holds specific tools, including but not limited to tweezers, cotton balls, paint brushes, cotton swabs, Pam spray oil, and rubbing alcohol; used when working on a set.

sizzle: (television, film) Preheating a skillet or pan so that it is very hot when the segment starts; the food sizzles for the soundtrack and creates smoke on camera.

slurry: (culinary) Viscous liquid usually made up of equal parts liquid and flour or cornstarch, and used for thickening sauces.

special effects: (photography, television, film) The illusions used in the film, television, or photography to simulate things that would otherwise be too difficult or impossible to get "in real life." In photography, this could mean adding flame, smoke, or splashes to a photograph in Photoshop.

stand-in: (all) Substitute or practice object used in place of the real one, so that the lighting can be adjusted before the hero is put in place and shot, preventing the hero from being ruined under hot lights while the correct lighting is achieved.

stinger: (television, film) A single live extension cord. When working on sets, the stylist calls for a stinger for a heat gun, microwave, or any other electrical equipment.

striking: (television, film) Breakdown process of a set and/or location.

style: (food styling) To bring a food component into conformity or to enhance the look of it by using a variety of techniques.

sweating: (culinary) Using low heat and fat to extract liquid from an item without adding color/browning.

taillights: (television) Time of day when everyone is expected to be driving away.

talent: (television, film) The actors or pitchperson in front of the camera.

tease: (television) A shot, under 30 seconds in duration, of the talent or of a finished plate shown at the top of the hour to promote an upcoming segment.

tracking shot: (television, film) Any shot made from a moving dolly; also called a dolly or traveling shot.

triplet: (styling, television, film) Having a third food item in addition to the twin. For example, if the cake is being frosted on camera, an additional finished cake is needed. See *twin*.

trussing: (culinary) To tie protein together to prevent it from falling apart and to hold its shape.

twin: (styling, television, film) Having a second food item to replace another. For example, pulling a finished baked cake out of an oven when the raw cake batter has just been placed inside the oven. The baked cake is the twin.

voiceover: (television, film) An off-camera recording or narration, taped separately and put together with the action in postproduction.

walk-through: (television, film) Thorough explanation of a scene, usually including a demonstration of each step or act in a process or scene.

Appendix B

Troubleshooting Common Food Styling Problems

Included here are some interesting questions we've gotten from clients and former students that provide a look inside the thought process and problem solving nature of food styling.

Problem: How do you fix a crack in hot dog or hamburger buns?
Solution: Cracks in buns are what Photoshop was made for. We avoid this problem by purchasing buns in bulk or ordering buns from a bakery. You can smooth wrinkles in buns with some gentle steaming (see page 181 for instructions).

Problem: My client wants to film a teabag going into a clear glass teacup of hot water, coloring the water, without the condensation or steam caused by hot water.
Solution: Obviously you can't use hot water in this case. If the tea is not sufficiently coloring the water on its own, then open the teabags and spread the tea onto paper towels. Place Kitchen Bouquet in a spray bottle and spray tea leaves until well coated. Stir and spray again. Scatter over clean paper towels and allow to dry. Place back into teabags. Immerse in cool water.

Problem: How do you keep corn tortillas from cracking?
Solution: Rub the outside surface of the tortillas with a thin layer of petroleum jelly.

Problem: I can't get condensation to stay on glasses; it just runs together and then runs off the glass.
Solution: Lightly spray the outside of the glass with Scotch Guard, making sure to mask the top of the glass with drafting tape (or post-its or anything that's just lightly sticky) at the fill line, because condensation naturally gathers only where there is chilled liquid. Let dry. Place in set and fill with liquid. Using a fine mist sprayer (an Evian sprayer works great), spray the glass, especially where the light shines on it. Remove tape. You can also make a mixture of 1 part glycerin to 4 parts water, shake very well, and spray on. The stickiness of the glycerin will cause the droplets to stay on longer. Or buy and use Aqua Gel according to package instructions. (Found at www.Trengove Studios.com)

Problem: How do I fix a crack in cooked fish?
Solution: Fill crack with petroleum jelly or white denture cream.

Problem: How do I fix a crack or hole in cooked meat?
Solution: Color petroleum jelly, white denture cream, or clear piping gel with Kitchen Bouquet to a dark brown and use to fill crack.

Problem: How do I bring a dried old piece of cooked meat back to life?
Solution: Rub surface of meat with dark or brown sugar Karo syrup.

Problem: When I put the top bun on my burger it looks like it's wearing a hat.
Solution: When the bun is sitting too high on the burger it tends to resemble a hat perched atop the burger. First, make sure your burger is relatively the same diameter as your bun and is flat, not rounded, on top. Assuming the burger is in proportion to the bun, pick away some of the bread from the inside of the top bun until enough has been removed so that the bun sits flat on the meat.

Problem: I built a beautiful hamburger but now that its lit, my meat looks dry, dry, dry.
Solution: If your lettuce and other condiments still look great and you just want to freshen up the meat, place a little oil in a cup and brush onto any exposed areas. You can also brush any dry areas with a little dark or brown sugar Karo syrup.

Problem: I made this great sandwich but the photographer wanted a couple of water droplets on the visible skin of the sliced tomato. I tried spraying with water but that didn't work. What should I have done?
Solution: Place a small amount of glycerin in a cup and, using the tip of a toothpick, dot glycerin where you want droplets.

Problem: My clients always want to taste the food I make for photo shoots. How do I nicely tell them that I'm not the caterer or craft service?
Solution: We run into this problem all the time! Point out to them that: a) the food has been sitting in your car overnight; b) you are not cooking in a health-department-approved facility and nothing is sanitary; c) your job is to make the food look great for the camera, which is a completely different process from making food for consumption; d) you don't have the time to scrub and sanitize your prep area so it is very likely that the food is contaminated; e) you've sprayed the food with Windex to keep the bees off; or f) you've sprayed the food with bathroom cleaner to keep the smell at bay.

Problem: My salads keep going flat.
Solution: Lettuce wilts as it sits, so it would help to false bottom your salad bowl with paper towels moistened with cold water. If using a salad dressing, don't add it until right before taking the shot. Keep styled salads moist by spraying often with water. Keep covered with damp paper towels until ready to shoot. If styling larger bowls of salad, wrap a blue ice or other cold pack in damp paper towels and bury in the bottom of the salad bowl.

Problem: The skin on sausages splits before it gets brown enough.
Solution: Before cooking, massage a little Kitchen Bouquet into the surface of sausages. Cook sausages in a hot nonstick skillet, rolling constantly so that outside cooks evenly. Stop cooking when there are no more visible raw spots. To add a sear mark, place sausage in a medium-hot skillet, rocking very slightly to make the sear mark thicker. Remove before skin begins to tear. Alternatively, you can get nice brown marks using a heat gun. We don't advise using a kitchen torch, as the skin will tear in an instant.

Problem: For a commercial, I need to make a plate that includes a dipping sauce. The sauce has to stay in the bowl when it's tipped back and forth. How do I do that?
Solution: Stir xantham gum into the sauce until it is sticky and thick enough to stay in place. Sauces treated this way cannot be dipped into but will turn solid enough to keep from running. Xantham gum will cloud sauces slightly. Use xantham gum sparingly, adding a little at a time. Alternatively, if you have a day to prep, make a gelatin mixture (3 to 4 times as strong as is usual) that looks like the sauce, using the actual sauce if you can. Pour into hero bowls and let set until ready to use. For both of these methods, you can add a little straight sauce in a thin layer to cover the top surface for a realistic look.

Problem: I cooked the steaks, chicken, shrimp, etc., but the client wants to save them to shoot the next day. How to I preserve them? How do I bring them back to life?
Solution: Spray product generously with Pam spray oil and cover with several layers of damp paper towels. Place in heavy-duty resealable plastic bags and leave at room temperature. When ready to plate, reheat for a few minutes in a 300 degree F oven or run a heat gun over the surface to warm up a bit. Touch up any raw-looking areas with a kitchen torch. For red meat, rub surface with dark or brown sugar Karo syrup. Spray with Pam spray oil.

Problem: How do you keep sliced deli meats from tearing when using for sandwiches?
Solution: The cheaper and more processed the sandwich meat, the less prone it is to tearing. If the look you want is ribbon-like folds of sandwich meat that swirls back and forth, purchase the cheapest, most pressed and formed kind you can find.

Problem: How do I keep guacamole from turning brown?
Solution: Fresh avocados are your enemy. They may be delicious but they turn brown in an instant. Use prepared guacamole with the most chemicals in the ingredient list and the least amount of actual avocado. Add freshly chopped avocado, onion, cilantro, tomato for garnish, replacing the pieces of avocado when necessary. Spray cut pieces of avocado with Pam spray oil or vodka to keep from browning.

Problem: How do I fix old fake ice cream if it's become too dry (or too sticky)?
Solution: To moisten fake ice cream that has become dry, using your hands, knead in a little light Karo syrup. Use sparingly and knead well. If your mixture is too sticky, knead in powdered sugar and a pinch or two of cornstarch.

Problem: My photographer asks me to darken mashed potatoes (whipped cream, yogurt) because it's too white for the camera.
Solution: Stir in just the tiniest drop of Kitchen Bouquet or spray with Coloring Spray for Poultry (see recipe on page 158) and stir to combine. Add coloring until desired color is reached. You just want to take the color from stark white to off-white.

Problem: Thin pancake syrup that soaks into pancakes before it has a chance to dribble down the sides.
Solution: Use cheap pancake syrup or Karo pancake syrup. Maple syrup is too thin. Place syrup in freezer before using to thicken it. Spray pancakes with Scotch Guard before using to create a moisture-repellent seal.

Problem: How do I get dark grill marks without overcooking meats?
Solution: Rub surface of meat with Karo syrup. Blot well with paper towels so the surface of meat is nearly dry. Cook on a very hot preheated grill pan without moving until the desired grill marks are achieved. Turn meat over and remove from heat. Cook any raw-looking parts with a kitchen torch. Darken meat with Coloring Spray (see recipe on page 170) if necessary. The Karo syrup burns quickly, making lovely dark grill marks.

Problem: My cooked vegetables turn gray after awhile. How do I avoid this?

Solution: Vegetables turn gray when they've been over-cooked. Cook vegetables just long enough so they don't look raw. Either blanch briefly in boiling water or sauté very briefly in a sauté pan. My basic method for many vegetables is to spray a sauté pan with Pam and sauté vegetables for just a minute, then sprinkle with a tablespoon or two of water and immediately cover and remove from heat. Let steam for a minute or less, then remove and let cool.

Problem: *Sautéed mushrooms turn dark when cooked.*
Solution: About halfway through sautéing, sprinkle with a teaspoon or so of lemon juice. Lemon juice in a spray bottle works well for this. Also, the mushrooms are probably overcooked. Cook only long enough so there is a nice golden color on one side.

Problem: *How to get rid of loose, raw-looking skin on poultry?*
Solution: Using a kitchen torch, very lightly heat any loose areas of skin. The heat will cause the skin to visibly tighten. Be careful: too much heat will make tears in the skin.

Problem: *I have a big piece of ugly white fat on an otherwise great-looking cooked steak. How to I get rid of it?*
Solution: If you can't cut it off, there are several ways. If it's a large area, you can brown it with a kitchen torch. You can paint it with straight Kitchen Bouquet or with Kitchen Bouquet mixed with denture cream, Vaseline, or clear piping gel. Or you can cover it with a light layer of dark Karo syrup. If it's still shining through, burn the Karo syrup with a kitchen torch.

Problem: *When I build sandwiches, the back tends to be lower than the front.*
Solution: Place small pieces of cosmetic wedges, cotton balls, or pieces of sandwich meat in the back side of the sandwich to build up the back.

Problem: *When I put sauce on pasta it looks messy!*
Solution: Pasta sauces need to be used sparingly or they make a bowl of lively, different ingredients look the same. Most of the time sauces should be painted or drizzled on after the plate is in front of the camera. In some instances, placing un-sauced pasta in the hero plate, then saucing about a third of the pasta separately and arranging it on top of the un-sauced pasta is the way to go. You can always add more sauce later.

Problem: *The surface of my coffee looks as dark and flat as a tar pit.*
Solution: Freshly poured hot coffee will have a few bubbles floating on top. Take a small cup half full with lukewarm coffee or fake coffee made with soy sauce (preferred) and add a small squirt of dish soap. Stir vigorously to make bubbles. Spoon bubbles on top of hero coffee.

Problem: *How do I use those dark purple greens that come in the mixed bags of lettuces?*
Solution: Unless your photographer is getting really close and using a strong backlight, don't use them, as they tend to go black on camera.

Problem: *How do you keep the crust on a pizza slice from drooping?*
Solution: Cut a piece of thin cardboard slightly smaller than the pizza slice and use it for a support.

Appendix C

Further Reading

These are the books we get information and inspiration from.

Informational Books

Bellingham, Lynda and Jean Ann Bybee. *Food Styling for Photographers: A Guide to Creating Your Own Appetizing Art*. Burlington, MD: Focal Press, 2008.

Carucci, Linda. *Cooking School Secrets for Real World Cooks*. San Francisco, CA: Chronicle Books, 2005.

Chalmers, Irena. *Food Jobs: 150 Great Jobs for Culinary Students, Career Changers and Food Lovers*. New York: Beaufort Books, Inc., 2008.

Child, Julia. *Mastering the Art of French Cooking*. New York: Random House, 1961.

Corriher, Shirley. *Cookwise: The Secrets of Cooking Revealed*. New York: William Morrow, 1997.

———. *Bakewise: The Hows and Whys of Successful Baking with Over 200 Magnificent Recipes*. New York: William Morrow, 1997.

The Culinary Institute of America. *The Professional Chef* (eighth edition). New York: Wiley, 2006.

Donovan, Mary. *Opportunities in Culinary Careers*. New York: McGraw Hill, 2003.

Dornenburg, Andrew and Page, Karen. *Culinary Artistry*. New York: Wiley, 1996.

———. *The Flavor Bible: The Essential Culinary Guide to Culinary Creativity, Based on the Wisdom of America's Most Imaginative Chefs*. New York: Little, Brown, and Company, 2008.

Herbst, Ron and Sharon Tyler Herbst. *The New Wine Lover's Companion* (second edition). Hauppauge, NY: Barron's Educational Series, 2003.

———. *Food Lover's Companion* (fourth edition). Hauppage, NY: Barron's Educational Series, 2007.

Herbst, Sharon Tyler. *The New Food Lover's Tiptionary: More Than 6,000 Food and Drink Tips, Secrets, Shortcuts, and Other Things Cookbooks Never Tell You*. New York: William Morrow Cookbooks, 2002.

Joachim, David and Schloss, Andrew. *The Science of Good Food: The Ulitmate Reference on How Cooking Works*. Toronto, Ontario: Robert Rose, 2008.

Labensky, Sarah, et al. *On Cooking: A Textbook of Culinary Fundamentals* (fourth edition). Upper Saddle River, NJ: Prentice Hall, 2006.

Manna, Lou. *Digital Food Photography*. Boston, MA: Course Technology PTR, 2005.

McGee, Harold. *On Food and Cooking: The Science and Lore of the Kitchen*. New York: Scribner, 2004.

Ostmann, Barbara Gibbs and Jane L. Baker. *The Recipe Writer's Handbook* (revised and expanded). New York: Wiley, 2001.

Parsons, Russ. *How to Read a French Fry: And Other Stories of Intriguing Kitchen Science*. Boston, MA: Houghton Mifflin Harcourt, 2003.

Business Books

Below is a list of business books to help you become profitable and enjoy your business.

Zingerman's Guide to Giving Great Service. New York: Hyperion, 2004. 144 pages.

Ann Arbor, Michigan is home to world-renowned Zingerman's Deli. Ari Weinzweig and partner Paul Saginaw opened the deli in 1982 and have since created a mini empire, including a full-service restaurant, creamery, bakehouse, mail-order business, and training company. Besides providing excellent food, Zingerman's impeccable service (authentically friendly, completely unhurried) sets them apart. It is an easy, entertaining and fun read that will inspire and empower you to develop real, long-term relationships with your clients.

Small Giants: Companies that Choose to Be Great Instead of Big. The Woodlands, TX: Portfolio Hardcover, 2005. 256 pages.

Small Giants profiles fourteen companies who have experienced tremendous financial success and acclaim without being "big." If your aim is to be lean, mean, and create a business that reflects your ingenuity, this is a must read!

Start Your Own Business (*Entrepreneur* magazine's start up). Newburgh, NJ: Entrepreneur Press; 4th edition, 2007. 700 pages.

This tome is perfect if, as a new business owner, you are worried about forgetting something. They cover it all: business forms, insurance, accounting. They even have a chapter on selecting the right office equipment. Having come from *Entrepreneur* magazine, the authors have a wealth of resources and perspectives that deliver a clear picture of what owning a business entails.

Appendix D

Resources

Below are places where we've found useful tools and supplies for styling. The national stores all have websites, as do most of the local stores. If you can't get there in person, you can always order online.

Hardware Stores

Hardware stores are fantastic resources for the food stylist. You'll find heat guns, charcoal starters, tool bags, paintbrushes, shims, museum wax, Scotch Guard, Exact-O knives, painter's tape, and many other useful items. Home Depot (www.homedepot.com) carries the Husky brand tool bags that we adore. Lowes (www.lowes.com) carries a comparable AWP tool tote but only in one size.

Art and Craft Supply Stores

These are great places to find rulers, paint brushes, matte cutters, foam core, gaffer's tape, styrofoam shapes and forms, florist's wire, modeling clay, sculptor's tools, and so many other fun things. Michaels (www.michaels.com), Ben Franklin (bfranklincrafts.com), JoAnn (www.joann.com), Pearl (www.pearlpaint.com), and Dick Blick (www.dickblick.com) all have multiple locations across the country as well as online shopping.

Big Box or Discount Stores

Another place to get many of the items listed above is a box or discount store like Big Lots (www.biglots.com). They have pens, pencils, rulers, pads of paper, tape, paint brushes, wooden spoons, spatulas, whisks, and much more for steeply discounted prices. At stores like Costco (www.costco.com) you can get Sharpie markers, transparent tape, and Post-its in bulk. Target (www.target.com) is an excellent place to get cooking equipment and utensils, stationery supplies, and some of your hardware. The 99 Cent Only Store (www.99only.com) can even have items for your kit.

Restaurant Supply or Culinary Stores

These fun stores have a huge selection of must-have things for your kit: sets of round cookie cutters, all the utensils you will ever need, pots and pans, plastic trays, piping gel, pastry bags and tips, sieves, ice cream scoops, parchment paper, food coloring gels, knives, steels, and just about anything else you can imagine. They now make collapsible rubber measuring cups, strainers, and colanders—great items to have in your kit because of their light weight, durability, and packability. Sur la Table (www.surlatable.com) and Williams-Sonoma (www.williams-sonoma.com) are two national cooking supply stores, but most cities will have local stores that carry an excellent array of products. Two of our favorites are Surfas Restaurant Supply (www.surfasonline.com) in Culver City, California, and Great News Discount Cookware (www.great-news.com) in San Diego, California.

Drug Stores

Your friendly neighborhood drug store or pharmacy is the best place to get cotton balls, cosmetic wedges, rubbing alcohol, and glycerin.

Specialty Equipment Suppliers

Trengove Studios (www.trengovestudios.com) is a wonderland of special effects products. They will custom make liquid spills, splashes, pours, drips, and bubbles. Also available are acrylic, glass, or rubber ice cubes in every shape and size, and the various powders and gels for creating beverage special effects.

American Scientific & Surplus (www.sciplus. com) is a wonderful site full of all sorts of stuff that you didn't know you couldn't live without. It has fabulous items like the Pencil Torch (a butane torch the size of a pencil), a watch repair kit (with great tiny tools), tweezers, scissors, and sculpting tools, to name a few.

Papa John's Toolbox (www.hobbytool.com) has a good selection of dental tools for non-medical use.

Indigo Instruments (www.indigo.com) also carries medical supplies for the hobbyist.

Plum Party (www.plumparty.com) has interesting items to put in your prop bag (it's always good to have a few props with you), like swizzle sticks and fun flatware and tableware. Indigo has just about anything else for a party you can imagine.

Oriental Trading Company (www.oriental-trading.com) is a party-supply, arts and craft, and holiday store. You can find just about anything there at very good prices. If you need Valentine candy in October, this is where you'll find it.

Professional Organizations

**International Association of
Culinary Professionals**
1100 Johnson Ferry Road, Suite 300
Atlanta, GA 30342
Direct: (404) 252-3663
Toll free: (800) 928-4227
info@iacp.com
www.iacp.com

Women Chefs and Restaurateurs
P.O. Box 1875
Madison, AL 35758
Toll free: (877) 927-7787
Direct: (256) 975-1346
admin@womenchefs.org
www.womenchefs.org

American Culinary Federation
180 Center Place Way
St. Augustine, FL 32095
Toll free: (800) 624-9458
Fax: (904) 825-4758
acf@acfchefs.net
www.acfchefs.org

American Institute of Wine and Food
26364 Carmel Rancho Lane, Suite 201
Carmel, CA 93923
Toll free: (800) 274-2493
Fax: (831) 622-7783
info@aiwf.org
www.aiwf.org

Photogaphy Credits

Photographers

Matt Armendariz: pages 14, 15, 173 (left), 146, and 147.

Ryan Beck: pages 163 (right), 205, 224, and 229.

Victor Boghossian: pages 138, 157 (top right), 219 (right), and 234.

Kent Cameron: page 151.

Rachael Coleman: pages 40 and 230.

Edward Covello: pages 7 (top left and bottom right), 8, 85, 86, 87, 88, 89, 90, 92, 93, and 95.

Jack Coyier: pages 160, 161, 162, 163 (left and center), 166, 167, 172, 178, 179, 180, 181, 182, 186, 187, 208, and 211.

Anita Crotty: pages 190, 191, 194, and 231 (bottom left).

Jon Edwards: Cover (front, back, and flap), pages 2, 6, 7 (top center, bottom center and left), 11, 13, 16, 17, 26, 41, 42, 44 (center and bottom), 46 (bottom), 47 (top right and bottom), 67, 83, 130, 131, 132, 133, 168, 136, 141, 142, 148, 149, 157, 159 (top and bottom left), 170, 171, 173 (right), 175, 184, 185, 188, 198, 199 (right), 200, 201, 203, 209 (right), 210, 212 (left), 213, 214 (right), 215 (left), 221, 225, 231 (top right), 232 (top and bottom right, top left), 235 (top row), 237, 245.

Laura Edwards: pages 51 and 69.

Ben Fink: pages 24 and 25.

Cindie Flannigan: pages 58, 59, 61, 82, and 228.

Kim Hudson: pages 30, 189, 195, and 196.

Jeff Katz: pages 47 (left and center right), 98, 114, 199 (left), 218 (right), 236, 238, and 239.

Diana Lundin: pages 68, 151, and 219.

Martin Mann: pages 35 and 50.

Ed Ouellette pages 18, 19, 22, 23, 46 (top left), 111, 115, 165, 169, 193, 209 (left), 214 (left), 215 (right), 216, 218 (left), and 231 (top left).

Jerome Pennington: pages 28, 29, 99, 156, 202, 212 (right), 220, 222, 226, 227, and 231 (bottom right).

R. Pratima Reddy: pages 21, 27, and 157 (bottom right).

Jeff Sarpa: pages 204 and 207.

Heather Winter: pages 43, 44 (top), 45, 137, 197, 235 (bottom), 240, and 241.

Prop Stylists

Matt Armendariz: pages 6, 26, 46, 47 (center right and bottom), 98, 111, 114, 131, 133, 136, 157 (top left), 168, 184, 185, 203, 209 (right), 210, 212 (left), 216, 225, 235 (top row), and 236 (left).

Laurie Bear: pages 16, 17, 42, 67, 149, 201, 236 (right), 238, and 239.

Brian Toffoli: page 232 (bottom left)

Robin Tucker: pages 29 (right), 99, 165, 169, 202, 215 (right), and 231 (bottom right).

Denise Vivaldo: pages 14, 15, 18, 19, 22, 23, 158 (top right and bottom left), 171, 188, and 237.

Kim Wong: front cover and page 231 (top right).

Clients

Photographs are provided by courtesy of the following clients and publications:

Tom Barber, Bradshaw International: pages 205, 224 and 229.

Bristol Farms: front cover and pages 16, 17, 26, 41, 42, 67, 111, 131, 133, 136, 149, 159, 173 (left), 185, 201, 216, 231 (top right), 232 (bottom right), and 235 (top row).

Cacique USA: pages 44 (top and bottom right), 173 (left), and 214 (right).

The Calorie Countdown Cookbook by Juan-Carlos Cruz: pages 115, 193, 214, and 231 (top left).

Tony Cimilino, GWT: page 245.

Cooking Well: Beautiful Skin by Elizabeth TenHouten: back cover (both) and pages 9, 157, 168 (left), 188.

The Date Night Cookbook by Meredith Phillips: pages 1, 8, 9, 11, 46 (bottom), 47, 141, (top right, bottom), 168 (left), 170, 198, 199 (left), 200, 203, (top left and right, bottom right), 209 (right), 210, 212 (right), 213, 215 (left), 225, and 232 (top left and right).

Denise Vivaldo: Cover back flap.

Do It For Less! Weddings by Denise Vivaldo: pages 14 and 15.

Eat Taste Heal by Dr. Thomas Yarema: pages 46 (top left), 215 (right), and 218 (left).

Fast and Easy by Suzanne Somers: page 232.

Fresh & Easy: page 13.

Intercourses: an Aphrodisiac Cookbook by Martha Hopkins and Randall Lockridge: pages 24 and 25.

Bill Kelly: page 171.

Mariel's Kitchen by Mariel Hemmingway: pages 47 (center), 98, 114, 199 (left), and 236 (left).

Jamie McMonigle: pages 174 and 237.

Somersize Chocolate by Suzanne Somers: page 47 (left).

Somersize Cocktails by Suzanne Somers: pages 236 (right), 238 and 239.

Somersize Desserts by Suzanne Somers: page 218 (right).

The 3-Hour Diet Cookbook by Jorge Cruise: pages 165, 169, and 209 (left).

Index